COOK, EAT, THRIVE

Vegan Recipes from Everyday to Exotic

Joy Tienzo

Cook, Eat, Thrive: Vegan Recipes from Everyday to Exotic
by Joy Tienzo
© 2012 Joy Tienzo

This edition copyright © 2012 PM Press All Rights Reserved

ISBN: 978-1-60486-509-7
Library of Congress Control Number: 2009901397

PM Press
PO Box 23912
Oakland, CA 94623
www.pmpress.org

Layout by Jonathan Rowland
Cover art by Tofu Hound and John Yates
Icons designed by Jess Deugan
Cover photos by Art Heffron

10 9 8 7 6 5 4 3 2 1

Printed on recycled paper by the Employee Owners of Thomson-Shore in Dexter, Michigan.
www.thomsonshore.com

Contents

Introduction

Drinks

Breakfasts and Brunches

Breads

Sauces, Dressings, and Condiments

Little Bites

Salads

Soups, Curries, and Stews

Entrées

Sides

Desserts

Index

Acknowledgments

First, thanks to Bob and Jenna Torres at Tofu Hound Press, who have been so intentional in finding new talent and encouraging vegans to be activists in a variety of ways. Without their generosity and belief in me, this book would not exist.

My gratitude to Jean Labo, for making me your pastry cook at such a daring time, and allowing me to take creative risks daily. Your trust in the kitchen was the best teacher. And to Jean's late husband Jim, who is missed by so many of us.

To Debora Durant, for her encouragement first to become vegan, and then to write a cookbook. You saw these things before even I did, and pressed me to pursue them.

Big gratitude to Jonathan Rowland, Gregory Nipper, and everyone at PM Press, for your initiative and persistence in bringing *Cook, Eat, Thrive* to print. It has been a pleasure working with you and being part of PM's vision.

My gratitude to Jess Deugan for her excellent icon design and ever-inspiring friendship. And to Art Heffron for his keen eye and beautiful photos.

To Dreena Burton and Dino Sarma Weierman, who I sometimes imagine sharing a kitchen with. Dreena, you've long set the standard for being a mom and vegan author, and I aspire to your thoughtfulness and creativity. Dino, your brilliance and vulnerability in the kitchen are embedded in your words, and I love that. I am fortunate to have such gifted authors lend their kind endorsements to this book.

I am ever grateful for both my mom and my dad. Their seeing me as I am—and with unwavering support—is such a remarkable thing, and has freed me to explore. And for my brother Jon, who is never without kind words for me or my food. You are all a continual source of encouragement.

For Ron, who just loves me so much and is behind everything I do. The fortune of our life together is the loveliest thing I know. And for our children, to whom I hope we leave a persistent legacy of compassion, freedom, and vibrant health. They are my best companions in the kitchen, and I'm convinced their presence on a hip or a counter is my primary source of culinary inspiration.

Thanks to God, for countless ways to express grace for people, animals, and this amazing world we all live in. It is a joy for me to practice a bit of this compassion everyday.

And especially to those who tested my recipes and graciously provided their feedback on the Vegan Freak forums: Pamela B, Lelly, Heather Blake, Sabrina Butkera, Debora Durant, Ida Fong, Mindy Getch, Vincent Guihan, Gary Loewenthal, Sandie Longs, Rachel Mandel, Beth Morrow, Christopher Plumb, Constanze Reichardt, Amy Ryan, Maralee Sanders, Andrea Weaver, and the fantastic Dino Sarma Weierman. Special thanks to tester Cassandra Greenwald, for your invaluable editorial assistance.

I am full of gratitude for everyone who has made this book what it is. And to you, the reader, for now becoming part of it.

For Ron, G, and Z.
I could not
imagine better people
to live my life with.

Introduction

Cook, Eat, Thrive

Cook

Do you remember the first thing you ever cooked?

I do. It was peach pie. I stood in the kitchen, scrawny and eight years old, as my mother helped me tumble fresh peaches into a dough-lined glass plate and flute the edges just so. Thinking of it, I can practically feel the pastry beneath my hands. And years later, the smell of a peach pie evokes a little sigh, and an involuntary upturn at the corners of my mouth.

Cooking isn't simply about the finished product but the experience of putting it all together: finding perfectly round peas at a farmer's market, kneading bread dough until it becomes stiff and elastic, and inhaling the deep fragrance of oven-fresh gingerbread. All of these things take time to learn.

My culinary education was quintessentially American: a jumble of steak-and-potatoes fundamentals, health food, junk food, and a sprinkle of international influence. (I grew up in Los Angeles, so the latter was particularly true.) As a child, my mother fed me homemade baby foods, pureed into velvety gold and green hues in the food processor. I remember eating yogurt pops mixed from aspartame and artificial chocolate flavoring, and cheese omelets made in the microwave. Cheerios and Kix were considered "sugar cereals," so

my brother and I once scaled the kitchen cabinets to lick the cloying shell from mysterious green prescription pills. Mom still cringes at the thought of this!

For celebrations, my mom was ace. Birthdays featured an assortment of themed food. My father's poker games merited bowls of hearty guacamole and fantastically mixed drinks, and picnics were graced by the most perfect potato salad. And of course, my father, who was responsible for every spaghetti noodle, pancake, and sautéed mushroom over the course of three presidential administrations.

For so many of us, these celebratory and everyday bits are an anchor. They allow us to be homemakers and international travelers, and give little rituals to display love. In the midst of such a common act, I learned what it meant to cook—not necessarily *how* to cook—but the simple significance of doing so.

Eat

Then I learned how to eat.

I remember my first visit to an Indian restaurant, my wide-eyed gaze fixed on every platter that floated by. I tilted my head back, inhaling tandoori smoke and spice, and eagerly sucking down a thick mango lassi. My sense of decorum had evaporated like the kitchen's fragrant steam, and my slack-jawed awe must have really been a sight!

I've since adopted a bit more restraint, although my otherwise demure countenance still turns giddy and starstruck in the face of new food. There is something powerful and lovely in recapturing a domestic side, and I feel it every time I eat: it is deliberate and calm, and evocative of mellow wine, honest polenta, good chocolate.

In Thailand I learned to recognize the smell of perfectly browned garlic, and to appreciate the pairing of crisp raw vegetables with cooked dishes. In Jerusalem, I eavesdropped around the corners of old city walls to discover which falafel vendor used the freshest oil. I developed habits of breakfast: biscuits in India, cherry compote in Turkey, fresh mango in Haiti.

Back home, I watched as a Turkish friend formed dough into thick rounds of *ekmek*, memorized her stippling the crust with a hundred indentations. As we sat down to bread and tea, I heard her stories of leaving home and felt again the deep connection of culture and food.

I baked wedding cakes four, five, *six* layers high, and learned how much sweeter the slices taste when celebrating a happy union. When I lived in a small apartment, I crammed guests into my kitchen for tea and chatter. In a mansion, I hosted brunches for forty. Whether we find ourselves living large or small, everyday or exotic, there are countless opportunities to come to the table.

Eating accompanies the stuff of life, whether significant or ordinary. And when that food is *good*, everything becomes full of flavor.

Thrive

And years later, I learned what it means to bring life into the act of cooking, to really thrive.

I came to veganism not out of ethical convictions or disdain of animal products, but out of desperation. After years of eating a fairly healthy diet and working as a pastry cook, my cholesterol level was a ridiculously high 327. A few days after discovering this, I found myself chatting with a friend, and mentioned that I was thinking of trying raw foods. I was referring to raw dairy, raw fish, that sort of thing. But she happened to be vegan, and pointed me toward vegan resources instead. The next day, I began eating a raw vegan diet.

After a few months, my cholesterol was reduced by half, and I felt better than ever before. Separate from the system of animal agriculture, I was able to see it really clearly, and to then decide that I wanted to be an ethical vegan. Most people first resolve to become vegan, gradually reducing their intake of animal foods. But sometimes, participation in a system prevents us from seeing things objectively. Reducing or eliminating the intake of animal products is good, but why not do it all at once? For me, going from omnivore to herbivore was really easy and enjoyable.

Eating a vegan diet is distinct from any other, in that it substantially reduces the amount of harm done to animals, people, and the world in which we live. From the way our bodies feel when properly nourished to the seas no longer taxed by overfishing, we are creating a world in which everyone and everything can thrive.

If that doesn't make food taste better, I don't know what does.

Redemption is also a vital part of eating vegan. The discipline of cooking has been historically connected to harming animals and using their products. A vegan diet completely departs from centuries of culinary harm—it gives us a fresh start. In every vegan meal, we affirm that the work of cooking and eating are fundamentally good. By separating this act from the mercilessness it once held, the whole process is redefined in a kinder way.

We're working with the best materials: fresh produce, hearty grains and legumes, rich spices, all ready for tinkering. And there's so much freedom. The rules aren't too fixed; departing from them is encouraged. I hope you'll find that here, as you develop and trust your intuition. I also hope you will discover that you really enjoy cooking, and feel confident doing it. I'm convinced domesticity is a vital thing, creating a space slow and large enough to take others into our lives. And when we adopt—even for a moment—the gastronomic and domestic practices of other cultures, we welcome them, too. This book is about creating global dishes while eating locally, bridging the gap between the exotic and the everyday...and inviting the neighbors over while you're at it.

Symbols

RAW

These foods are as close to their natural state as possible and have not been heated over 105° F.

The agave nectar and apple cider vinegar I use in this book are always raw, although this is not always noted. I include spices, oils (cold-pressed), and mustards, which are sometimes raw, sometimes not. If you are a strict raw-foodist, you may choose to omit these things from your diet.

LOW FAT

These recipes contain less than 3 grams of fat per serving (as with FDA labeling laws), and are often fat-free.

SOY-FREE

Free of all soybean products, including soybean oil, soy sauce, and fermented soy.

WHEAT-FREE

Free of all wheat products. These recipes are not all considered gluten-free, as they can contain oats, which are often dangerous to those with celiac disease.

TASTY FOR ALL

These recipes contain little or no vegan specialty ingredients, and are generally enjoyable to mainstream palates.

QUICK ● FIX

Can be prepared in 30 minutes or less.

Food Language

Many cookbooks use terms like "cheeze" or "mylk." You won't find that here.

First, those words are silly. Significant movements don't fuss with terms that merit ridicule. Vegan food isn't novel or cutesy; it's important culinary stuff, and vegan chefs these days are doing arguably some of the most inventive and tasty work around. That should be taken seriously, and should not require a separate system of naming.

More importantly, dairy or egg-laden versions of things don't deserve the monopoly on food. If we humans never consumed animal products, it's likely we would at some point create a drink made from soaked, blended nuts, or ferment that beverage into a cultured cream. Those products could rightly be called "milk" and "yogurt." When we see the word "cheese," dairy instantly comes to mind, because after years of dominance by the egg and dairy industries, exploitation is inherent in our vocabulary. These industries have plenty of control over governments and individuals. They don't deserve to have it over food as well.

Let's retrieve a bit of that power. Rather than relegate vegan fare to the fringe, accept it as a valid food choice. When talking about food, specify whether something is cow, goat, coconut, or cashew based. The vegan version is no less legitimate, and can stand up next to its animal-based cousins.

Now, on to equipment and food.

Kitchen Equipment

When it comes to kitchen equipment, use your budget and priorities as a guideline. Consider how much you cook, how often you entertain, and the importance you place on food in general. I won't spend over $15 on a pair of jeans, but I own enough All-Clad to equal the GDP of a small country. Still, some of the best equipment can be discovered at thrift stores and estate sales. Use this guide to determine whether you want to splurge or save.

You should have

Baking pans
Purchase sturdy pans at cooking supply or thrift stores. At minimum, you should have 6 and 9-inch round pans, a 9 by 4-inch loaf pan, a 9 by 9-inch square pan, a 3-quart glass casserole dish, and a 10-inch tartlet pan with a removable bottom.

Baking sheets
Look for large rimmed sheets. I prefer those free of nonstick coating, as they have greater longevity.

Blender
An inexpensive blender will handle most tasks, although it may take a bit longer. I recommend going very cheap, or upgrading to a high-speed blender straightaway.

Cake pans
These are great for roasting vegetables, holding cleaned ingredients, and of course, baking cakes. The best and most durable are found at cake supply stores.

Cast-iron skillet
A good skillet will meet many of your stovetop needs, and prices at home stores are very reasonable. Cast-iron used for years of cooking animal products will contain them, so unless you can secure a good vegan hand-me-down, purchase new. Season your cast-iron by rubbing with shortening or vegetable oil and heating in a 300° F oven for several hours.

To clean cast-iron, rinse with hot water and shake dry. Toss in a handful of coarse salt and rub with your fingertips to dislodge any attached bits. Rinse again, and wipe dry with a kitchen towel. Coat with a thin layer of vegetable oil and store in a pilot-light-heated oven to enhance the patina, if you like.

Citrus reamer
A small wooden variety—with one end a handle and the other a star-shape—is all you need.

Cutting boards
I prefer the flexible plastic ones for foods with a heavy odor, and bamboo for everything else. If you use any kind of wood, treat it frequently with a thin coating of neutral food-grade oil (olive oil is perfect).

Food processor
Any decent brand will do, provided it has a dough attachment.

Grater and rasp

A small hand grater is useful, although you can always use your food processor's attachment, if you have one. A fine zester or rasp is indispensable for removing fine shards of citrus zest, while leaving the bitter white pith behind.

Hand mixer

If you don't plan to double or triple a recipe for batter or dough, a hand mixer is suitable.

One good knife

I have a single, excellent knife. It's heavy and well balanced, with speed grooves and my name engraved by my husband. I also have others (hand-me-downs from past roommates): a long, thin knife for paring, and a cleaver for coconuts. But one excellent knife will handle most of your cutting.

Measuring cups and spoons

Look for sturdy metal construction in these indispensable kitchen pieces, as plastic can wear out quickly and leach into food. A 2-cup glass measure with a pouring lip makes measuring and combining liquid ingredients an easy task.

Mixing bowls

Choose different sizes, in a nonporous material. My favorites are old-fashioned milk glass, which is very sturdy, heat-resistant, and attractive. The best can be found at thrift stores.

Mortar and pestle

When you find the right one, it's like love, so wait for it. I discovered mine at a bustling market in Thailand, and will use it for the next thirty years. Whether you prefer wood or stone, look for sturdy construction that has a pleasant heft and comfortable feel in your hands.

Parchment paper

Parchment provides a nonstick layer that protects baked goods from scorching and sticking. Place rounds or rectangles in oiled, floured cake pans to guarantee a quick release. The parchment can also be reused at least once, making it an economical addition to your baking repertoire. Waxed paper is a fine substitution but cannot be reused.

Spatulas

Thin metal offset spatulas are just the tool for spreading frosting or freeing a muffin from its tin, and can be found at specialty kitchen and baking supply stores.

Flexible, heat-resistant silicone spatulas are essential for stirring puddings or scraping a peanut butter jar. Several firm metal ones are also useful for frosting cakes and releasing pancakes from pans.

Stainless steel cookware

You should have small and medium saucepans, a sauté pan or skillet, and a large stockpot. Look for heavy cookware with a firmly affixed handle, preferably metal, which will allow you to transfer foods directly from stovetop to oven. Discount stores often carry cookware that is excellent and sturdy. I prefer cast-iron to nonstick pans and don't own any nonstick (but don't ditch them just yet; nonstick can be useful for quick sautés and other tasks).

Steamer insert

Steamer inserts are inexpensive and easy to find. I recommend one with a handle that fits directly over a saucepan rather than resting inside of it. They cost a bit more, but are worth it, and will prevent soggy vegetables and ensure complication-free draining.

Strainer

If you have a handled steamer insert, it will conveniently double as a vegetable strainer. Otherwise, look for a lightweight handheld version.

A small, fine strainer is essential for making juices and sauces smooth.

Kitchen tongs

These make simple work of flipping pizza crusts on the grill and turning roasting red peppers over a flame, as well as for serving salads and crudités.

Vegetable peeler

A simple peeler, preferably one with a blade that swivels slightly, will do.

Whisks

Forget using a sifter; try a wire whisk to aerate dry ingredients. These are also essential for combining liquids quickly and thoroughly. I also like a small whisk for use in a 2-cup measure.

You might want

Bamboo mats

For rolling sushi.

Blowtorch

No, not a kitchen torch. A *blowtorch*. Ideal for brûléeing, they can be found for under $10 at a home improvement store, and are superior to the smaller kitchen versions.

Cocktail shaker

Stainless steel is the best choice for creating cold shaken drinks. Alternatively, use a glass jar filled with ice, and strain liquid through the slightly parted lid.

Cookie and biscuit cutters

The best and most unusual can be found at thrift and antique stores. Use an overturned glass if you don't have any on hand.

Juicer

There are three types of juicers: centrifugal, masticating, and triturating. The first two tend to be reasonably priced but produce juice that oxidizes (darkens) and loses its nutrients quickly. A triturating juicer is superior in quality, but expensive. If you frequently drink fresh juice or like to make your own nut butters, it may be worth the investment.

French pin

Unlike typical rolling pins, which feature a roller surrounding a central rod, a French pin is simply a thin wooden baton. The ends are often tapered, allowing for dent-free pastries. I highly recommend these.

Alternatively, use a long, slender glass jar, or even an aluminum can (remove the label and wipe it down first).

High-speed blender

Consider a high-speed version if you frequently make nut or seed milks and want incomparably smooth sauces, or if you want a machine that grinds grains into flour.

Melon ballers and ice cream scoops

These are useful for removing seeds from the interiors of fruits and vegetables or serving small scoops of something.

Otherwise, use spoons of various sizes to make egg-shaped portions known as *quenelles*.

Muffin tins

For cupcakes and muffins. To keep it simple, you can instead purchase paper cups reinforced with foil, which can be placed directly on a cookie sheet.

Pastry brush

Use a natural fiber paintbrush or clean fingers if you don't want to bother with a pastry brush.

Ramekins

For miniature desserts, these are just the thing. Ramekins are also handy for mixing small amounts of sauces, or keeping vinegars and spices ready to toss into a recipe.

Rice cooker

I consider this indispensable for cooking rice, grains, and even beans. If you are watchful and patient (which I am decidedly not), it isn't necessary; just use a heavy, lidded pan.

Silpat

These French nonstick silicone mats are great for creating stick-free baked goods if you don't want to keep purchasing parchment paper.

Spice grinder

Set aside a coffee grinder specifically for this purpose. A mortar and pestle is a fine substitute.

Stand mixer

Stand mixers are excellent for quantity baking. Otherwise, a hand mixer will do.

Ingredients

The Pantry and Icebox

Don't you just love the word *pantry*? It means preparedness and possibility, and the chance to make an incredible array of dishes simply because you keep the right provisions on hand. The list below represents an ideally stocked cupboard, and should allow you to make nearly anything in this book.

When stocking the icebox, select the freshest ingredients possible, and aim for quick turnaround. Produce loses its nutrients and decreases in quality on refrigeration, so frequent shopping and purchasing small quantities is ideal.

Flours and leavenings
All-purpose flour, whole wheat flour, whole wheat pastry flour, rice flour, spelt flour, kamut flour, active dry yeast, baking powder, baking soda, vital wheat gluten.

The all-purpose flour frequently called for in this book is always unbleached and organic, if possible. Store flour in airtight containers at room temperature. For larger amounts or storage longer than 3 months, wrap well and freeze. As a general rule, up to half of the amount of all-purpose flour can be substituted for another in most baked goods.

Canned and jarred foods
Beans, coconut milk, jams, crushed tomatoes, tomato sauce, tomato paste, canned fruits.

Dried fruits
Apricots, dates, raisins, shredded and flaked coconut, prunes, mango slices.

Dried fruits are best kept at room temperature to avoid condensation, but may be frozen for longer storage. Purchase sulfite-free fruits with no added sugar, if possible.

Frozen goods
Breads such as tortillas, pita, sandwich loaves, and unbaked dough, fruit for smoothies, puff pastry, stocks, vegetables, cookie dough.

Produce is usually frozen in-season, so it is preferable to use good-quality frozen stuff rather than out-of-season fresh. If you plan to cook them, frozen corn, green beans, and asparagus are comparable to fresh. I keep pizza dough and cookie dough on hand for quick suppers and freshly baked treats.

Nondairy milks
Almond, soy, hemp, rice, hazelnut, oat, raw seed milks and nut milks.

Seek out unsweetened versions if a recipe specifies it; otherwise, regular and vanilla flavors can usually be used interchangeably.

Nuts and seeds
Almonds, cashews, chia seeds, hazelnuts,

hemp seeds, macadamias, peanuts, pecans, pine nuts, pistachios, pepitas (pumpkin seeds), sesame seeds, sunflower seeds, walnuts.

To avoid stocking both raw and toasted nuts, I prefer to purchase untoasted or raw and heat them as necessary. Refrigeration protects the volatile oils in nuts and seeds and prevents them from going rancid. If keeping for over 2 months, cover tightly and place in the freezer.

Vinegars
Balsamic, fruit-flavored, red wine, rice, white wine, raw apple cider.

Condiments
Dijon mustard, barbecue sauce, hoisin sauce, soy sauce, fresh horseradish, capers, liquid smoke, miso, mayonnaise.

Always refrigerate after opening and use vegan mayonnaise.

Salts and spices
Kosher salt, sea salt, fleur de sel, black peppercorns, cayenne pepper, dried dill, ground cinnamon, whole cumin, whole nutmeg, ground allspice, curry powder, turmeric, bay leaves, cardamom, mustard seeds, ground cloves, dried basil, dried oregano, dried sage, dried thyme.

Purchase the freshest spices you can find. Ethnic markets often have quick turnover.

Sweeteners
Evaporated cane juice or sugar, brown sugar, agave nectar, maple syrup, stevia, molasses, powdered sugar, dates, simple syrup.

For the sugar listed in this book, my choice is evaporated cane juice. It is unrefined and therefore always vegan as opposed to most sugars which are refined using bone char. For liquid sweeteners, agave nectar provides a clean taste, while maple syrup and molasses lend rich, pointed flavors.

Extracts and flavorings
Vanilla, almond, and peppermint extracts, cocoa powder, flavored sugars, semisweet chocolate.

Spirits
Light and dark rum, brandy, vodka, gin, amaretto, Kahlua, Scotch whiskey, Port, sherry, tequila, vermouth, champagne, red and white vegan wines, vegan beers.

The ingredients for liqueurs tend to be consistent for decades, so remembering what isn't vegan (Irish cream or Campari, for example) is simple. Because wine and champagne formulas vary from year to year, look for those specifically labeled vegan or search the internet for an updated list.

Grains, rice, and pasta
Brown basmati rice, cornmeal, couscous, jasmine rice, rice noodles, millet, oats, pearl barley, polenta, quinoa, rye, teff, soba, udon, wheat berries, whole wheat noodles, wild rice.

Beans
Black, cannelloni, chickpeas, kidney, mung, and pinto beans, red and Le Puy lentils, various heirloom beans.

Oils
Extra virgin olive, canola, safflower, sunflower, coconut, almond, hazelnut, toasted sesame, flaxseed oil,

hempseed oil, solid vegetable shortening, margarine.

Store frequently used oils, like olive, at room temperature. Keep others in the refrigerator. Since most margarine contains animal products, any margarine referred to in the recipes is always vegan and nonhydrogenated.

Teas

English breakfast, chai, lapsang souchong, hibiscus-based herbal, chamomile, jasmine, gunpowder, sencha, rooibos.

I generally have at least thirty kinds of tea on hand. Try to at least keep a black, a green, and an herbal tea in your cupboard. Or, find one signature tea you really like. Keep it stocked, and serve it hot or iced whenever tea is called for.

Drinks

From smoothies that start the day to night-
caps that finish it, drinks announce and define
the meals we share. Whether you choose a
refreshing cocktail to enliven a party, or a sul-
try hot chocolate to share with someone you
love, these concoctions will set the tone for
your best occasions.

Basic Nut Milk

Makes about 2 cups

Commercial nondairy milks can be heavily processed and laden with sugar. This version is raw, mildly sweet, and very simple.

Use this anywhere nondairy milk is needed—it works in all of this book's recipes. For a creamier drink with a boost of omegas, add 1 teaspoon flax or chia seeds along with the nuts.

2 cups water
¼ cup almonds
¼ cup cashews

1 teaspoon agave nectar or 1 date
Pinch of sea salt

Combine all ingredients in the jar of a blender and soak at least 2 hours, or overnight in the refrigerator.

Blend as smooth as possible; this may take several minutes. Strain through a straining bag or a fine sieve into a jar, and adjust the sweetener if necessary. The milk will keep, refrigerated, for up to 3 days.

Super Seed Milk

Makes about 2 cups

Made with barley, flax (telba), or sunflower (suff), the seed- and nut-based drinks of Ethiopia are refreshingly creamy and served cold (nice over ice).

This calcium- and omega-packed version can be enjoyed over ice, on cereal, or as a base for smoothies. Unlike conventional milks, it contains no soy or nuts, and is a good choice for those avoiding these common allergens. Toss the ingredients into a blender the evening before you make it, and whiz it up in the morning. Nothing could be simpler.

2 cups water
¼ cup sunflower seeds
2 tablespoons sesame seeds
2 tablespoons shelled hemp seeds

1 tablespoon flaxseeds
1 tablespoon agave nectar or 1 date
Pinch of sea salt
Pinch of cinnamon (optional)

Combine all ingredients in the jar of a blender and soak for at least 2 hours, or overnight in the refrigerator.

Blend as smooth as possible; this may take several minutes. Strain through a straining bag or a fine sieve into a jar. The milk will keep, refrigerated, for up to 3 days.

Flaxseeds

One tablespoon of flaxseeds contains 100 percent of the recommended daily allowance of omega-3 fatty acids, as well as dietary fiber, antioxidants, lignans, and protein. They add creaminess to blended liquids and a pleasantly gooey texture to nondairy cheeses.

Golden or brown flaxseeds can be used interchangeably in any of the recipes in this book. They are nutritionally identical and are simply grown in different areas.

Orange Cream Green Smoothie

Makes 1 smoothie

Much as I love leisurely brunches, a quick and healthy smoothie is my usual morning drink. Using this flavor combination, the green taste is almost indistinguishable, made so by a fresh orange punch. It's also a great way to get more greens into children, who love its snappy green color. If you're new to green smoothies, start with a smaller amount of spinach and add more next time.

1 banana, frozen
Juice of 1 orange
½ teaspoon orange zest (just estimate; it's about a quarter of the orange's skin)

Generous handful (1 to 2 cups) spinach
½ cup water
1 cup ice

Combine all ingredients in a blender until completely smooth. Drink.

Strawberry-Apple Virgin

Makes 4 servings

This alcohol-free libation is perfect for your teetotaling celebrations. Lime juice and Granny Smith apples add tartness, while frozen strawberries are reminiscent of a daiquiri or margarita. Filled with fresh fruit and juice, it's a healthy, refreshing addition to any cocktail party.

The Virgin is best made with freshly juiced green apples. If you don't have a juicer or juice bar nearby, purchase "fresh pressed" apple juice and use the substitution below. Avoid regular filtered, pasteurized apple juice, as the end result will be completely different.

Margarita salt, for serving (optional)
1½ cups fresh green apple juice (from 3 to 4 Granny Smith apples), or 1½ cups fresh-pressed apple juice plus 1 teaspoon fresh lime or lemon juice

2 cups frozen strawberries
1½ cups ice
¼ cup fresh lime juice
½ teaspoon lime zest (about ½ a lime)
2 tablespoons agave nectar
⅛ teaspoon sea salt

Run a lime rind around the rim of four serving glasses, and dip them into the margarita salt. Transfer to the freezer to chill.

Combine everything in a blender and process until very smooth. If you prefer a thinner drink, add additional water or juice by the tablespoon. Pour into the prepared glasses and serve immediately.

For raw use raw agave nectar and unpasteurized juice

Bloody Mary

Makes 1 drink

Serve this at your next brunch: multiply the quantities by your number of guests and allow them to help themselves from a large pitcher at the table.

¾ cup tomato juice

2 tablespoons vodka

Juice of ½ lime or lemon

½ teaspoon grated fresh horseradish

Generous pinch of black pepper

Pinch of sea salt

1 to 3 dashes hot sauce

1 short celery stick, leaves included,
   for serving

Whisk together all ingredients. Serve over ice, garnished with a celery stick.

Horseradish

Horseradish is evocative of a bygone era, when vodka-soaked men wore unreasonably high pants and smoked cigarettes for breakfast.

You might not have occasion to use this assertive root often, so it can be stored in the freezer. To use, thaw slightly, shave off the brown exterior, and grate.

To make a spread perfect for slathering on your portabella burger, combine 1 tablespoon horseradish with ¼ cup mayonnaise.

Steeping Tea

Although loose tea is generally preferable to bagged, today's tea blenders are creating excellent versions of the latter. Regardless of what you choose, look for largish leaves, unbroken flowers and herbs, and no signs of moisture or deterioration.

Begin by preparing your teapot: pour about ¼ cup of near-boiling water into an empty pot and swish to distribute the heat. Meanwhile, gently spoon tea leaves into a strainer or tea ball. For each cup of tea, use 8 ounces of water and 1 level teaspoon of tea leaves. Discard the warming water in the teapot. Add strainer or tea ball to the pot, and top with fresh boiling water. Cover, and steep for the recommended amount of time. Gently remove tea. Do not press the leaves to extract residual liquid, as this will produce a brew with more tannins than the blender intended.

The caffeine in tea is water-soluble, and nearly all of it seeps into water within the first 30 seconds of brewing. To decaffeinate tea naturally, steep tea leaves in half the amount of water for just under a minute. Strain, reserving the leaves and discarding the first infusion. Proceed as usual with the process above. This technique may compromise the tea's intensity a bit, so allow an additional minute when preparing the second infusion.

Store tea in airtight containers at room temperature. Unlike coffee, which stores well in the freezer or refrigerator, tea leaves absorb moisture and odor when chilled.

Unless the packaging indicates otherwise, follow these general guidelines for brewing:

White teas
180° F
3 to 5 minutes

Red teas (rooibos)
212° F
3 minutes

Green teas
180° F
1 to 2 minutes

Black teas (plain or flavored)
212° F
3 minutes

Oolong teas (jasmine, and other partially oxidized varieties)
180° to 215° F
1 to 5 minutes

Herbals
212° F
5 minutes

Limoncello Slush

Makes 2 large drinks

Limoncello, a lemon-infused liqueur, can be made at home by soaking lemon rinds with sugar and vodka. This summery drink has the clean bite of the liqueur, without the wait.

⅓ cup fresh lemon juice (about 3 lemons)
1 teaspoon lightly packed lemon zest
3 tablespoons agave nectar or Simple
    Syrup (page 186)

3 tablespoons vodka
½ cup water
3 cups ice
Pinch of sea salt

Process all ingredients in a blender until completely smooth. Pour into 2 glasses and garnish with lemon slices, if desired.

Hibiscus Cooler

Makes 2 drinks

When the weather is hot, few things are lovelier than cold gin and tangy hibiscus over ice. Drink this rosy blend after a day of yard work, when you're covered in sweat and smudges of earth. Whether sipped on a wraparound porch or a fire escape, it tastes infinitely better when enjoyed outside.

To brew hibiscus tea, pour boiling water over dried hibiscus flowers in a ratio of 1 cup to 1 heaping teaspoon. Allow it to steep 5 minutes, strain, and chill in the refrigerator.

If you can't find loose hibiscus blossoms, substitute tea in which hibiscus is the main ingredient. (Tazo Passion or Celestial Seasonings Red Zinger are fine choices.)

2 cups cold hibiscus tea
2 ounces gin
½ teaspoon orange flower water

1 tablespoon agave nectar or Simple
    Syrup (page 186)
2 orange slices, for garnish

Combine tea, gin, orange flower water, and agave nectar or syrup in a cocktail shaker or lidded glass jar full of ice, and shake until thoroughly mixed. Strain into 2 chilled, ice-filled glasses. Serve immediately, garnished with orange slices.

White Melon Sangria

Makes 2 large pitchers full

Spend some time at a farmer's market this summer, walking among the juice-heavy fruit and grassy herbs, and choose several melons in blushing shades of pale green, orange, and pink. After you've scooped out enough melon for the recipe, hack the rest up roughly. Stand outside and eat heartily, sweet juice dripping down your forearms, no thought to the nearest sink.

For the wine, choose a good white: crisp pinot grigio, chardonnay, or pinot blanc; or choose gewürztraminer or riesling for a sweeter drink.

Some Sangrians (hardcore sangria makers, that is—we're working on a constitution and other acts of nationbuilding) macerate the fruit in alcohol overnight. I skip this step because—apart from taking hours longer—it muddles the idea of sangria for me, infusing the fruit with alcohol instead of the other way around.

3 cups melon balls, from a combination
   of different melons
1 (750 ml) bottle white wine

1 (750 ml) bottle white grape juice
4 cups sparkling water
Juice of 1 lime

Gently combine all ingredients in a large pitcher and refrigerate until thoroughly chilled. To serve, fill the largest wine glasses or tumblers you have with some ice. Ladle in the sangria, being sure to include several pieces of the colorful melon in each glass.

White Peach Sangria

Substitute 3 white peaches, very thinly sliced, for the melon, and lemon for the lime. Continue and serve as directed.

Dirty Martini

Makes 1 drink (double or triple as needed)

Gin is ideal in many drinks, but for an exceptional martini, vodka—"dirtied" with olive juice—is just right.

- 1 ounce good-quality vodka
- 1 to 2 drops vermouth
- Dribble of olive juice

- 3 to 5 large pimento-stuffed green olives

Combine all ingredients except the olives in an ice-filled cocktail shaker or glass jar. Strain into a martini glass, add olives, and serve.

Moroccan Mint Tea

Makes 2 servings (double or triple as needed)

While living in Jerusalem, I regularly visited the long row of shopkeepers' stalls in the Old City, eventually becoming acquainted with a number of merchants there. We students were apparent immediately: sweaty, smiling westerners clad in cargo pants and sandals, usually with satchels slung across our unshowered bodies. Unlike tourists, we stayed for months or years, and became familiar with the dry, bright surroundings. On entering a merchant's shop, we were often greeted with a small cup of hot, sweetened mint tea. It seemed odd, considering the heat. Now I recognize its value (hot drinks encourage sweating, which cools the body), and a cup of this steaming mint infusion is one of my favorite summer drinks.

- 2 heaping teaspoons loose green tea (any green variety will do)
- 2 cups boiling water

- 2 rounded tablespoons sugar
- 4 sprigs fresh mint

Place tea leaves in a teapot or saucepan. Pour boiling water over, cover, and steep for 5 minutes.

　　Strain into another pot containing the sugar and half the mint, stirring until the sugar is dissolved. Pour into 2 small cups, and serve immediately, garnished with the remaining mint.

Venezuelan Hot Chocolate

Makes 4 servings

Rich, dark, and spicy.

4 cups almond milk
1 whole star anise or ½ teaspoon
   whole fennel seeds
2 allspice berries or ¼ teaspoon
   ground allspice
1 cinnamon stick or ¼ teaspoon
   ground cinnamon

¾ teaspoon orange zest
1 tablespoon brown sugar or
   maple syrup
6 ounces semisweet chocolate,
   roughly chopped
¼ cup dark rum

Combine the almond milk, anise, allspice, cinnamon, zest, and brown sugar or maple syrup in a medium saucepan over medium heat. Cook, stirring, until the mixture just begins to boil. Lower the heat and simmer for 5 minutes. Remove from the heat, cover, and allow it to steep for 10 minutes.

Strain the mixture into another saucepan. Add the chocolate and rum, and return to the stove over low heat. Whisk until chocolate is completely melted. Serve hot.

Mexican Hot Chocolate

4 cups almond milk
¼ teaspoon ground cinnamon
Pinch of cayenne powder

1 tablespoon brown or granulated sugar
6 ounces semisweet chocolate,
   roughly chopped

Heat almond milk, cinnamon, cayenne, and sugar over medium heat. When bubbles appear at the edges, reduce the heat to low. Add chocolate, whisking gently until completely melted. Serve hot.

Breakfasts and Brunches

Over the years, I have lent my pajama-clad loyalty to various breakfasts: oatmeal with caramelized apples, scrambled tofu on sourdough, green smoothies, toast and tea...I'll favor one for weeks, then move on to the next, determined the new breakfast is my absolute favorite. The beauty of morning meals is that they start fresh every day, allowing for new choices each time.

Many of the recipes that follow are made to withstand the slow morning haze that settles over kitchens everywhere, and can be prepared in advance or quickly tossed together.

Tropical Granola

Makes about 4 cups

Kissed with vanilla and coconut, and studded with macadamias, this granola is a sublime taste of the tropics. Sit on your porch and have a bowl. You'll believe you've been transported to Hawaii, where ginger, mac nuts, and pineapple grow casually in backyards.

Left whole, the gingered macadamias make a lovely and indulgent snack or holiday gift.

½ teaspoon minced fresh ginger

1 tablespoon agave nectar

¾ cups macadamia nuts, coarsely chopped (Brazil nuts are a fine substitution)

3 cups old-fashioned rolled oats

⅓ cup coconut or vegetable oil

⅔ cup agave nectar

1 teaspoon vanilla extract

¾ cup dried flaked coconut (see note below)

¾ cup dried diced pineapple

Heat the oven to 350° F. Lightly oil a large, rimmed baking sheet.

In a small bowl, toss together the ginger, agave nectar, and macadamia nuts, stirring to coat. Place the mixture on the prepared baking sheet, transfer to the oven, and toast, stirring every 2 to 3 minutes. The macadamias should be a bit moist to the touch, and a pale golden color. This will take 6 to 10 minutes. Remove from the oven and set aside to cool and dry. Keep the baking sheet within reach, as you'll use it again to bake the granola. Reduce the heat to 250° F.

In a large bowl, stir together oats, oil, agave nectar, and vanilla. Spread evenly on prepared baking sheet, and bake 65 to 75 minutes, stirring every 15 minutes or so.

Remove the granola from the oven and allow it to cool completely. Break into pieces by hand. Stir in the gingered macadamias, flaked coconut, and pineapple chunks.

Store in an airtight container in the cupboard, refrigerator, or freezer.

Coconut and Coconut Oil

Be sure to use flaked rather than shredded coconut in this recipe. While both can be found unsweetened, larger flakes are more suitable.

Once believed to be extremely unhealthy, coconut oil is actually high in fatty acids and has antimicrobial properties. Consumption of unprocessed coconut oil has also been linked to a reduced risk of heart disease. It adds a luxurious flavor to foods and can be substituted for shortening or oil in equal parts in most recipes.

Virgin, unrefined coconut oil comes from fresh coconuts and has a distinct coconut flavor. It can be substituted for margarine in any of the recipes in this book.

Refined oil is extracted from dried coconut meat and lacks the health benefits of unprocessed oil. It has a higher smoking point, and is suitable for frying or other high-heat cooking methods.

Blueberry-Flax Granola

Makes about 6 cups

It's simple to make your own breakfast cereal, and homemade granola is much more economical than store-bought. An afternoon of cereal-making is well spent and will fill your home with the wonderful aroma of ripe blueberries. Enlist the help of a nearby child, if you like. Granola is a great introduction to cooking.

If you don't have all of the spices, just omit what you're missing.

This recipe doubles excellently.

3 cups old-fashioned rolled oats

1 cup crisped rice cereal (brown rice version if available)

½ cup raw cashews, coarsely chopped

⅓ cup golden or brown flaxseeds

½ cup fresh or frozen blueberries

¼ cup vegetable oil

⅔ cup agave nectar or maple syrup

2 tablespoons cornstarch dissolved in ¼ cup cold water

1 teaspoon vanilla extract

¼ teaspoon ground cardamom

¼ teaspoon ground nutmeg

¼ teaspoon ground fennel

¼ teaspoon sea salt

1 cup dried blueberries (preferably the crispy sort)

Heat the oven to 250° F. Lightly oil a large, rimmed baking sheet or several cake pans of any shape.

In a large bowl, combine the oats, crisped rice cereal, cashews, and flaxseeds, and set aside. In a blender or food processor, process the fresh or frozen blueberries, oil, agave nectar, cornstarch mixture, vanilla extract, spices, and sea salt until just combined. Pour into the dry mixture, and stir well.

Spread evenly onto the prepared baking sheet. Bake for 65 to 75 minutes, stirring every 15 minutes or so to prevent uneven browning. The mixture will be fairly moist for much of the baking, then will turn pale golden when nearly done. If you're not sure of doneness, remove a chunk and taste after it rests for a moment. The granola will crisp further on cooling, so keep this in mind.

Remove from the heat and allow it to cool slightly. While still warm, break or stir into chunks. When granola has cooled completely, stir in dried blueberries.

Store in an airtight container in the cupboard, refrigerator, or freezer.

Savory Farina

Makes 2 breakfast servings

Growing up, my father rose early to prepare wheat cereal, and I woke to steaming bowls of the stuff. He was a single dad and always found a moment to talk over the salty, comforting porridge before running off to work.

Since then, I've been convinced grits and farina should be savory, rather than sweet.

To the basic version, you can add chopped mushrooms, onions, or any other vegetable you like when sautéing the garlic, and cook 4 to 6 minutes before adding the herbs.

The cereal can be made using quick-cooking or regular farina, or by substituting grits.

1 teaspoon margarine or olive oil
3 cloves garlic, minced
¼ teaspoon ground black pepper
⅛ teaspoon thyme
⅛ teaspoon oregano
2 cups water
½ cup farina
½ teaspoon sea salt

1 teaspoon margarine, for serving (optional)
½ cup unsweetened nondairy milk (I prefer almond)
2 green onions, thinly sliced, white parts included
Dash of paprika, for serving

Heat a medium saucepan over medium heat. Add margarine or olive oil and garlic and cook, stirring constantly, until the garlic just begins to darken, about 1 minute. Add the pepper, thyme, and oregano and cook 30 seconds more.

Pour in the water, scraping the bottom of the saucepan to remove any sticky bits. Bring the mixture to a low boil, and add the farina in a steady stream, whisking swiftly to prevent lumps. Whisk in sea salt. Cook, and keep whisking, until the cereal has thickened, about 2 minutes. Remove from the heat and adjust the seasonings if necessary.

Pour the farina into two bowls and dot with margarine. Evenly divide the milk between bowls. Sprinkle the green onions over them, add the paprika, and serve hot.

To serve as leftovers, slowly reheat the refrigerated farina, adjusting the consistency with a bit of nondairy milk or water.

Alternate serving suggestions: the farina can also be spread ½ to ¾ inch thick on a plate before refrigerating, then fried or baked like polenta. Heat 1 teaspoon olive oil in a cast-iron skillet, cut cooled farina into slices, and cook until browned on both sides. Alternatively, bake in a 350° F oven until golden. Smother with sautéed mushrooms and onions or marinara sauce for supper.

Buttermilk Pancakes

Makes 10 to 12 pancakes

This is the thing to serve at 2 a.m., when friends have stumbled into your small apartment after an evening of imbibing. The pancakes are quick and easy to whisk together, even in a half-tipsy condition. And there's a charming innocence in asking, "Can I make you some pancakes?" that has the power to remove hours of alcohol-tinged debauchery. Eat them leaning against your kitchen sink and laughing, preferably with strong coffee.

Equipment

To effortlessly release the pancakes before flipping, you'll need a very thin metal spatula. It should be wide enough to slide under the pancake, and flexible for easy handling.

1 teaspoon vegetable oil
1 cup nondairy milk
½ cup coconut milk or soy creamer
1 tablespoon apple cider vinegar
½ cup water
1 tablespoon agave nectar or
    maple syrup

1 teaspoon vanilla
1½ cups all-purpose flour
2 teaspoons baking powder
¼ teaspoon baking soda
¼ teaspoon sea salt
Margarine, for serving

Heat a cast-iron skillet over medium-high heat. Brush lightly with the vegetable oil.

In a bowl or 2-cup measure, combine the milks, vinegar, water, agave or maple syrup, and vanilla and allow it to sit for 5 minutes. Meanwhile, whisk together the flour, baking powder, baking soda, and sea salt in a medium bowl. Pour the liquid mixture into the dry and mix with a spatula, using a light hand to prevent tough pancakes. The batter will bubble up some; give it a good stir after this happens to dissipate any lumps.

Pour batter into the prepared pan using a ½ cup measure, spreading it slightly. When bubbles begin to form and burst on top, slide a thin spatula underneath and release the pancake all around. It's likely the cakes will stick a bit, but a quick loosening makes them manageable. Flip the cake, and continue to cook until slightly golden on the bottom, about 1 minute more.

Stack high on a plate, with smears of margarine between the cakes. Serve warm, topped with syrup, peanut butter, chocolate sauce...

Waffles

These make excellent waffles with a crisp exterior and fluffy interior. Simply prepare as directed and cook in a waffle-maker according to the manufacturer's instructions.

Chocolate Chip Pancakes or Waffles

Add ⅔ cup miniature chocolate chips with the dry mixture, tossing well to coat. Continue with recipe as directed.

These are particularly good—and very pretty—topped with raspberry jam and a dusting of cocoa powder.

Blueberry Pancakes

Gently rinse 1 cup of fresh blueberries. Once the pancake has been poured into the pan, drop 8 to 10 blueberries directly into the batter. Wait for the bubbles to burst, then flip and continue to cook as directed.

Spiced Pear or Apple Pancakes

Peel and core 2 firm pears or apples. Slice the fruit crosswise into ¼-inch-thick rings, and toss them together in a bowl with: 1 tablespoon maple syrup, ¼ teaspoon cinnamon, ⅛ teaspoon ground ginger, and ⅛ teaspoon fresh ground nutmeg.

Heat and oil the skillet as directed. For each pancake, place a fruit ring in the middle of the skillet and allow it to cook, undisturbed, for 1 minute. Flip, then ladle ⅓ cup batter into the center of the ring, allowing it to overflow slightly. Using a small metal spatula, spread the batter evenly over the fruit, making a concentric ring of batter around it. From the center outward, you should have a smallish pancake center, a ring of spiced pear or apple, and a ring of pancake. Cook and flip as directed.

Serve with maple syrup and a dollop of vanilla nondairy yogurt or whipped coconut cream with nutmeg or cinnamon mixed in.

Perfect Potatoes

Makes 2 servings (double or triple as needed)

These potatoes bear no resemblance to the wrinkled, oil-saturated bits that often clutter breakfast plates. Instead, they bake into crisp, golden morsels perfect for any meal. I make them in large quantities to enjoy throughout the week: serve the first batch at brunch, then toss the leftovers into a breakfast burrito, or smash into croquettes with legumes, vegetables, and seasonings.

Parboiling potatoes reduces cooking time, and enables you to prepare them up to several days in advance. Unlike raw potatoes, they won't brown when in contact with air—particularly nice if you're pressed for time and don't want to occupy the oven too long.

1 pound potatoes (about 2 medium), cut into ¾-inch chunks	1 tablespoon fresh rosemary, or 1 teaspoon dried
1 tablespoon olive oil	½ teaspoon sea salt
1½ teaspoons all-purpose flour	¼ teaspoon fresh pepper

Place potatoes in cold salted water to cover, and cook over medium-high heat until just slightly tender, 15 to 20 minutes. Reduce the heat slightly if the potatoes begin to boil over.

While cooking the potatoes, prepare the oven and pan. The key to perfect potatoes is a really hot pan, so ensure enough time for the metal to get scorching hot. Heat the largest pan you have (I prefer a giant cake pan) in the oven at 450° F. Several cast-iron or nonstick skillets would also work. You want the potatoes to sizzle against, rather than adhere to, the surface.

Meanwhile, make the coating. Whisk together olive oil, flour, rosemary, sea salt, and pepper until it's a nice, emulsified slurry. Pour this over the parboiled potatoes, stirring to coat and blur the edges a bit. Spread evenly in the piping hot pan, taking care not to burn your fingers. Bake 20 to 30 minutes, stirring every 10 minutes or so for even browning. When done, the potatoes should be fork-tender and very crisp. Serve immediately.

You can also dish up the potatoes as a side for supper, along with a roasted portabella mushroom and some sautéed greens. Tossed with dressing, they are an excellent and substantial addition to cold salads.

Potatoes

Regardless of the variety, choose firm, minimally blemished potatoes. Store in a cool, dark area; a basket atop the refrigerator or in a pantry is ideal. Just before using, remove any sprouted eyes or blemishes with a paring knife and scrub clean under hot running water.

Quick Scrambled Tofu

Makes 4 servings

Serve this fast, protein-rich breakfast with potatoes and sautéed tomatoes, in a breakfast burrito, or on its own. To add a different character to the scramble, replace the sea salt, paprika, turmeric, cumin, and pepper with one of the spice rubs on page 70.

1 tablespoon olive oil
1 medium onion, finely diced
4 cloves garlic, minced
1 pound firm or extra firm tofu,
    drained and patted dry
2 tablespoons nutritional yeast

1 teaspoon sea salt
1 teaspoon paprika
½ teaspoon turmeric
½ teaspoon ground cumin
½ teaspoon freshly ground pepper

Heat the olive oil in a cast-iron skillet over medium-high heat. Toss in the onion and garlic, then crumble the tofu over it, squeezing it through your fingers to break it up into small pieces. Cook, stirring, for 2 minutes. Add the nutritional yeast, sea salt, paprika, turmeric, cumin, and pepper. Continue stirring, until the mixture is well combined and the spices are incorporated, about 2 minutes. Cook it for 4 to 6 minutes more, until the onions are tender.

Tofu Brouillé (French-Style Scrambled Tofu)

The French prefer a creamier scramble. The addition of tahini and nondairy yogurt or mayonnaise gives it a luscious, satiny finish.

Omit the cumin. When finished cooking, remove from the heat and stir in 1 teaspoon tahini mixed with 1 tablespoon unsweetened nondairy yogurt or mayonnaise. If using mayonnaise, reduce overall salt by ¼ teaspoon.

This is delicious drizzled with truffle oil and served on whole-grain toast.

Simple Breakfast Ideas

Since vegans cannot live on lattes alone, spend a few extra minutes in the kitchen preparing a proper meal that will see you through the day.

Seared Breakfast Burritos

The burritos are excellent at warm room temperature; heat the fillings in advance for a warmer version. Don't worry if you don't have the exact amounts called for—this isn't a precise sort of recipe.

½ recipe Quick Scrambled
Tofu (page 35)
½ recipe Frijoles Mezclados
(page 105)
½ recipe Perfect Potatoes
(page 34)

4 to 6 whole wheat or white tortillas
1 cup good jarred salsa
Salsa, cilantro, and guacamole,
for serving (optional)

Heat an ungreased cast-iron skillet or grill pan. While it heats, prepare the burritos.

Place a tortilla on a work surface and fill with about ½ cup Scrambled Tofu, ½ cup Frijoles Mezclados, and several tablespoons salsa. Tuck in the sides and tightly roll into a burrito.

Place each burrito in the hot skillet and allow it to it for cook to a golden brown, about 3 minutes. Flip and cook for 3 minutes on the other side. The burritos will be crisp and toasty.

Yogurt Parfait

Layer nondairy yogurt, granola (try the Blueberry-Flax Granola, page 30), and berries in a pretty glass, repeating to make two layers. Top with more berries and fresh mint.

Fruit-Topped Oatmeal

Cook apples or peaches with a bit of brown sugar and a flavorful oil, such as hazelnut, or margarine until softened and lightly golden. Serve over oatmeal or steel-cut oats (see the Guide to Grains, page 162) and sprinkle with omega-rich walnuts.

Tofu Scramble Muffin

Layer an English muffin with Quick Scrambled Tofu (page 35), Seitan Bacon (page 41), and fresh sliced tomato or spinach leaves. Split halves of Buttermilk Biscuits (page 37) make an excellent sandwich bread as well.

Blended Raw Chai

For caffeine-free energy, blend about 2 cups Basic Nut Milk (page 17) with 3 large dates, ½ teaspoon ground cinnamon, ¼ teaspoon ground cloves, and a generous pinch of cardamom. Serve over ice, or add 2 cups of ice cubes, and continue blending until frothy.

Frugal Breakfast

Put leftover rice to good use by frying it simply with oil, sea salt, and fresh garlic. Or toss cooked brown rice with peanut butter and raisins for a protein- and iron-rich meal.

Buttermilk Biscuits

Makes 9 to 12 biscuits

These are quick to put together, and the dough can be made in advance and refrigerated. The key to light, fluffy biscuits and scones is to work the dough as little as you can manage, preventing the development of gluten. The more the dough is handled, the tougher it will become, so use a light hand. It's also important to keep the ingredients as cold as possible, using the freezer method below. Following these tips will yield tender, flaky biscuits that can only be improved by a dunking in Southern-Style Gravy (page 40).

¾ cup nondairy milk

1 tablespoon apple cider vinegar

2 cups all-purpose flour

2 teaspoons baking powder

½ teaspoon baking soda

½ teaspoon sea salt

3 tablespoons very cold margarine, cut into small pieces

3 tablespoons cold nonhydrogenated shortening, cut into small pieces

Nondairy milk (optional, for a deeper color)

Heat the oven to 450° F. Have a large, ungreased baking sheet ready.

Combine nondairy milk and vinegar and set aside while you get on with the dough.

In a large bowl, whisk together the flour, baking powder, baking soda, and sea salt. Place in the freezer while you measure the shortening. Using a pastry cutter or fork, cut in the margarine and shortening until the texture resembles something between peas and bread crumbs. Return to the freezer for several minutes, or up to 30.

Pour the liquid in, and—using a light hand—briefly agitate the mixture until everything is almost moistened. Scrape the sides of the bowl with a flexible spatula, folding the dough together until nearly all loose flour is part of the dough. If making the dough in advance, form into a ½-inch-high disk, wrap in plastic, and refrigerate for up to 2 days.

Turn the dough out onto a lightly floured surface, and pat or roll to ½-inch thickness. Dip the edge of a biscuit cutter or glass in flour, and cut biscuits from the dough. Reroll the scraps only once. Alternatively, shape the dough into a large square ½ inch thick, and cut into squares 2½ inches wide.

Place 2 inches apart on the baking sheet, or almost touching for biscuits with soft sides. If you like, brush with nondairy milk. Bake until puffed and golden, 10 to 12 minutes. Serve hot.

Gluten

Gluten, contained in the endosperm of most grains, is what makes pizza crusts and soft pretzels desirably chewy. When flour—in combination with liquid—is agitated, the gluten develops and enhances a dough's strength. This quality, however, is not preferred for all baked goods.

For light, airy foods (biscuits and scones, cakes, or muffins), thoroughly mix liquid and dry ingredients *separately*, then stir minimally once combined. The gluten won't be activated much, and the crumb will remain tender. Keeping ingredients cold and first coating the flour in fat—as with biscuits and scones—further enhances this effect.

For chewy breads with some heft (pizza dough, unleavened flatbreads, or cinnamon rolls), knead or process the finished dough well. This allows the gluten to develop, resulting in a more elastic texture. Breads with a high gluten content often shrink or tear when shaped too aggressively, so allow them to rest.

Peach-Almond Pain Ressuscité

Makes 4 servings

Pain perdu, the true name for French toast, literally translates to "lost bread," and I think it's a shame to regard anything so heavenly as having given up its soul.

This is what I imagine French toast should be: heavy slices of custard-soaked bread cooked over a hot skillet until golden on the outside, creamy inside. Topped with amaretto syrup, fresh peaches, and almonds, it truly is "resurrected bread."

¾ cup almond or other nondairy milk

½ cup coconut milk

½ cup nondairy yogurt (or ½ cup additional coconut milk plus 1 teaspoon vinegar)

1 tablespoon maple syrup (any liquid or granulated sweetener will do)

1 tablespoon amaretto (optional)

½ teaspoon almond extract

¼ teaspoon sea salt

Margarine or oil, for the cooking surface

8 slices sturdy bread (French or leftover Challah, page 46, are ideal; white or sourdough are fine choices)

¾ cup maple syrup

1 tablespoon amaretto

2 fresh juicy peaches (or use apricots if they're in season)

¼ cup slivered or coarsely chopped almonds

In a wide, shallow pan or dish, whisk together almond milk, coconut milk, nondairy yogurt, maple syrup, amaretto, almond extract, and sea salt. The custard will be thick. Place bread in the pan, turning once to cover completely. Allow it to it for absorb the liquid for at least 15 minutes and up to 1 hour.

Heat a cast-iron skillet or griddle over medium-high heat. Run a bit of margarine or oil over the surface. Take a slice of bread from the custard, using the edge of the pan or dish to remove excess liquid. Place in skillet or on griddle, and cook the bread for a minute or so, peeking underneath to check for doneness. When the bottom is golden with patches of brown, flip. Continue cooking until both sides are golden. Keep cooked slices warm in a 200° F oven, or simply cover with a clean kitchen towel.

To serve, stir the amaretto into the maple syrup and set aside. Assemble pain on a plate in overlapping slices. Thinly slice peaches and mound them across the center. Scatter almonds atop the peaches and drizzle syrup over everything. Then hurry into the next room with your plate of velvety goodness, ready to receive accolades.

Coconut Pineapple Macadamia Pain

Omit almond extract, and replace amaretto with dark rum.

Soak and cook the bread as directed. Substitute ½ medium pineapple, cut into ½-inch chunks, for the peaches. Instead of the amaretto syrup, combine ⅓ cup maple syrup with ⅓ cup coconut milk, and drizzle over. Top with ¼ cup chopped macadamia nuts.

Banana-Pecan French Toast

Omit amaretto and almond extract. Instead of the peaches, amaretto syrup, and almonds, top with 2 sliced bananas, plain maple syrup, and ¼ cup roughly chopped pecans.

Grand Marnier French Toast

Omit almond extract and substitute 1 tablespoon Grand Marnier for the amaretto. Add 1 tablespoon orange zest to the custard. Serve with fresh raspberries and dust with powdered sugar.

Pain Perdu aux Neufchatel et Marmalade

Substitute vanilla extract for almond extract. Spread half of the cooked slices with Chèvre (page 64) or nondairy cream cheese, and the other half with orange marmalade. Gently press the toast together and cut in half to serve. Top with fresh sliced strawberries and maple syrup.

Southern-Style Gravy

Makes about 3½ cups

A fine vegan gravy can be made simply, by mixing a béchamel of fat and flour, then whisking in vegetable stock.

This is entirely different: a creamy pale version, made protein-rich with beans and savory with herbs. It's ideal over biscuits and scrambled tofu, but wouldn't be altogether awful on mashed potatoes or a roast, either.

1 teaspoon olive oil
1 medium onion, diced
4 cloves garlic, minced
8 ounces mushrooms, finely chopped
½ teaspoon fennel seeds
¼ teaspoon dried thyme
¼ teaspoon black peppercorns
⅛ teaspoon dried rosemary
⅛ teaspoon dried sage

1 (16-ounce) can great northern or other white beans, drained and rinsed
1 tablespoon all-purpose flour
¼ cup cashew butter (or ⅓ cup cashews, soaked overnight, drained, and blended smooth)
1 teaspoon sea salt
½ cup plus 1 cup water

In a cast-iron skillet over medium heat, combine the olive oil, onion, garlic, and mushrooms. Cook, stirring constantly, until vegetables are slightly browned, 10 to 12 minutes. If they begin to stick but aren't yet soft and translucent, reduce the heat. Otherwise, don't mind the browned bits. In a mortar and pestle, crush together the fennel, thyme, black peppercorns, rosemary, and sage. Set aside.

Meanwhile, in a blender, combine the beans, flour, cashew butter, sea salt, and ½ cup of the water, processing until completely smooth. Reduce the heat to low. Pour the bean mixture into the vegetables along with the reserved spice mixture, and whisk together, scraping up any browned vegetables on the bottom. Add the remaining 1 cup water, and continue whisking until the mixture thickens slightly, about 5 minutes. If you find it too thick, add water by the tablespoonful until it reaches the desired consistency.

Serve hot, or cover and refrigerate for up to 4 days.

Seitan Bacon

Makes 8 ounces

There are so many uses for this: serve alongside scrambled tofu, pancakes, and all that. Chop it up and add to a wrap, filled with roasted tomatoes and arugula, and slathered in Tahini-Lemon Sauce (page 76). Thinly slice and toss with cooked pasta, olive oil, and garlic. Layer on an English muffin or biscuit, topped with scrambled tofu and gravy...

8 ounces seitan, sliced into ⅛-inch thick strips

3 tablespoons soy sauce

1 tablespoon neutral vegetable oil

1 tablespoon maple syrup

2 cloves garlic, smashed with the side of a knife

¼ teaspoon liquid smoke

Dash of cayenne pepper (optional)

Press seitan strips between paper towels to remove as much moisture as possible.

In a large bowl or shallow pan, whisk together everything except the seitan. Add seitan, cover, and marinate at room temperature for 2 to 4 hours, or refrigerate overnight.

Place a baking sheet inside the oven and heat to 450° F. Shake excess marinade from seitan. Working quickly and carefully, open oven and place strips on the hot sheet. Kitchen tongs are an excellent tool for this, and will spare your fingers. Bake until crisp on the bottom, about 8 minutes. Flip with kitchen tongs, and return to oven until well browned on both sides, 5 to 8 minutes more.

The seitan will keep, refrigerated, for up to a week.

Red Pepper–Chèvre Frittata

Makes 4 largish or 6 smaller servings

Tart Chèvre balances the sweetness of red pepper in this comforting breakfast dish. Add up to 2 cups chopped mixed vegetables to boost its nutritional content. Regular (Chinese-style) tofu can be substituted for silken, giving the frittata a less smooth, more substantial texture.

1 (12.3-ounce) package silken tofu
¼ cup all-purpose flour
¼ cup nutritional yeast
¼ cup water
1 tablespoon fresh lemon juice
1 teaspoon baking powder
¼ teaspoon turmeric
¼ teaspoon ground cumin
¼ teaspoon paprika

½ teaspoon sea salt
¼ cup loosely packed fresh basil
    leaves, coarsely chopped
1 red pepper, diced
½ cup Chèvre (page 64) cut into
    roughly ½-inch pieces
1 tablespoon olive or other vegetable
    oil, for skillet

Heat the oven to 375° F.

In a blender or food processor, combine silken tofu, flour, nutritional yeast, water, fresh lemon juice, baking powder, turmeric, cumin, paprika, and sea salt. Process until completely smooth, scraping down the sides as necessary.

Transfer to a medium bowl, and fold in the basil, red pepper, and Chèvre.

Heat a large cast-iron skillet over medium-high heat. Add oil and rotate pan to distribute evenly. Pour in batter, smoothing the top. Cook on the stovetop until slightly firm, 8 to 10 minutes.

Transfer the frittata to the preheated oven. Bake 15 to 20 minutes, until the top is golden and puffed slightly. Allow it to it for set for 5 to 10 minutes before serving.

Leftovers make a lovely lunch, cold or at room temperature, with a green salad alongside.

Breads

Baking bread is both art and science. There's a bit of precision involved—we're dealing with chemical reactions, after all—but at the heart of it, crafting a satisfying loaf is a very creative act.

This chapter includes yeasted, quick, and flat breads, giving you a variety of mediums in which to practice. Once you feel comfortable with a technique, make the bread your own by adding your favorite herbs, flavors, or toppings.

Pizza Dough

Makes 4 individual or 2 12-inch pizzas

This dough is incredibly versatile and can be used for pizza, calzones, dumplings, or even dessert pizza (use a neutral oil, rather than olive).

An additional bit of wheat gluten gives the dough more malleability when shaping, and a nice chewiness when baked; don't be tempted to omit it. You can replace up to half the all-purpose flour with buckwheat, whole wheat, kamut, brown rice, rye, or spelt flours.

1⅓ cups room-temperature water

1 package active dry yeast (2¼ teaspoons or ¼ ounces)

Pinch of sugar

3½ cups all-purpose flour

2 tablespoons vital wheat gluten

1 tablespoon sea salt

1 teaspoon sugar or other granulated sweetener

1 tablespoon olive oil

Additional water, as necessary

In a medium bowl or 2-cup measure, combine the water, yeast, and sugar. Allow it to it for stand and proof while you prepare the flour mixture.

In the bowl of a food processor or standing mixer with a dough hook, combine flour, wheat gluten, sea salt, and sweetener. If you don't have a food processor, you may also combine the ingredients with a small hand mixer and then, once incorporated, transfer the mixture to a bowl and knead by hand for 8 to 10 minutes until dough reaches the proper texture.

After 5 minutes or so, the yeast should be mostly dissolved and slightly frothy on top. With the food processor or mixer running, slowly pour in the yeast mixture, then drizzle in the olive oil. Process for several minutes, until the dough cleans the sides completely and is fairly stiff and smooth in consistency. Be careful not to let the dough get too warm, particularly when using a food processor.

Shape the dough into a ball and place into a well-oiled bowl, turning once to coat. Cover with a clean kitchen towel and allow it to it for rest in a warm, draft-free place. If your climate is particularly dry, cover loosely with plastic wrap instead. Allow it to double in size; this will take 45 to 90 minutes, depending on temperature, altitude, and so on.

Punch down the dough in the center, then gather the sides, deflating the mass. Divide into 2 or 4 portions, and allow them to rest for 15 minutes before shaping and baking.

Use in Grilled Pizza (page 142), Rosemary-Fig Focaccia (page 58), or as desired.

If preparing the dough in advance, simply refrigerate or freeze in a plastic bag after punching down and dividing. Bring to cool room temperature before using.

> ## Yeast
>
> Yeast is a living organism (yes, it *is* vegan), and lifeless yeast results in bread that doesn't rise. "Proofing" yeast is simply making sure the yeast is active. To do this, add a pinch of sweetener when dissolving dry yeast in liquids. Wait 5 minutes. If the mixture is slightly frothy on top, the yeast is active. If not, feed it another pinch of sugar, and wait 5 minutes more. If the top of the liquid is flat, it's time to start over with fresh yeast.

Sweet Potato Challah

Makes 1 loaf

Challah reminds me of Shabbat dinners while at school in Jerusalem. On those evenings, the students all gathered together, and the everyday dining hall seemed sacred and beautiful in the shifting light.

Walking through the cobbled streets after the meal, Sabbath candles still shone from windows, and a quiet lull settled over the neighborhood. Despite its heaviness, the air carried the aroma of challah, the Sabbath loaves. It was unimaginable that this was a place of unrest during the day.

You don't have to be observant to enjoy the rich heft of this artful braid. Its melt-in-the-mouth quality and faint sweetness will make you feel at once calm and indulgent, down to the last crumb.

Dough

⅓ cup water, at room temperature

1 package active dry yeast (2½ teaspoons or 1¼ ounces)

1 cup nondairy milk

4 tablespoons margarine, melted and cooled slightly

½ cup sweet potato puree, or cooked mashed sweet potato

4½ cups all-purpose flour

½ cup sugar

2 tablespoons vital wheat gluten

¼ teaspoon sea salt

Wash

1 tablespoon nondairy milk

1 teaspoon maple syrup or agave nectar

½ teaspoon margarine, melted

1 tablespoon nigella (black caraway), sesame, or poppy seeds

In a small bowl, combine the water, yeast, and a small pinch of sugar to proof the yeast; after 2 to 5 minutes it should appear slightly foamy. While waiting, whisk together the milk, margarine, and sweet potato. Stir in the yeast mixture, and set aside.

Place the flour, sugar, wheat gluten, and sea salt in the bowl of a food processor. On the dough setting, pulse dry ingredients several times. With the processor running, slowly pour the liquid mixture into the feed tube. Pulse until the dough clumps together and begins to clean the sides of the processor. Don't allow the dough to overheat, since this will kill the yeast and prevent rising. Alternatively, use a handheld mixer to combine the liquid ingredients with the dry. Either way, once it gets unwieldy, turn it out and knead by hand for 4 to 6 minutes, until smooth and elastic. The dough will be very sticky.

BREADS

Place dough in a large oiled bowl, turning once to coat. Cover with a clean kitchen towel and allow it to double in size (this will take 1 to 3 hours, depending on temperature, altitude, and so on).

Punch the dough down, and gather the risen edges into the punched center; you'll have a ball with an indentation in the center. Divide into thirds, cover, and allow them to rest for 10 minutes.

Roll each piece of dough into a 20-inch rope. Place the three strands on a baking sheet 1 inch apart and, beginning from the center, braid the Challah as you would hair. Pinch ends together, then tuck them under.

Cover with a clean kitchen towel, and allow the Challah to double in size, about 20 minutes. Meanwhile, heat the oven to 375° F, and prepare the wash by whisking together the nondairy milk, maple syrup or agave nectar, and margarine.

Before baking, brush wash over the Challah, getting it well into the crevices. Sprinkle with nigella, sesame, or poppy seeds. Bake for 35 to 40 minutes, covering loosely with foil if the Challah browns too quickly. During the last 10 minutes of baking, brush additional wash over the loaf to intensify the finish.

Transfer to a wire rack, cool, and slice.

Sweet Potato Rolls

Reduce sugar to ⅓ cup. After punching dough down, allow it to rest for 10 minutes. Pinch off pieces of dough the size of golf balls, and place in a well-oiled 9 by 9-inch square pan, and a 9 by 5-inch loaf pan. You should have 16 balls of dough in the square pan (4 across, 4 down), and another 5 in the loaf pan (lined up through the center). Brush with the wash, cover, and allow them to double in size. Before baking, brush with more wash. Bake 15 to 20 minutes, rotating halfway through baking for evenly golden tops. Turn out of the pans, pull apart, and serve immediately.

Cinnamon Rolls

Makes 16 large rolls

For rolls with a surprising likeness to the gooey brand found in malls worldwide, look no further.

This recipe has absurd amounts of everything, from margarine to cinnamon. Trust it, and you'll be rewarded with sweet, yeasty dough swirled with syrupy filling.

Keep dental floss at hand for easily slicing the dough into rolls.

Dough

⅓ cup water, at room temperature

1 (¼-ounce) package yeast

1 cup nondairy milk

½ cup sweet potato puree, or cooked mashed sweet potato

1 teaspoon vanilla

½ cup (1 stick) margarine, melted and cooled slightly

4 ¼ cups all-purpose flour

½ cup sugar

3 tablespoons vital wheat gluten

¼ teaspoon sea salt

Filling

½ cup margarine, at room temperature

1 cup brown sugar

4 tablespoons cinnamon

Icing

4 ounces nondairy cream cheese

½ cup (1 stick) margarine

2½ cups powdered sugar

½ teaspoon lemon zest

Generously grease a 14-inch round, 2 9 by 9-inch square, or 2 9-inch round baking pans, and set aside.

Make the dough: combine the water, yeast, and a small pinch of sugar to proof the yeast (see page 1). After 2 to 5 minutes it should appear slightly foamy. Add nondairy milk, sweet potato, margarine, and vanilla in that order, stirring well to combine. Set aside.

Place the flour, sugar, wheat gluten, and sea salt in the bowl of a food processor. On the dough setting, pulse dry ingredients several times. With the processor running, slowly pour the liquid mixture into the feed tube. Pulse until the dough clumps together and just begins to clean the sides of the processor. Allow it to rest 2 minutes for the gluten to relax and the dough to absorb its moisture. Continue processing until the dough is sticky and shiny, but not too warm, as this can kill the yeast and prevent rising. Alternatively, use a handheld mixer to combine the liquid ingredients with the dry. Once it gets unwieldy and stiff, turn it out and knead by hand for 4 to 6 minutes. The dough will be sticky and a bit difficult to manage; resist the temptation to add extra flour.

Place dough in a large oiled bowl, turning once to coat. Cover with a clean kitchen towel or plastic wrap, and allow it to double in size (this will take 1 to 3 hours, depending on temperature, altitude, and so on).

Punch the dough down, and gather the risen edges into the punched center; you'll have a ball with an indentation in the center. Allow it to rest for several minutes, and get on with the assembly.

Make the icing: with a handheld mixer, beat the nondairy cream cheese and margarine until smooth. Gradually add the powdered sugar, and continue beating for 10 to 12 minutes. Stir in lemon zest. The icing can be made several days in advance and refrigerated.

To assemble: on a lightly floured surface, roll the dough into a 15 by 24-inch rectangle, with the long side facing you. If the dough shrinks, let it rest for 3 to 5 minutes; this will allow the gluten to relax. Spread with softened margarine, keeping a clean 1-inch border at the edge closest to you. Let the dough relax again while you prepare the rest of the filling.

In a medium bowl, combine brown sugar and cinnamon. Scatter this mixture evenly over the dough, keeping the 1-inch edge clean. Using your hands or a rolling pin, gently press the sugar mixture into the margarine.

Beginning at the end farthest from you, tightly roll toward yourself, lifting and stretching as you go. Start at one side, and roll to the other, then back again. You should end up with a 24-inch-long log of dough.

Get some dental floss (any flavor will do). Slide it under the log about 1½ inches, then pull the ends together to create neat edges. Repeat at 1½-inch intervals. You should have 16 rolls.

Place the rolls 1 inch apart in prepared pans. Cover with a clean kitchen towel, and allow them to double in size, about 1 hour. At this point, the rolls can be covered loosely in plastic and refrigerated overnight.

Bake in a 350° F oven for 15 to 20 minutes (5 more if refrigerated), until cinnamon rolls are lightly browned and still soft. Allow them to cool 5 to 10 minutes, then slather with icing while warm. Serve right away.

Vital Wheat Gluten

Don't be tempted to omit the vital wheat gluten. Also the key ingredient in seitan, it adds elasticity to the dough that can't be duplicated. Look for it in the flour or dry goods section of health food stores.

Pepita-Flax Cornbread

Makes 1 loaf

This sunny, mildly sweet cornbread is encrusted with spicy pepitas (pumpkin seeds) and flaxseeds. Serve it with chili or any of the heartier soups in this book.

Topping

2 tablespoons flaxseeds

3 tablespoons raw pepitas

1 teaspoon sugar

¼ teaspoon sea salt

¼ teaspoon oil

Generous pinch of chili powder
or cayenne

Bread

1 cup all-purpose flour

1 cup cornmeal

3 tablespoons sugar

1 tablespoon baking powder

⅛ teaspoon sea salt

1¼ cup nondairy milk

5 tablespoons shortening, melted

1 teaspoon apple cider vinegar

Heat the oven to 400° F. Oil a 9 by 4-inch loaf pan and set aside. Stir together topping ingredients in a small bowl, and set aside.

In a medium bowl, whisk together flour, cornmeal, sugar, baking powder, and sea salt. In a 2-cup measure or small bowl, combine nondairy milk, shortening, and apple cider vinegar. Make a well in the dry ingredients, and fold in the liquid mixture until no streaks of flour remain and batter is minimally lumpy. Pour into prepared pan and sprinkle evenly with the pepita-flaxseed topping.

Transfer to oven and bake until the top springs back when pressed, 25 to 30 minutes. Slice and serve warm, or allow it to cool completely in the pan.

The cornbread will keep for 2 days at room temperature, or 4 days in the refrigerator.

Earl Grey–Carrot Muffins

Makes 12 muffins

Perfumed with bergamot and sweet carrots, these muffins are a lovely addition to a lunch of soup and salad. They are also excellent for breakfast, spread with nondairy cream cheese or jam.

1½ cups all-purpose flour	¼ teaspoon sea salt
1 teaspoon Earl Grey tea, pulverized to a powder in a mortar and pestle or coffee grinder	1 cup sugar
	1 cup finely grated carrots (2 to 3 medium)
1 teaspoon baking powder	½ cup water
½ teaspoon baking soda	½ cup vegetable oil

Heat the oven to 350° F. Line a muffin mold with 12 baking cups, and set aside.

In a large bowl, whisk together the flour, tea, baking powder, baking soda, and sea salt. Set aside.

In a medium bowl or 2-cup measure, stir together the sugar, carrots, water, and vegetable oil. Add wet ingredients to dry, and fold with a flexible spatula just until no streaks of flour remain. Be careful not to overmix. Divide evenly among muffin cups, and transfer to oven. Bake 20 to 25 minutes, until the tops spring back and your kitchen is lightly fragranced with Earl Grey tea.

Earl Grey–Carrot Bread

Bake the batter in an oiled and floured 9 by 4-inch loaf pan for 55 to 65 minutes, until the top springs back when pressed or a knife inserted near the center comes out clean. Remove from the oven, and run a thin metal spatula around the edge of the pan. Cool in the pan 5 minutes, then turn out onto a wire rack top side up to cool completely. The bread can be kept at room temperature, well wrapped, for up to 3 days.

Savory Sticks

Makes about 2 dozen

Quick and simple to make, these breadsticks are the perfect accompaniment to a bowl of Tomato-Coconut Curry (page 119). Add fresh or dried herbs, sprinkle with sesame, caraway, or poppy seeds, or add fresh cracked pepper. The water in the recipe can be replaced with an equal amount of vegetable juice, tinting the sticks with whimsical hues of carrots, beets, or spinach.

BREADS

2 cups all-purpose flour	½ teaspoon sea salt
1 tablespoon baking powder	3 tablespoons shortening
2 teaspoons nutritional yeast	⅔ cup cold water
1 teaspoon dried herbs (optional)	

Heat the oven to 350° F. Have 2 ungreased baking sheets ready, and a clean surface for rolling.

In a food processor, pulse together the flour, baking powder, nutritional yeast, herbs, and sea salt. Add the shortening and pulse again until no large pieces remain. With the processor running, slowly pour in the water. The dough might appear grainy but will come together easily when mounded into a ball.

Pinch a walnut-sized piece of dough from the larger mass. Using your open palms, roll the dough on a clean surface, pulling gently in both directions to elongate it. Continue rolling until the stick is about 14 inches long. Transfer to the prepared baking sheet, pressing the ends into it to keep them straight while baking. Repeat with the remaining dough, placing the sticks 1 inch apart. They will appear misshapen and all different, as they should be.

Bake 15 to 18 minutes, depending on the degree of crispness you prefer; the minimum time will yield a soft interior, while the maximum will make it crisp throughout. Eat immediately, or cool and wrap loosely in a plastic bag.

The sticks will keep for several days, and can be refreshed by heating in a 300° F oven for 3 to 5 minutes.

Cream Scones

Makes 1 dozen

I am not an early riser by any stretch, but as a pastry cook I loved waking before the light and tiptoeing into the kitchen to bake these scones fresh every day. Hours later, they would be slathered with lemon curd and jam, and enjoyed with steaming cups of tea, which is just what I hope you will do.

These are quick to put together, and the dough can be made in advance and refrigerated. It's important to keep the ingredients as cold as possible, using the freezer method below.

For the most gorgeous strawberry shortcakes, omit the dried berries and coconut milk glaze. Split in half crosswise, and fill with sliced strawberries and Vanilla Custard (page 180).

½ cup nondairy milk

2 teaspoons apple cider vinegar

2 cups all-purpose flour

¼ cup sugar

2 teaspoons baking powder

½ teaspoon baking soda

¼ teaspoon sea salt

6 tablespoons cold nonhydrogenated shortening, cut into small pieces

¾ cup dried cranberries or cherries

¼ cup coconut milk

¼ cup crystal sugar (large-grained sugar; regular is a fine substitute)

Heat the oven to 400° F. Have a large, ungreased baking sheet ready.

Combine the nondairy milk and vinegar, and set aside while you get on with the dough.

In a large bowl, sift or whisk together the flour, sugar, baking powder, baking soda, and sea salt. Place in the freezer while you measure the shortening. Using a pastry cutter or fork, cut in the shortening until the texture resembles something between peas and bread crumbs. Return to the freezer for several minutes, or up to 30.

Pour the liquid in and—using a light hand—briefly agitate the mixture until everything is almost moistened. Scrape the sides with a flexible spatula, folding the dough together until nearly all loose flour is incorporated.

Shape dough into a 2½-inch-wide log, and slice into about 10 rounds. Dip the top of each scone into coconut milk, then press into a shallow plate of crystal sugar to coat liberally. Place 2 inches apart on prepared baking sheet, and bake until puffed and golden, 10 to 12 minutes. Cool slightly on a wire rack before serving.

Lemon Scones

Omit dried fruit. Substitute fresh lemon juice for apple cider vinegar, and add 1 teaspoon lemon zest with the nondairy milk mixture.

Pumpkin Scones

Makes 8 scones

When the weather cools and trees are tipped with gold, these are the perfect match for a hot drink and a brisk walk. On stepping into a warm kitchen, a plateful will make wind-burned cheeks and cold fingers a distant memory.

BREADS

Scones

⅓ cup nondairy milk

2 teaspoons apple cider vinegar

⅓ cup canola oil

½ cup canned pumpkin puree

½ teaspoon vanilla extract

2 cups all-purpose flour

⅓ cup brown sugar

1 tablespoon baking powder

¼ teaspoon baking soda

½ teaspoon ground cinnamon

¼ teaspoon ground nutmeg

¼ teaspoon ground ginger

¼ teaspoon ground allspice

Pinch of sea salt

Glaze

1 tablespoon margarine, melted

2 tablespoons orange juice

1 teaspoon orange zest

1 cup powdered sugar

Heat the oven to 400° F. Lightly oil a baking sheet or line it with parchment, and set aside.

In a medium bowl or 2-cup measure, whisk together the nondairy milk, vinegar, oil, pumpkin, and vanilla. Set aside.

In a large bowl, sift or whisk together the flour, brown sugar, baking powder, baking soda, spices, and sea salt.

Make a well in the center of the dry mixture and pour in the liquid mixture. Using a flexible spatula or your hands, make a scraping-scooping-pressing sort of motion to gently combine the two. When you have only a few streaks of flour left in the dough, remove it to a lightly floured surface. Pat the dough evenly into a circle 6 inches in diameter and about 1½ inches high. Using a sharp knife, cut the mound into eight wedges. It should be fairly sticky and a bit misshapen; that's okay. Transfer wedges to prepared baking sheet.

Bake until firm and just baked through (insert a knife; if it comes out clean, they're done), 12 to 15 minutes. Transfer scones to a wire rack while you quickly make the glaze.

Whisk all the glaze ingredients together. For the perfect glaze consistency, lift a spoonful and drizzle it into the remaining glaze; ribbons should just disappear on the surface.

For scones with a delicate finish, drizzle lightly with glaze while slightly warm. For more generously glazed scones, pour glaze into a shallow bowl and dip the tops into the glaze, pressing it into the nooks. Turn upright, and return to rack.

While best fresh-baked, the scones will keep in an airtight container at room temperature for 2 to 3 days (although the glaze will cause them to soften slightly).

For faux-fresh scones, leave unglazed and crisp in a 350° F oven for 3 to 5 minutes. Glaze as directed.

Chapati

Makes 6 chapati

This simple Indian flatbread brings to mind traveling through Tamil Nadu as part of a caravan full of children on a holiday trip. We stopped at nightfall, and women flowed from the jeeps and busses, settling into the corners of a many-roomed building. They prepared daals, vegetables, and breads while sitting gracefully on the floors and laughing with happy ease.

Thinking of that evening, I like to sit on the floor while mixing chapati. I chat with my tiny daughter while we practice sitting like lotuses and laughing together. So I recommend hunkering down with a neighbor, a cat, or whoever is at hand, while working the pliable dough.

Make it fresh and use the still-hot chapati to pinch between your fingers and scoop up daals or curries.

2 cups whole wheat flour
¼ teaspoon sea salt

1½ cups water

In a medium bowl, combine flour and sea salt. Make a well in the mixture, and add water. Using a flexible spatula, scrape and scoop the mixture into itself to form a firm but spongy dough. Continue kneading with the spatula for about 3 minutes. The dough should feel quite sticky when touched, but should clean the sides of the bowl. If it does not, add flour by the teaspoon until the dough is suitably dry. Cover the bowl with plastic (this is ideal) or a wet cloth, transfer to the refrigerator, and allow it to rest for an hour.

Heat a griddle or cast-iron skillet over very high heat. Divide dough into 6 pieces. Roll a piece into a round as thin as you can manage without tearing. Toss onto the hot skillet and cook for 1 minute. Using tongs or your fingertips, flip the chapati. Press it gently with a towel or spatula, and cook 1 minute more. The bottom should be spotty brown, and the chapati fragrant.

Repeat with the remaining dough, rolling the next flatbread as you cook the previous one. Stack finished chapati and cover with a clean kitchen towel. Serve immediately.

Chapati are best made just before a meal. In the unlikely event you have leftovers, store them in a plastic bag at room temperature for up to a day. Reheat on a hot griddle or in a 300° F oven before serving.

Mildred's Bread

Makes 1 loaf

For the last 30 years of their lives, my grandparents were vegetarians. My grandmother, a college English professor, volunteered tirelessly and was an environmentalist before it was fashionable. My grandfather had the rough hands and practical gentility that comes from growing up on a farm. He learned Mandarin in his spare time and spoke Spanish with the neighbors. Evenings, they played Scrabble over hot coffee, and were the only people I knew who didn't have a television.

Their midday meal was eaten on a modest table, shaded by a loquat tree in their Los Angeles backyard. It always featured a loaf of whole wheat bread, which my grandmother had baked earlier in the day. At those suppers, rich with vegetables and quiet conversation, their care for us was always evident.

My grandmother understood every moment as a teachable one, and from her I have learned that it is infinitely rewarding to bake your own bread. I hope you will discover this unfussy fortune as well.

Up to half of the flour can be substituted with another variety: spelt, kamut, and so on. The recipe is very forgiving and accepts additions such as raisins, nuts, or seeds very well.

1⅓ cups water, lukewarm
1 package (2¼ teaspoons) active
   dry yeast
3 tablespoons agave nectar
¼ cup vegetable oil

3 cups whole wheat flour
1½ teaspoons sea salt
½ cup oats
¼ cup sunflower seeds

Oil a 9 by 4-inch loaf pan, and set aside.

In a 2-cup measure or medium bowl, combine the water, yeast, and agave nectar. Allow the dough to proof for 5 minutes while you mix the dry ingredients. Small bubbles will appear on top. Stir in vegetable oil and set aside.

In a large bowl, stir together the whole wheat flour and sea salt. Add yeast mixture, and stir well with a spatula or sturdy wooden spoon. Knead by hand for 2 to 3 minutes; the mixture will be sticky, but should clear the bowl's sides. Knead in the oats and sunflower seeds until well combined.

Cover dough with a clean kitchen towel (there's no need to transfer it to another bowl), and allow it to double in size. This will take 45 minutes to an hour or more, depending on altitude, humidity, and so on.

Punch dough down, pulling the sides toward the center. Gather the dough into a ball and pull into a taut, oblong shape. The top should be smooth. Transfer to the prepared loaf pan and sprinkle the top with additional oats, if desired. Allow it to double in size once more while you heat the oven to 375° F.

Bake 35 to 40 minutes. Unlike most loaves, it will not sound hollow when tapped, so insert a clean knife into the center if you need to check for doneness. Transfer to a wire rack to cool for 15 minutes. Slide a small offset spatula around the edge of the pan, then remove to a wire rack and cool completely.

The bread is especially good toasted and spread generously with margarine.

Rosemary-Fig Focaccia

Makes 8 pieces

This is exactly the sort of sweet-savory treat I want to accompany soup or a salad: lush figs paired with pungent rosemary, and Spiced Balsamic Syrup dappling everything in a burnished glaze. Use whatever variety of fig you enjoy: black mission, calimyrna, brown turkey... Dried figs can be substituted for fresh, and will lend a different character to the focaccia. Soak them in water for 5 minutes before using, then quarter and proceed as directed.

This recipe will make a thin, chewy focaccia. For a thicker version suitable for sandwiches, use a full recipe of dough. Once baked, slice in half crosswise.

Half-recipe Pizza Dough (page 45)
1 tablespoon olive oil
1 6-inch (or so) sprig fresh rosemary, needles removed

8 ounces fresh figs, quartered (or 4 ounces dried)
2 tablespoons Spiced Balsamic Syrup (page 183)
½ teaspoon coarse sea salt

Heat the oven to 400° F. Pour half the olive oil into a 9 by 9-inch square or 9-inch round cake pan, and spread to coat the bottom and sides.

After the dough's second rising, press it evenly into the prepared pan. Spread remaining olive oil over the top. Using your fingertips, make deep impressions on the surface at 1-inch intervals. I simply use my index and middle fingers, held 1 inch apart, and go at it. With your still-oily fingers, scatter figs evenly over the dough, then sprinkle with rosemary. Gently press it all into the dough with open palms.

Drizzle syrup over everything and allow it to rest for 10 minutes. Transfer to the oven and bake 20 to 25 minutes, until puffed and golden. Remove to a wire rack, and sprinkle with sea salt. Run a small metal spatula around the edge to free any caramelized bits, and allow it to cool for at least 10 minutes in the pan.

Pry the focaccia loose with the spatula, sliding it under to release it completely, and turn out onto a cutting board. Slice into 8 pieces with a serrated knife, and serve.

The focaccia can be kept, covered, at room temperature for 1 day, or refrigerated for several. Rewarm in a 300° F oven.

Figs

When using fresh figs, look for heavy fruit that are lush and swollen rather than smaller and wrinkled. Pinch off the stem close to the fruit to avoid its white sap.

When using dried figs, note the appearance when you cut it open; it should look dense and moist. If the interior is dry or crumbly, discard it.

Sauces, Dressings, and Condiments

Condiments are more than clinking bottles brought to the table just prior to eating. They add nuance and character to the entire meal, and can elevate an entrée to something really divine. Don't be afraid to experiment beyond what's recommended here. The best dishes come from combining tastes and techniques in brave new ways.

Fresh Herb Vinaigrette

Makes about 1 cup

This cookbook could be carried on the strength of this recipe. I created it with my mom in mind. She eats more fresh vegetables than anyone I know, and should have something really delicious to adorn them with.

The vinaigrette can be prepared up to several days in advance. Give it a good shake before serving. Do try to use fresh basil, even if the other herbs are dried. Otherwise, the dressing has lots of flexibility: substitute up to a tablespoon of balsamic or apple cider vinegar for the wine vinegar, or reduce the amount of oil, if you like.

2 cloves garlic, minced

2 tablespoons fresh lemon juice

3 tablespoons wine vinegar (red, white, or a combination)

2 tablespoons Dijon mustard

1 teaspoon any liquid or granulated sweetener

3 tablespoons chopped fresh herbs, or 1½ tablespoons dried: basil, thyme, oregano, tarragon, dill

¼ teaspoon sea salt

¼ teaspoon ground black pepper

½ cup olive oil

In a smallish bowl or 2-cup measure, combine everything except the olive oil. If you have other kitchen faffing to look after, allow the mixture to sit for several minutes so the flavors meld.

Whisk the oil into the vinegar mixture in a steady stream until completely incorporated. The vinaigrette will keep, tightly covered and refrigerated, for up to 2 weeks.

Salad Dressing Basics

Experimenting with salad dressings is one of the most rewarding things to do in the kitchen. Use these guidelines to create inventive and flavorful elixirs to top your best produce.

Most salad dressings have 3 main components: acid, emulsifier, and oil. Traditionally, seasonings and emulsifiers are added to an acid to allow flavors to meld before whisking in the oil. But you can begin with these basic elements, then layer the flavors to suit your taste. In creating your own dressings, a good ratio is:

3 parts acid • 1 part emulsifier • 3 parts oil

Acids

Any plain or flavored vinegar: red wine, balsamic, apple cider, rice vinegar, and so on

Citrus juice: lemon, orange, lime, grapefruit

Emulsifiers

Dijon mustard
Mashed roasted garlic
Pureed avocado, mango, papaya, even cooked sweet potato
Miso
Tomato paste
Mayonnaise, pureed silken tofu, or Cashew Crema (page 65)

Oils

Extra virgin olive
Hazelnut
Almond
Sesame
Grapeseed
Walnut

Add finely chopped fresh ingredients, if you like

Garlic
Onion
Fennel
Shallots
Ginger
Herbs

Then, seasonings

Poppy seeds
Dried herbs and spices
Cumin
Paprika
Horseradish or wasabi

And a sweet note

Orange juice
Pureed mango
Agave nectar
Maple syrup
Sugar

Finally, the essentials, to taste

Sea salt
Ground black pepper

The dressing should keep in the refrigerator for up to 2 weeks. While the oil and vinegar may separate, they can be re-emulsified simply by whisking or shaking.

Peppercorn Ranch Dressing

Makes about 1 cup

½ cup mayonnaise

2 tablespoons nondairy milk, preferably unsweetened

2 cloves garlic, minced

2 tablespoons apple cider vinegar

¼ teaspoon dried basil, or ½ teaspoon finely minced fresh basil

¼ teaspoon dried parsley, or ½ teaspoon finely minced fresh parsley

¾ teaspoon freshly ground pepper

Whisk together all ingredients in smallish bowl. Store in a jar in the refrigerator for up to a week.

SAUCES, DRESSINGS, AND CONDIMENTS

Hazelnut Vinaigrette

Makes about ½ cup

This vinaigrette can be used in Fresh Kale Salad (page 103), or drizzled over mixed vegetables before roasting.

3 tablespoons white wine vinegar

2 tablespoons hazelnut oil

1 shallot, minced

1 tablespoon Dijon mustard

1 tablespoon maple syrup

⅛ teaspoon sea salt

Whisk everything together. Store in a jar in the refrigerator for up to a week.

For raw use cold-pressed oil and substitute raw agave nectar for maple syrup

Chèvre

Makes 2 8-inch cylinders

Chèvre is a French cheese with a semisoft texture and distinctive, tart flavor. As with classic chèvre, this is pleasantly salty, and uses acid (vinegar and lemon juice) to coagulate and intensify the cheese. Serve dabbed on crackers, fresh vegetables, or sandwiches. Its creamy tang is also excellent as a substitute for cream cheese.

SAUCES, DRESSINGS, AND CONDIMENTS

3 cups water, boiling
1½ cups raw cashews
2 tablespoons agar flakes
½ cup plus ½ cup water

2 tablespoons fresh lemon juice
1 tablespoon raw tahini
1 tablespoon apple cider vinegar
1¼ teaspoons sea salt

Pour boiling water over cashews, and soak for at least an hour, or up to overnight.

In a small saucepan off the heat, combine the agar and ½ cup of the water. Set aside to dissolve while the cashews soak. The agar flakes will enlarge slightly and take on a pale cast.

Line a shallow container (a 9 by 9-inch or 9 by 13-inch casserole dish is ideal) with plastic wrap, allowing it to hang over the sides slightly. Set aside.

Place the agar mixture over low heat, stirring occasionally as you put together the cashew mixture.

Drain the cashews, rinse, and drain again. In a blender, combine cashews, the remaining ½ cup water, lemon juice, tahini, vinegar, and sea salt. Blend until completely smooth, scraping down the sides as necessary. This process should take about 5 minutes while the agar mixture bubbles away.

Once the cashew mixture is smooth, scrape the agar mixture into the blender with the machine running. Continue blending until the texture is silky. Scrape into the plastic-lined container, smoothing the top. Cover loosely and refrigerate until firm, about 1 hour.

Once fairly solid, divide the Chèvre in half. Using the plastic, shape each section into a cylinder about 2 inches in diameter and 8 inches long. Wrap tightly in plastic, and chill until ready to use. It can be stored in the refrigerator for up to a week.

Herbed Chèvre

After forming the Chèvre into cylinders, roll in a mixture of ¼ cup finely chopped fresh parsley, 2 tablespoons finely chopped fresh basil, and 1 teaspoon finely chopped fresh thyme or oregano. Add 1 teaspoon dried lavender for a distinctive French flavor.

Peppercorn Chèvre

After forming the Chèvre into cylinders, roll in 2 tablespoons coarsely ground peppercorns.

Raw Chèvre

If you have a high-speed blender, the Chèvre can be made raw: soak cashews in lukewarm water instead of boiling water, and soak the agar for at least 1 hour. Use raw apple cider vinegar. Skip the step of heating the agar and continue with everything else as directed.

Cashew Crema

Makes about ¾ cup

Crema Mexicana, a thick cream similar to crème fraiche, and crema agria, a tangier sort, are both familiar additions to the Mexican table. This cashew version is like the tangier agria.

   Double or triple the recipe and keep it on hand for whenever sour cream is called for.

1 cup water, boiling
½ cup raw cashews
¼ cup water

3 tablespoons fresh lime juice
1 teaspoon apple cider vinegar
1 teaspoon sea salt

Pour boiling water over cashews and soak for at least an hour, or up to overnight.

   Drain cashews, rinse, and drain again. In a blender, combine the cashews, water, lime juice, vinegar, and sea salt. Blend until completely smooth, scraping down the sides as necessary. This will take a while; be patient. Scrape the crema into a small bowl, cover, and refrigerate until chilled.

   The crema can be stored in a jar, refrigerated, for 3 to 4 days.

Avocado Crema

Once crema is blended smooth, add half an avocado, and blend again. Store as directed.

For raw substitute warm water for boiling and use raw cider vinegar

Guacamole

Makes about 3 cups

4 avocados, pitted and skinned
⅓ cup diced red onion
2 cloves garlic, minced
1 jalapeño, minced

¼ cup cilantro, roughly chopped
Juice of 1 lime
1 teaspoon sea salt

Tumble everything into a medium bowl as you chop it up. Using a tablespoon or serving spoon, slice through the mixture, turning it under as if you were folding cake batter. The texture should be combined but mostly chunky; keep going through it if you prefer a smoother guacamole.

SAUCES, DRESSINGS, AND CONDIMENTS

Spicy Dipping Sauce

Makes about ⅔ cup

Serve with Buttermilk Onion Rings (page 94), or any fresh or fried vegetables.

½ cup mayonnaise
2 teaspoons ketchup
1½ teaspoons peeled and grated
    fresh horseradish
2 teaspoons apple cider vinegar, or
    lime or lemon juice

½ teaspoon paprika
¼ teaspoon pepper
Generous pinch of cayenne
Pinch of dried oregano

Whisk together all ingredients. Adjust cayenne to taste. Chill until ready to serve.

Look for heavy, firm avocados free of blemishes. The skin should yield slightly to pressure from your thumb, perhaps leaving a slight indentation. If the avocado feels very soft or hollow under your fingers, avoid it; the fruit is overripe.

To cut an avocado, slice through the skin and flesh all the way around the seed, turning as you go. Grasp both sides, and gently twist apart. Using a large knife, firmly whack the blade into the pit, and wiggle to remove it. Tap the knife against a trash bin to discard the pit.

Using a large spoon, scoop fruit from the halves, or score into squares and scrape free.

Avocado Aioli

Makes about 1½ cups

This mayonnaise features a base of rich, nourishing avocado, made tangy with lemon, Dijon mustard, and apple cider vinegar. It can be used anywhere mayonnaise is called for and is a great alternative to soy-based spreads. Add chopped herbs, ground pepper, horseradish, or wasabi as you like.

1 avocado, cut roughly into quarters
2 tablespoons fresh lemon juice
1 tablespoon raw apple cider vinegar
1 teaspoon Dijon mustard

1 clove garlic
½ teaspoon sea salt
3 tablespoons extra virgin olive oil

In a food processor or blender, combine all ingredients except extra virgin olive oil until completely smooth, scraping down the sides as necessary. With the processor or blender still running, add olive oil in a thin stream. The mixture will emulsify immediately, but continue blending for another 30 seconds or so to incorporate extra air. The aioli should be light and creamy in consistency and pale green in color.

Use immediately, or refrigerate for up to 2 days.

Ras el Hanout

Makes about ¼ cup

Ras el Hanout, a combination of up to fifty different spices, can be purchased at Middle Eastern markets. The time-honored version contains ingredients such as rose petal and black fly (yes, the aphrodisiac). The latter has been banned from inclusion since the 1990s, but this version has love-inspiring powers as well.

Use the spice blend as a rub for seitan or tempeh, a seasoning for roasted vegetables, or to add a unique flavor to soups.

SAUCES, DRESSINGS, AND CONDIMENTS

1 tablespoon ground ginger

1 teaspoon ground allspice

1 teaspoon ground cardamom

1 teaspoon ground cinnamon

1 teaspoon ground nutmeg

1 teaspoon ground turmeric

1 teaspoon ground black pepper

½ teaspoon ground coriander

¼ teaspoon ground cloves

⅛ teaspoon cayenne pepper

Combine all ingredients. The Ras el Hanout can be jarred and stored with your other spices for several months.

Moroccan Preserved Lemons

Makes 1 jar

Be sure to use organic lemons, as this condiment is composed primarily of their skin.

8 small to medium lemons
½ cup sea salt or kosher salt
1 stick cinnamon, or 4 whole cloves
    (optional)

1 dried chile pepper, left whole
    (optional)
Additional fresh lemon juice,
    as needed

SAUCES, DRESSINGS, AND CONDIMENTS

Thoroughly clean a wide-mouthed 25-ounce jar and lid. Set aside.

Scrub the lemons under hot water and dry well. Using a paring knife, remove the small nub at the stem end. Starting at the opposite end, cut the lemon in quarters, leaving ½ inch connected at the bottom. The lemon should look like a blooming flower with four long petals.

Rub about 1 tablespoon sea salt onto the cut sides of each lemon; don't be stingy. As you go, place each lemon into the jar, smashing to release the juice and sea salt. Add cinnamon, cloves, or chile, if desired. Press everything down once more, and tightly replace the lid. Shake well, and give the jar a place of honor in your kitchen.

Each day, press the lemons down to release more juice, replace the lid, and shake again. Once the lemons are completely submerged in their own juice, there is no need to press them down, but do shake the jar occasionally. If the lemons are not immersed in liquid by the third day, add enough additional fresh lemon juice to cover. The lemons will be ready in about a month, when the skins have softened and melted into a delicious, salty muddle.

As you remove lemons from the jar or use the juice, be sure you have enough liquid to cover; just squeeze in additional fresh lemon juice as needed. Once preserved, refrigerate the lemons, to be on the safe side.

To use: remove a section of lemon and rinse well. Scrape away pulp (use it in salad dressing, to brighten a soup, or eat it on the spot, as I do). Slice the rind into thin slices, and serve as a condiment or use in recipes.

Suggested uses

Mince, and serve a spoonful atop a finished bowl of soup.
Add the juice to vinaigrette for a sunny flavor.
Stir chopped bits into a salad of beans and fresh vegetables.
Chop up with parsley, drizzle with olive oil, and toss with pasta.

Spice Rubs
for Seitan, Tempeh, or Tofu

For 1 (8-ounce) package seitan, 1 (8-ounce) package steamed tempeh, 1 (16-ounce) package tofu, or 8 ounces rehydrated texturized vegetable protein.

These mixtures are infinitely versatile, and serve as a base for loads of recipes. Process seitan, tofu, or steamed tempeh in a food processor until crumbly, then sauté with a few teaspoons of oil and one of the blends below. (Texturized vegetable protein is already crumbled; just reconstitute, add the spices, and sauté.) Chunks or slices of protein can also be coated with the spice rub and braised, baked, or stir-fried.

To store, combine spices in a jar and keep at room temperature. Add garlic or onion just before using.

Italian

1 teaspoon sea salt
1 teaspoon fennel seeds, coarsely crushed
1 teaspoon dried basil
½ teaspoon dried oregano
½ teaspoon red pepper flakes
½ teaspoon ground black pepper
2 cloves garlic, minced

Mexican

2 tablespoons chopped fresh cilantro
1 teaspoon sea salt
1 teaspoon ground cumin
1 teaspoon lime zest
¼ teaspoon chili powder
2 cloves garlic, minced

Indian

1 teaspoon sea salt
1 teaspoon turmeric
½ teaspoon ground coriander
½ teaspoon ground cumin
½ teaspoon fennel seeds, coarsely crushed
2 cloves garlic, minced

French

1 teaspoon sea salt
½ teaspoon dried rosemary, crumbled
½ teaspoon dried marjoram
½ teaspoon dried thyme
½ teaspoon dried basil
Pinch of lavender flowers (optional)
2 cloves garlic, minced

Chinese

1 teaspoon sea salt
1 teaspoon ground ginger
½ teaspoon ground black or white pepper
½ teaspoon anise seeds, coarsely crushed
½ teaspoon red pepper flakes
¼ teaspoon ground cinnamon
⅛ teaspoon ground cloves
2 cloves garlic, minced

Caribbean

1 tablespoon shredded coconut
1 teaspoon sea salt
1 teaspoon lime zest
½ teaspoon red pepper flakes
¼ teaspoon allspice
1 tablespoon minced onion

Charmoula

Makes about ¾ cup

Serve this hot and flavorful relish with Vegetable-Chickpea Tagine (page 133) any North African dish, or as part of the Fresh Melon Carpaccio with Sweet Chili Relish (page 85).

1 teaspoon coriander seeds
1 teaspoon cumin seeds
½ teaspoon red pepper flakes
½ teaspoon whole peppercorns
½ cup firmly packed parsley
½ cup firmly packed cilantro
2 cloves garlic

½ medium onion
3 tablespoons fresh lemon juice
2 teaspoons olive oil
1 teaspoon paprika
½ teaspoon sea salt
¼ teaspoon cayenne pepper

In a coffee grinder or with a mortar and pestle, grind the coriander, cumin, red pepper, and peppercorns into a fine powder. Transfer to a small bowl.

Place the parsley, cilantro, garlic, and onion on a cutting board, and go at it with a knife until finely chopped. Add to spice mixture.

Add the remaining ingredients, and stir well to combine. Drizzle additional olive oil over the top before serving. To store, refrigerate the charmoula in a glass jar, covered completely with olive oil, for up to 2 weeks.

Lemon-Dill Dressing

Makes about ¾ cup

This light, springy dressing is particularly good as a dip for crudités or on salads such as the Curtice Street (page 108) that combine vegetables and fruit.

½ cup mayonnaise

1 tablespoon Dijon mustard

1 tablespoon dried dill, or
   2 teaspoons fresh

1 tablespoon fresh lemon juice

1 teaspoon lemon zest

¾ teaspoon fresh pepper

Whisk everything together.

Agave, Mustard, and Poppy Seed Dressing

Makes about ½ cup

Serve this simple, fat-free dressing over a giant salad of baby romaine, shredded carrots, grape tomatoes, avocado, red onion, sunflower seeds, and raisins.

3 tablespoons agave nectar

2 tablespoons Dijon mustard

1 tablespoon apple cider vinegar

2 teaspoons poppy seeds

Whisk everything together in a small bowl.

Roasted Mustard Dressing

Omit the poppy seeds. Roast 1 head garlic according to directions on page 88. Once cool, squeeze roasted cloves into a small bowl, and mash thoroughly before whisking in the ingredients above.

Muffaletta Spread

Makes about 1½ cups

For the peppers, look for deeply colored nightshades with tight skins and no puckering or shrinkage.

I try to avoid—and never cook with—green peppers. Their unripe, twangy flavor makes me think of eating a grasshopper, and I remain unconvinced of their culinary merit.

1 red pepper, roasted, or ¾ cup jarred
 roasted red peppers
1 cup pitted black olives
1 cup green olives stuffed
 with pimento
5 cloves garlic, minced
⅓ to ½ cup olive oil

¼ cup packed fresh Italian parsley,
 coarsely chopped
2 tablespoons apple cider vinegar
½ teaspoon lemon zest
½ teaspoon dried oregano
½ teaspoon freshly ground pepper
⅛ teaspoon sea salt

Dice the roasted red pepper into ¼-inch pieces. Roughly chop the black and green olives into similar-sized pieces. Be patient; it's worth it.

Combine the pepper and olives in a medium bowl. Stir in garlic, olive oil, parsley, vinegar, zest, oregano, sea salt, and pepper. Allow the flavors to meld for at least 15 minutes before serving. Store in the refrigerator, tightly covered, for up to a week.

Roasting Red Peppers

Grill method

Place peppers on a rack just over hot, greying coals (this is an excellent way to make use of dying coals, as you can roast peppers when you've got a grill on and store them in the refrigerator). With kitchen tongs, turn the peppers as the grill-side blackens.

Gas stovetop method

Stab the bottom of a pepper with a dinner fork or two-prong cooking fork. Using a pot holder to protect your skin from the heat, place it directly over a gas flame on medium-high heat, an inch or two from the flame, turning slowly. The skin will blister and blacken; continue turning until all skin is blackened.

Broiler method

Line a broiler pan with aluminum foil and heat the broiler to its highest setting. Place peppers on the foil and broil, turning with kitchen tongs when the skin beneath the broiler is blackened.

In all cases, once blackened, place peppers in a bowl and cover with a plate, or simply wrap a kitchen towel around the whole pepper. The steam will loosen the skin, which can be scraped away with a knife several minutes later. Flay peppers open with a vertical slit down one side and open the things up. Remove membranes and seeds with a knife. Don't rinse the peppers; this removes some of the wonderful, smoky flavor, and you don't need any additional liquid on their flesh.

Edamame Pesto

Makes about 1½ cups

When spring arrives, I always eat more raw foods and green things. Everything outside has burst into color, and my body begins to crave it too. Sprightly all-purpose pesto is the perfect way to celebrate this verdant season, and it comes together in a flash. Rich in vitamins and minerals, its bright flavor is perfect on crudités, spread on a sandwich, tossed with pasta, or spooned into hot bowls of soup.

If you have concerns about using raw edamame, briefly steam the soybeans before using.

2 cups frozen shelled edamame, thawed

2 cloves garlic

1 tablespoon extra virgin olive oil

1 cup fresh basil leaves

½ teaspoon sea salt

1 to 3 tablespoons water

In a food processor, combine all ingredients except water, and process until well blended. The pesto should be dense and pasty, and not quite smooth. Drizzle in water by the tablespoon and continue blending until pesto reaches the desired consistency.

The pesto can be refrigerated for up to 4 days, or frozen for up to a month.

Ti Malice

Makes about ⅓ cup

Use this blistering Haitian relish as you would hot sauce.

1 tablespoon olive oil

1 onion, minced

1 habañero chili (2 jalapeños are a
 fine substitution)

3 medium shallots, minced

2 cloves garlic, minced

¼ cup fresh lime juice

¼ teaspoon sea salt

In a medium saucepan, combine all ingredients over medium heat. Bring to a boil, and stir constantly for 2 to 3 minutes. Remove the sauce from the heat and allow it to cool.

Stored in a jar, it can be refrigerated for up to a month.

SAUCES, DRESSINGS, AND CONDIMENTS

Sharp White Cheddar Sauce

Makes about 2 cups

Serve this rich, tangy sauce over pasta or pizza, as a dip for crudités, or on Broccoli-Cheese Bruschetta (page 89).

The best tool for creating a satiny-textured sauce is a high-speed blender, like a Vita-Mix. If you don't have a high-speed blender, a regular blender is preferable to a food processor.

SAUCES, DRESSINGS, AND CONDIMENTS

1 cup raw cashews, soaked in boiling water for 1 hour and drained

1 cup water

1 clove garlic

4 teaspoons tahini, preferably raw

4 teaspoons nutritional yeast

½ teaspoon ground flaxseed

2 tablespoons fresh lemon juice

1 teaspoon sea salt

In a blender or food processor, combine everything and blend until completely smooth. This will take several minutes. Be sure to stop the machine as needed to scrape down the sides. Pour the mixture into a medium saucepan and cook, whisking constantly, for 2 minutes. The sauce will thicken slightly. Remove from the heat, and allow it to cool 5 minutes. Add extra lemon juice to taste if a sharper sauce is desired.

Use immediately, or pour into a glass jar and refrigerate for up to a week. The sauce will thicken on refrigeration, so gently rewarm it in a saucepan or microwave before using.

Raw White Cheddar Sauce

Soak cashews in warm water instead of boiling. Substitute raw tahini for roasted, decrease blending water to ½ cup, and increase flaxseed to 1½ teaspoon. Instead of cooking the sauce, allow it to stand for 15 minutes. It will become thicker and gooier on resting.

Tahini-Lemon Sauce

Makes about ¾ cup

2 cloves garlic, minced

2 tablespoons fresh lemon juice

¼ teaspoon sea salt

¼ cup tahini

¼ cup water

In a small bowl, stir together the garlic, fresh lemon juice, and sea salt. Add tahini, whisking until it thickens, lightens in color, then smoothes out completely. Slowly whisk in water. To use as a salad dressing, stir in an additional tablespoon of water.

For raw use raw tahini

Infusing Oils and Vinegars

Impart any oil with the essence of spices, herbs, or other flavorings (see Salad Dressing Basics on page 62 for ideas). Simply combine the oil of your choice with dried chiles, sprigs of rosemary, or other pungent ingredients, and allow it to sit at room temperature for about a day, until their flavor has been absorbed. Before serving, remove the flavor element, and replace with a fresh one.

Vinegar is essentially liquid in which the sugars have fermented and turned sour due to their exposure to air. To make your own, simply store leftover wine or champagne at room temperature in a wide-mouthed jar loosely covered with a clean towel for several weeks. Once sour, the vinegar will keep indefinitely.

To add summer ripeness to your dressings, simmer vinegar with overripe fruit (peaches and blueberries are excellent here) in a large saucepan. Puree briefly, then strain through cheesecloth into clean jars, where it will keep for a month in the refrigerator.

For herby infusions, add lavender, tarragon, or whole peppercorns to a bottle of vinegar. Cover tightly and steep in a cool place for 1 to 2 weeks. Refrigerate for several months.

Garlic-Infused Olive Oil

Makes about ½ cup

Slather onto pizza while on the grill, or whisk in vinegar for a quick dressing.

½ cup extra virgin olive oil
2 cloves garlic, minced
½ teaspoon sea salt
½ teaspoon fresh pepper

1 tablespoon chopped mixed fresh herbs (rosemary, basil, oregano, thyme), or 1½ teaspoons dried

Combine all ingredients. Use on Grilled Pizza (page 142), or brush on bread and grill for garlic toast, drizzle over mashed potatoes, mix with an equal amount of vinegar for salad dressing...

Cilantro-Lime Gremolata

Makes about ½ cup

Gremolata, an Italian relish similar to the French persillade, is stirred into finished dishes or served raw as condiment. This version is bright with the Latin-Caribbean flavors of lime and cilantro. Dollop into soups, toss with cold soba noodles, or thin with vinegar and use as a salad dressing. The gremolata also makes an excellent rub for baked tempeh or seitan.

For a traditional gremolata, replace the lime zest with lemon, the cilantro with parsley, and continue as directed.

2 tablespoons grated lime zest (from about 4 limes)
½ cup firmly packed cilantro

2 cloves garlic
¼ teaspoon sea salt
1 teaspoon olive oil

Tumble the lime zest, cilantro, and garlic onto a cutting board, and chop away until combined and no large chunks remain. Transfer to a small bowl, stir in the salt and olive oil, and refrigerate until ready to serve.

Hummus

Makes about 2½ cups

When I want hummus, I want it this way: sour, with raw tahini and lemon, and reeking of garlic. Add an extra clove if you're bent toward isolation, as it will certainly provide the opportunity.

SAUCES, DRESSINGS, AND CONDIMENTS

1 (25-ounce) can chickpeas, or 2½ cups cooked
⅓ cup tahini, preferably raw
⅓ cup fresh lemon juice

2 cloves garlic, peeled
1 tablespoon olive oil
1½ teaspoons sea salt
½ cup water

Dump everything into a food processor or blender and process until smooth, scraping down the sides as necessary. The hummus will be whipped and fluffy, and should have no lumps whatsoever. If you have a high-speed blender, this is an excellent time to use it, as it will create a smooth texture that can't be replicated in a food processor.

Little Bites

Small is beautiful: the miniburger, the sliver of pâté, the tumbler of soup. Apart from being tasty, the best appetizers are easy to eat, and distinctive without being pretentious. Serve a few little bites to pique the appetite before something more substantial, or compose a meal exclusively of several diminutive dishes.

Pepita-Lime Apple Tiers

Makes 4 appetizer servings

Tart Granny Smith apples are layered with spicy Pepita-Lime Cheese and cilantro in this light, fresh starter.

Pepita-Lime Cheese

1 cup raw cashews

½ cup water

¼ cup raw pepitas (pumpkin seeds)

3 tablespoons lime juice

4 teaspoons raw tahini or raw
    sesame seeds

4 teaspoons nutritional yeast

2 teaspoons flaxseeds

1 teaspoon sea salt

half a jalapeño pepper, seeds and
    membranes removed

1 clove garlic

To Assemble

2 Granny Smith apples

1 cup cilantro, coarsely chopped

1 jalapeño pepper, sliced into very
    thin rings

daikon or broccoli sprouts, or frisée
    lettuce, for serving

Whole coriander seeds, roughly
    crushed (as you would with
    cracked pepper)

Make the cheese: in a blender or food processor, process all ingredients until smooth. Remove to a bowl and allow it to rest at room temperature while you prepare the apples.

Slice the apples across the seeds into ⅓-inch slices, and remove the seeds from the center of each slice. I use the bottom of a cake decorating tip for this, as it makes perfect circles, but you can also use a paring knife. If you won't be eating the tiers immediately, brush the cut sides with a bit of lime juice to prevent browning.

Place the bottom slice of an apple on a serving plate and spread with about 2 tablespoons of the cheese mixture. Sprinkle with cilantro and jalapeños, and top with the next slice, building the apple from the bottom up. Repeat with the cheese, cilantro, and jalapeños, finishing the top with an apple slice. Repeat with the other apple and remaining fillings.

To serve: mound sprouts or frisée around each apple tier, and scatter any additional cilantro or jalapeño over the top, along with the cracked coriander seeds. The tiers can be cut into like layer cakes, or enjoyed by simply lifting each topped slice.

Soba Cabbage Wraps

Makes 4 appetizer servings

Fresh cabbage leaves hold sesame-coated soba noodles and cool pineapple relish in this light appetizer.

Soba Noodles

6 ounces soba (buckwheat) noodles

Spicy Sesame Dressing

½ small Thai pepper, seeded and minced
   (jalapeño is a fine substitution)
½ teaspoon freshly grated ginger root
2 cloves garlic, minced
1 scallion, thinly sliced, green parts only
2 tablespoons soy sauce

2 tablespoons rice vinegar
1 tablespoon sesame oil (canola is a
   fine substitution)
2 teaspoons maple syrup
1 teaspoon toasted sesame oil

Pineapple Relish

¼ medium pineapple (1½ to 2 cups),
   peeled, tough core removed,
   and diced
½ medium cucumber, seeded and diced

½ red pepper, diced
¼ cup tightly packed fresh cilantro,
   roughly chopped

For Serving

8 to 12 large cabbage leaves, washed
   and patted dry

Additional cilantro leaves,
   for garnish (optional)

Prepare the soba noodles according to package directions. Drain, rinse with very cold water, and drain again. Set aside.

In a measuring cup or small bowl, whisk together all ingredients for the dressing. Alternatively, place them in a jar and shake to combine. Pour the dressing over the cold soba noodles and stir slightly. Allow the noodles to absorb the dressing while preparing the relish.

In a medium bowl, combine the pineapple, cucumber, red pepper, and cilantro. Set aside until ready to serve. At this point, the dressed noodles and relish can be refrigerated separately overnight and assembled the next day.

To serve, evenly distribute the soba noodles among the cabbage leaves. Top with equal portions of the relish. Garnish with the additional cilantro leaves and serve.

Raw Cabbage Wraps

Substitute 4 zucchini, sliced into noodles as you would Raw Zucchini Noodles (page 168), and allow them to absorb the dressing while preparing the Pineapple Relish. Make the Spicy Sesame Dressing, substituting Nama Shoyu for soy sauce, cold-pressed sesame oil for toasted, and raw agave nectar for maple syrup. Everything else goes as directed.

Palm Heart Ceviche

Makes 8 appetizer servings

Served in many Latin American coastal areas, ceviche is "cooked" with a piquant marinade. Ceviches vary widely according to region: in Peru, where it's considered the national dish, ceviche is served alongside sliced sweet potatoes, while Ecuadorians use bitter Seville oranges and a garnish of crisp corn. The Mexican version is accompanied by raw onion slices and mounded on toasted tortillas.

This ceviche uses hearts of palm instead of fish, and fuses several traditions. A blend of citrus juice mimics the pucker of Seville oranges. Be sure to strain the juice, as the pulp (particularly lime pulp) can add undesired bitterness.

1 (14-ounce) can palm hearts
¼ cup fresh lemon juice
¼ cup fresh lime juice
¼ cup fresh orange juice
2 cloves garlic, minced
1 tablespoon red onion, minced and
    rinsed well in cold water
1 tablespoon coarsely chopped cilantro

1 Roma or plum tomato, diced
½ jalapeño pepper, seeded and minced
½ teaspoon sea salt
2-inch piece of nori, ground to a
    powder in a coffee grinder or
    mortar and pestle
Dash of paprika (optional)
Romaine lettuce, for serving

At least 2 of the following garnishes

1 ear corn, kernels cut
½ pound cooked sweet potatoes, cut
    into ½-inch chunks
½ cup diced red pepper

½ cup loosely packed cilantro,
    roughly chopped
Hot and Sweet Popcorn (page 90)

Cut hearts of palm into ¾-inch slices and place in a large bowl.

Whisk together the citrus juices, garlic, onion, cilantro, tomato, jalapeño, pepper, sea salt, nori, and paprika. Pour over the palm hearts and gently toss to combine. Refrigerate, and allow flavors to meld for at least 2 hours, or overnight.

Serve in small glasses or martini glasses lined with romaine leaves, garnishes alongside.

Mushroom Pâté en Croûte

Makes 8 appetizer servings

This evokes the decadence of that oozy classic, brie en croûte, sans fromage. Don't be daunted; it's actually really easy, and the elements can all be made in advance. Plus it'll really impress your party guests. Serve it as part of an hors d'oeuvres buffet, or with champagne and truffles for a New Year's indulgence.

⅓ cup pecans

2 tablespoons margarine or olive oil

1 pound (about 5 cups) mixed mushrooms (portabella, white button, shitake, cremini), finely chopped

2 cloves garlic, minced

1 teaspoon fresh thyme, or ½ teaspoon dried

2 tablespoons sherry or dry white wine

½ teaspoons sea salt

½ teaspoon ground pepper

2 tablespoons finely chopped flat-leaf parsley

1 teaspoon fresh lemon juice

⅛ teaspoon paprika

4 ounces Chèvre (page 64) or nondairy cream cheese

1 sheet puff pastry, thawed

¼ cup nondairy milk, soy creamer, or water

Crackers, French bread, or sliced apples, for serving

Toast pecans in a hot skillet, stirring constantly, until they become fragrant and golden. Transfer to a cutting board, chop finely, and set aside.

Line a 6-inch round pan or 9 by 5-inch loaf pan with plastic wrap, leaving the extra to hang over the sides. Set aside.

In a cast-iron skillet over medium heat, combine the margarine, mushrooms, garlic, and thyme. Cook, stirring occasionally, 8 to 12 minutes. The mushrooms will soften, release their liquid, and then begin to dry slightly. Add the sherry, sea salt, and pepper, and continue cooking for 6 to 8 minutes, or until the skillet goes dry again.

Remove from the heat, and add the pecans, parsley, lemon juice, paprika, and Chèvre or cream cheese, stirring well to combine. Turn mixture into the prepared pan, cover with plastic, and refrigerate for at least 4 hours and up to 3 days.

Puff Pastry

Puff pastry is composed of dough (made simply from flour, water, and yeast) which is thinly layered with fat. When baked, the fat expands, causing hundreds of layers of dough to puff up, and creating the light, flaky pastry we all love.

Most packaged puff pastry is vegan. Look for dough made with all-vegetable shortening or oil, free of animal-based dough conditioners. Lots of varieties are available, including organic and whole wheat.

LITTLE BITES

Joy Tienzo | Cook, Eat, Thrive

The puff pastry will likely be folded into thirds. Once thawed, it should be just pliable enough to roll out. Roll into a 15 by 15-inch square. From it, cut a 6-inch circle and a 10-inch circle. Reserve the scraps. Place the 10-inch circle on a baking sheet. Center pâté on the 10-inch circle, folding the sides neatly up and over. Brush a bit of nondairy liquid around the edges, then place the 6-inch circle evenly over the top, pressing gently to affix it. Cut shapes from the scraps (I do a vine studded with leaves), and affix them to the pastry with a bit of the wash. Refrigerate, loosely covered, for at least 30 minutes and up to 2 days.

When ready to serve, heat the oven to 425° F. Brush the pâté once more with liquid. Bake until golden, between 20 and 35 minutes. Transfer to a plate, and serve warm.

Fresh Melon Carpaccio with Sweet Chili Relish

Makes 4 appetizer servings

This unconventional pairing of flavors: sweet, delicate cantaloupe and piquant herb sauce, makes an ideal first course for an elegant dinner.

½ medium cantaloupe, chilled in the refrigerator for at least an hour
1 teaspoon agave nectar or other liquid sweetener

½ cup Charmoula (page 71)
Freshly ground black pepper, for serving

In a small bowl, stir together the Charmoula and sweetener. Set aside.

Being gentle with the succulent fruit, scoop out the cantaloupe's seeds with a spoon, and peel using a sharp knife. Be sure to remove all the skin, shaving off any bits with a green cast. Using a mandoline or vegetable peeler, start with a cut side and shave off thin slices of cantaloupe. Pile the carpaccio directly onto four chilled plates, or into one large platter. Dollop the relish evenly around the perimeter of each plate, and over the carpaccio. Sprinkle each serving with a pinch of black pepper and serve immediately. Pass additional relish on the side.

Mediterranean Rolls

Makes about 2 dozen rolls

These rolls are a twist on sushi, filled with tahini-sauced rice and wrapped in grape leaves instead of nori. They're the perfect addition to a table spread with Italian, Lebanese, or Greek cuisine.

Half an 8-ounce jar grape leaves
2 cups cooked long-grain rice,
    at room temperature
¾ cup Tahini-Lemon Sauce (page 76)
1 cucumber, peeled, seeded, and
    sliced into thin strips
½ red onion, thinly sliced

1 portabella mushrooms, sliced into
    ¼-inch strips
¼ cup packed fresh basil and fresh mint
    (I do half of each), finely chopped
Balsamic vinegar, for dipping
Additional Tahini-Lemon Sauce, for
    serving (optional)

Place a sushi mat on a workspace. Alternatively, cut out a 10 by 8-inch piece of cardboard or paper (about the size of a sheet of nori). This will be your template for the rolls. Cover the sushi mat or template with a sheet of plastic wrap that extends beyond the template's borders, and have more plastic available.

Gently unroll the grape leaves. Place in a bowl and completely submerge in water to remove some of the brine. Pinch off the nubby stems if they are still attached.

While the leaves rest, fold the sauce into the cooked rice in a medium bowl. Transfer to the refrigerator to chill until you are ready to assemble the rolls.

Set everything up on your workspace so it is easily accessible. Place the cucumber, onion, portabella, and herbs into individual bowls.

Transfer the leaves to a strainer. Place several leaves on a clean kitchen towel and gently blot dry. Place leaves vein-side up, with the leaf tips pointed away from you, over the plastic-lined template. Overlap the leaves, using as many as necessary to cover the template completely (about 4). Tear additional leaves into pieces to fill in any gaps, if needed.

Using your hands, thinly spread about ¾ cup of the rice mixture over the template, leaving a clean 2-inch edge on the side farthest from you. At the edge closest to you, arrange cucumber, onion, and portabella slices, as you would with traditional sushi. An ideal amount is 2 cucumber strips, 2 portabella strips, and a scant handful of onion slivers. Sprinkle 1 tablespoon of the herb mixture over the filling.

Starting at the end nearest you, roll up the grape leaves as tightly as possible. At the end of the roll, gently press in the leaves to secure it, and tamp in any rice or fillings protruding from the ends. Wrap in plastic and refrigerate until ready to cut. Repeat with the remaining grape leaves and fillings. You should have 3 finished rolls, and some of the grape leaves and fillings left over.

LITTLE BITES

Cut the rolls just before serving. Using a very sharp knife, slice straight through the plastic wrap at 1-inch increments. Gently tease the plastic away from the cut rolls and arrange them on a plate. Serve with balsamic vinegar and additional Tahini-Lemon Sauce, if desired.

Muffaletta Sandwich

Makes 4 entrée or 12 appetizer servings

This is my very favorite sandwich, and has made me the envy of many at picnics, outdoor concerts, and sporting events.

1 loaf (1 pound) ciabatta
1 cup Muffaletta Spread (page 73)
¾ cup Chèvre (page 64)

4 ounces (about half a can, or 5 small) artichoke hearts
½ cup packed fresh basil leaves
Sea salt and ground black pepper

Split ciabatta crosswise with a serrated knife, and lay the top and bottom on a workspace. Using your fingers, remove just enough of the doughy insides to create a slight well on either side (several handfuls' worth).

Spread the halves evenly with Muffaletta. Drop small pieces of Chèvre onto the bottom half, then use an offset spatula to spread it out. The Chèvre will be thick and may adhere to the spatula a bit; just keep working at it. Break up the artichoke hearts and layer over the Chèvre. Arrange basil leaves, still whole, over the artichokes. Top with the remaining half of ciabatta.

Wrap the sandwich in parchment or waxed paper and secure with rubber bands, kitchen twine, or dental floss. Place under a large book or cast-iron skillet, and weight with several cans or additional books. Allow the package to press for at least an hour, and up to a day. Transfer to the refrigerator if pressing for more than 2 hours.

When ready to serve, unwrap the sandwich and slice into pieces on a diagonal. I often bring the sandwich on picnics, unsliced, and dig in with a good pocket knife.

A Clean Kitchen

You use the purest ingredients in your cooking. Why not use them in your kitchen, too? These natural cleaning agents will make things sparkle, and are significantly less expensive than commercial products.

Use dish soap made with coconut-derived surfactants and with no artificial fragrances added.

Fill a spray bottle with water and several tablespoons of vinegar for a simple all-purpose cleaner. Use vinegar full-strength for particularly greasy jobs. (Be careful when using acids on grout and marble, as it can etch their surfaces.)

Remove stains with a sprinkling of baking soda and a good scrubbing. For oily or baked-on residues on cookware, mix equal parts baking soda and dish soap directly on the item, and scour away.

To reduce sink odors, toss a leftover halved lemon into the disposal. Pour hot water in, and process until clear. The clean fragrance of citrus will fill your kitchen.

Most conventional kitchen cleaners can be replaced by baking soda, vinegar, or some combination of both. Experiment with these elements, and you may never need store brands again.

Everything Cleanser

I created this all-purpose spray to remove kitchen odors, and quickly realized its many uses. Ideal for cleaning everything from glass to counters to showers, it freshens the air, removes wrinkles from clothes, and is completely nontoxic (well, no more than any other alcohol). Replace the alcohol with white vinegar for a disinfecting countertop cleaner.

½ cup vodka or gin
5 drops peppermint oil

5 drops lavender oil
1½ cups water

Put the vodka or gin and the oils in a spray bottle. Swirl to combine. The liquid will appear cloudy but should mix without much effort. Pour in water, replace cap, and give the mixture a final shake. The cleanser stores indefinitely at room temperature.

LITTLE BITES

Roasted Garlic Bowl

Makes 4 appetizer servings

Sop up this intensely garlicky muddle with good French bread, crudités, or crackers.

4 heads garlic
Pinches of sea salt
3 tablespoons extra virgin olive oil
¼ cup chopped fresh herbs (I like basil, oregano, rosemary, and thyme)
½ teaspoon sea salt

½ teaspoon ground black pepper
2 tablespoons good-quality balsamic vinegar

Heat the oven to 375° F. Remove as much papery skin from the garlic heads as possible, while still keeping the cloves secured at the center. Using a very sharp or serrated knife, cut about ½ inch from the top (pointy end) of each head. Then go around the head, slicing the very top from each of the lower cloves.

Place a head on a sheet of foil at least 10 inches or so across. Sprinkle with a pinch of sea salt, and drizzle with a few teaspoons of water. Gather the foil together so you have some space within the bundle, but it's sealed tightly. Repeat with the remaining garlic.

Roast 45 to 50 minutes, until bundles are very soft when squeezed. Inside, the garlic will be syrupy and golden when done. Allow it to cool slightly, then squeeze the cloves onto a shallow bowl or platter. Drizzle with oil, herbs, sea salt, and pepper, then return to the oven for 5 minutes.

Drizzle with balsamic vinegar, and serve immediately.

Broccoli-Cheese Bruschetta

Makes 16 starter or 8 open-faced sandwich servings

Far from the usual broccoli and cheese, this appetizer combines the assertive flavors of caramelized broccoli and sharp cheddar.

2 cups Sharp White Cheddar Sauce (page 75)

1 recipe Caramelized Broccoli (page 164), left as is or coarsely chopped

8 slices good-quality bread (sourdough wheat and pumpernickel are excellent choices)

Lightly toast the bread in a toaster or skillet over medium heat. Set the bread on a workspace and spread each slice with several tablespoons of the sauce. Top each slice with ⅛ of the broccoli. Slice each bruschetta into quarters on a diagonal. Serve.

Broccoli and White Cheddar Panini

For 4 sandwiches, cover 4 slices with cheddar sauce and broccoli as directed above. Top with the remaining 4 slices of bread. Toast the sandwiches in a panini press until golden and grill-marked. Alternatively, toast them in a cast-iron skillet, weighted with another cast-iron skillet or other heavy object.

Hot and Sweet Popcorn

Makes about 10 cups

This spicy-sweet snack is the perfect contrast to Palm Heart Ceviche (page 83). Eaten by the handful, it is completely addictive.

Microwave popcorn is a fine choice here. If you live in an area with high humidity, or the day is particularly damp, be sure to store the popcorn as soon as it cools.

Vary the spices for a warm holiday treat: omit the cayenne, cumin, and paprika, and use ¼ teaspoon each of cinnamon, cloves, and nutmeg.

10 cups unsalted popped popcorn
½ cup sugar
¼ cup water
½ teaspoon vinegar (any kind will do)

½ teaspoon sea salt
¼ teaspoon cayenne
¼ teaspoon cumin
¼ teaspoon paprika

Place the popcorn in a very large bowl or baking pan and set aside. Line a counter surface with a sheet of parchment or waxed paper.

In a small, high-sided saucepan, combine the sugar, water, vinegar, and sea salt, stirring briefly to dissolve. Clip a food thermometer to the side and place over high heat. Cook, without stirring, until the mixture reaches 260° F, hard-ball stage. (If you're without a thermometer, closely watch the mixture. The hard-ball stage is achieved just before carmelization begins, which means you'll need to remove it the instant the edges begin to turn golden.)

Meanwhile, stir together the spices in a small bowl and keep it close at hand.

When the stovetop mixture reaches 260° F, immediately remove from the heat, whisk in spice blend—it will bubble up—and quickly drizzle over popcorn. Use a spatula or large spoon to stir, evenly coating the popcorn with the spice mixture. At this point, threads of sugar may become visible as you toss; this is normal.

Turn the popcorn out onto prepared parchment or waxed paper to cool completely. Break into clusters, and serve or store.

The popcorn will keep in an airtight container or sealed plastic bag for up to a week. If it becomes tacky, place on a rimmed baking sheet in a 350° F oven for 5 to 10 minutes, stirring once. Once cool, the popcorn will return to its original crispness.

Corn

Most corn grown in the United States is genetically modified, and the seed that grows it is controlled primarily by one company. We don't know the long-term effects of growing and consuming GMO foods, and the monopoly on seed creates problems worldwide, particularly in countries where corn is a native crop. For these reasons—and a number of others—it's important to make corn one of the foods you buy organically. Corn is found in many products you wouldn't expect, so check labels too.

Salmon-Safe Pâté

Makes about 2 cups

Many vegetarians and vegans have an instant in which they realize they're not going to consume animals anymore. For me, this defining moment happened while catering a retreat in Southern California. I had been eating a vegan diet for months, but only for health reasons. I thought ethical vegans were gluttons for deprivation.

One night while preparing dinner, I looked down at a piece of salmon in my hand, deep orange and glistening. As I turned it to slough off the skin, I stopped. Across the scales were intricate patterns, a million facets of light, and shades of silver I had never seen. I imagined the fish in a lake somewhere, leaping from the water, its luminous skin flashing back the sun. As I stared, I knew the fish would have been better alive, doing his own fish things.

"I'm never going to eat meat again," I said aloud. And that was that. Oddly, fish is the only animal thing I've thought about eating as a vegan. A bit of this salad every few months does the trick.

3 tablespoons dulse, preferably smoked
1 (15-ounce) can chickpeas
1 cup shredded carrots
2 tablespoons minced onion
2 tablespoons mayonnaise

2 tablespoons apple cider vinegar or
    fresh lemon juice
1 tablespoon chopped fresh parsley
    (optional)

Soak the dulse in fresh water for 10 to 15 minutes.

Pulse the remaining ingredients in a food processor until well combined but not pureed. Squeeze the excess water from the dulse, add to the processor, and pulse again. Transfer to a medium bowl, and refrigerate at least 15 minutes to allow the flavors to meld.

Serve as a sandwich filling, or with an assortment of vegetables. Celery and red bell pepper are particularly good for scooping it up.

Dulse

This recipe uses dulse, a type of seaweed prized for its high mineral content and intense flavor. Look for the dried, whole variety rather than dulse that has been ground into flakes or powder. If using flaked or powdered dulse, reduce the amount above to 2 tablespoons, and do not soak before using. If you can find it, applewood-smoked dulse is delicious.

Smoky Corn and Date Empanaditas

Makes 2 dozen

Empanadas are flaky Argentinean pastries stuffed with a variety of fillings depending on the region: raisins, potatoes, olives, rice. These smaller, savory-sweet empanaditas borrow from several South American traditions, and feature chipotle pepper, corn, dates, and pepitas.

Many empanada doughs use wheat flour instead of white. In this recipe, up to half the amount of flour can be substituted with whole wheat.

Dough

2 cups all-purpose flour

2 teaspoons sugar

5 tablespoons nonhydrogenated
    vegetable shortening

4 tablespoons margarine, chilled and
    cut into pieces

3 to 4 tablespoons ice water

Filling

1 tablespoon canola or corn oil

2 cloves garlic, minced

1 small onion, diced

1 chipotle pepper in adobo, minced

2 cups fresh or frozen corn (about 2
    cobs' worth)

⅓ cup pepitas, roughly chopped

¾ cup dates (6 to 8 large medjool),
    snipped into small pieces with
    kitchen shears

½ teaspoon ground cumin

¼ teaspoon cinnamon

¼ teaspoon sea salt

½ cup water

Glazing

Nondairy milk

Make the dough: in a food processor, pulse together the flour and sugar. Add shortening and margarine, and pulse again until only small lumps remain. With the machine running, add the ice water a bit at a time, allowing it to run until the dough is roughly combined or forms a ball (this shouldn't take long at all). Shape the dough into a disk. Wrap in plastic and refrigerate for at least 30 minutes. The dough can be kept, well-wrapped, for up to 2 days before assembling the empanaditas.

Make the filling: in a medium saucepan over high heat, sauté the garlic and onion in canola oil until translucent, 3 to 5 minutes. Add the chipotle pepper, corn, dates, pepitas, cinnamon, cumin, and sea salt. Cook, stirring, for 2 more minutes, mashing the dates with a spatula as you go. Pour in the water, then continue cooking until liquid is absorbed and dates are soft, about 5 minutes. Remove from the heat and allow them to cool before using. The mixture can be refrigerated up to 2 days before assembling the empanaditas.

To assemble and bake: heat the oven to 375° F. Line a baking sheet with parchment or waxed paper, and set aside.

On a lightly floured surface, roll out the dough to $^1/_{16}$-inch thickness. Using a 3-inch cookie cutter, drinking glass, or small bowl, cut rounds. Reroll the dough only once. Place one tablespoon filling in the center of one of the rounds. Using your finger, dampen one half of the round with a bit of nondairy milk. Fold the other side over. With the tines of a fork, crimp the rounded edge of the empanadita to seal and create a *repulgue*, or pattern. Place on prepared baking sheet. Repeat with the remaining dough rounds and filling. At this point, the dough can be wrapped carefully and frozen for up to 3 months.

To bake, brush the tops of empanaditas with a bit of nondairy milk. Bake until piping-hot and golden, 15 to 20 minutes. Allow them to cool slightly before serving.

Cutting Dates

To cut the dates: once pitted, make a lengthwise cut down each side of the date; you should have four long quarters. Press them somewhat back together, and snip the dates into bits with kitchen scissors. Be careful, as the flesh of fingers has a texture quite similar to dates, and it's easy to mistake the two.

LITTLE BITES

Buttermilk Onion Rings with Spicy Dipping Sauce

Makes 4 conservative or 2 generous appetizer servings (about 24 rings)

I'd really like to be modest about this recipe, but these onion rings are absurdly delicious. The batter adheres wonderfully to the onions, and they have a beautiful golden exterior that shatters when you take a bite. The coating is also great for frying zucchini, skewered chunks of seitan, or vegan candy bars.

Vidalia or Maui onions will produce onion rings with a nice sweetness; if you can locate them, use them here. Otherwise, any yellow or white variety will work. It's important that the oil be hot enough to create the right texture, so consider investing in a frying thermometer, which can be found for under $10.

1 white or yellow onion

2 to 5 cups vegetable oil, for frying

½ cup all-purpose flour, plus ⅓ cup flour for dredging

1 tablespoon cornstarch

1 teaspoon baking powder

½ teaspoon sea salt

¼ teaspoon ground pepper

½ cup nondairy milk

1 tablespoon cider vinegar

1 teaspoon oil

Several dashes hot sauce (optional)

⅔ cup Spicy Dipping Sauce (page 66)

Slice the onion across the center into even ½-inch rounds. If you prefer more ring and less onion, slice them into ¼-inch rounds. The center slices will be most desirable, but the smaller ones are fine, too. Gently separate into rings. You should have about 24 rings of various sizes. If using Vidalia or Maui onions, get on with the flour dredging. If you are using regular onions and want to decrease the bitterness, place them in a medium bowl, cover with cold water, and allow them to rest for 15 to 30 minutes. Drain well and pat dry.

Heat the oil to 365° F while you prepare the batter. The amount of oil will vary widely, depending on the size pan you use. I prefer a smaller pan, as it doesn't require as much, and gives greater control over the process. Whatever size you use, pour the oil about 2 inches deep.

Dredge the onion slices in ⅓ cup of the flour, using a very light coating, and set aside.

Whisk together the remaining ½ cup flour, cornstarch, baking powder, sea salt, and pepper. Slowly add the nondairy milk, whisking constantly until smooth. Stir in the vinegar, oil, and hot sauce.

Tap an onion to remove excess flour, then dip in batter, turning thoroughly to coat. Place the onion in the oil as soon as it has been battered, then repeat with the remaining rings.

LITTLE BITES

Fry the rings several at a time, until deep golden. The size of your pan will determine how many can be cooked at once. It's fine if they touch, just don't allow them to overlap. Using kitchen tongs, remove to a plate lined with paper towels or pieces of brown paper bags. Allow them to drain for a moment before serving, if you have the willpower.

Tea-Smoked Tofu or Tempeh

Makes 1 pound

In this simple dish, tofu or tempeh is immersed in a sort of poaching liquid of tea, soy sauce, and spices.

The dish is a nice accompaniment to steamed or sautéed vegetables; cut it into narrow strips and scatter over the top, cooked in sesame oil, or as is. Thin slices also make an ideal sushi filling.

Look for loose tea with a dark, smoky flavor. If you can't find loose tea, empty the contents from 3 to 4 teabags.

16 ounces firm or extra firm tofu, or 8 ounces steamed tempeh

1 teaspoon sea salt

2 tablespoons soy sauce

2 star anise blooms, or 1 teaspoon anise seeds

2 tablespoons loose black tea (Earl Grey or lapsang souchong are ideal)

2 cups water

1 tablespoon black sesame seeds, for garnish (plain sesame seeds are a fine substitution)

If using tofu, make several slashes across the top to help the liquid penetrate and add flavor. Flip tofu, and repeat on the opposite side. Set aside, and make the smoking liquid.

In a medium saucepan, combine the sea salt, soy sauce, anise, tea, and water. Stir, and bring to a boil. Remove the mixture from the heat, and submerge the tofu or tempeh in poaching liquid. Add water if necessary to cover. Allow it to cool completely, then refrigerate, covered, at least 8 hours and up to 4 days.

If serving right away, slice into thin slivers, and sprinkle with sesame seeds, or add to a stir-fry or hors d'oeuvres platter. Otherwise, keep refrigerated in poaching liquid until ready to use.

Tea-Smoked Tofu or Tempeh Sandwiches

Crumble one recipe Tea-Smoked Tofu or Tempeh together with 3 tablespoons mayonnaise, 1 thinly sliced onion, 2 teaspoons rice vinegar, ½ teaspoon sea salt, ¼ teaspoon ground pepper, and ¼ teaspoon dry mustard powder. Mash everything together to combine well. Spread 8 slices of white bread thinly with mayonnaise and top with filling. Halve sandwiches diagonally, spread edges with mayonnaise, and coat with black or regular sesame seeds.

Serve immediately or cover with a layer of slightly damp paper towels followed by a layer of plastic wrap. Leave at room temperature for up to an hour, or refrigerate if serving several hours later.

Salads

On first glance, salads seem so virtuous and austere. But no, the greens featured here are anything but. Slathered with creamy dressing or filled to the brim with flavorful roasted vegetables, these composed dishes are proof that salads needn't be boring. And yes, some of them are healthy, too.

Barbecue Ranch Salad

Makes 4 entrée-sized or 8 appetizer servings

You will really enjoy this, I just know it.

8 cups mixed greens (romaine, spinach, whatever you have on hand)

½ cup packed cilantro, coarsely chopped

3 medium tomatoes, diced

2 ears corn, kernels cut

½ pound jicama, peeled and cut into ½ inch chunks

1 (16-ounce) can black beans, drained and rinsed

¼ cup barbecue sauce (store-bought is fine; look for a brand free of honey)

1½ cups corn chips

¾ cup Peppercorn Ranch Dressing (page 63)

1 medium avocado, diced

Cilantro sprigs, for serving

In a large bowl, toss together the greens, cilantro, tomatoes, corn, jicama, and beans. Add ranch dressing and barbecue sauce, and gently toss again. Crumble the corn chips over everything. Top with diced avocado and additional cilantro, and serve.

Barbecue Tempeh Ranch Salad

Before whisking together the dressing, toss 16 ounces of cubed tempeh with ¼ cup barbecue sauce in a casserole dish. Transfer the foil to a 350° F oven and cook, stirring once, for 15 minutes. Remove it from the oven and allow it to cool slightly. Chop coarsely and add to salad with the ranch dressing.

Salade Niçoise

Makes 6 entrée servings

With a good loaf of bread and crisp white wine, this French bistro-style salad is a great casual meal. For something more substantial, add 1½ cups great northern beans, tossed with several tablespoons of the vinaigrette.

1 pound potatoes (about 3 medium, any variety will do), cut into ¾-inch chunks

1 pound green beans, strings removed, cut into 1½-inch segments

1 pound tomatoes (about 3 medium), or 1 pound grape tomatoes

1 pound mixed greens (spring mix, chopped romaine, chopped red or green leaf lettuces)

3 tablespoons capers

¾ cup Niçoise olives

Fresh Herb Vinaigrette (page 61)

Steam potatoes until tender when pierced with a fork, about 15 minutes. Shake dry, and transfer to a medium bowl. Gently toss with about ⅓ cup of the vinaigrette, and set aside.

Steam green beans until bright green, 2 to 3 minutes. Remove from the heat, top with a handful of ice cubes, and rinse under cold water to stop cooking. Shake dry, then transfer to a medium bowl. The green beans can also be left raw giving a crisper, texture and more intense flavor. Toss with about ¼ cup of the vinaigrette and set aside. If using medium tomatoes, slice them into eighths.

Mound the mixed greens in a large bowl or deep platter. Arrange potatoes, green beans, and tomatoes in individual mounds or concentric circles over the lettuce. Sprinkle capers and olives over the top. Serve with the remaining vinaigrette on the side. Any leftovers will keep well.

Potato Salad Niçoise

For a flavorful potato salad, cook the potatoes and toss with vinaigrette as directed. Add the olives and capers, and toss in 2 tablespoons diced red onion and several handfuls arugula. Drizzle with a more vinaigrette, if you like, and serve warm or chilled.

Ice Bath Shortcut

While superior for stopping cooking and sealing in color, an ice bath does take a moment to assemble. Save time by cooling directly in the strainer: top the drained, cooked vegetables with a few handfuls of ice cubes. Run cold water over everything, tossing by hand until thoroughly cold, and drain again. Your vegetables will be crisp and colorful in an instant.

Caramelized Onion and Lentil Salad

Makes 6 entrée or 8 appetizer servings

Seek out Le Puy lentils, which are very small and dark, and worth looking for. If you cannot find Le Puys, use French lentils, which are preferable to the regular green sort.

For the dried fruit, I like a combination of pears, peaches, apples, and cranberries. Prunes, cherries, plums, or golden raisins are also nice. Use a variety of whatever you have available.

This salad can be prepared up to 2 days in advance, but don't add the lentil mixture to the greens until ready to plate it. Served hot without greens, the salad makes a hearty yet refined side dish.

1 cup Le Puy lentils
Water or vegetable stock, to cover
  (3 to 6 cups)
2 white or yellow onions, sliced into
  thin half-moons
2 tablespoons margarine
Generous pinch of sugar

Generous pinch of sea salt
1 cup mixed dried fruit, finely chopped
¼ cup white wine
1 teaspoon apple cider vinegar
¾ teaspoon sea salt
½ teaspoon ground black pepper
8 cups spring greens, for serving

In a medium saucepan over medium heat, cook lentils in water or stock until tender, 45 to 60 minutes. Drain and transfer to a medium bowl.

Meanwhile, caramelize the onions: in a cast-iron skillet, combine the onions, margarine, sugar, and sea salt. Begin with medium-low heat, stirring often. Once the onions go translucent, reduce the heat to low and stir only enough to prevent browning. Very gradually, the onions will take on a pale golden color, which deepens to a more coppery color. The process will take at least 30 minutes, and up to an hour. Transfer caramelized onions to the bowl containing lentils, and set aside.

Return skillet to medium heat and add the dried fruit and white wine. Simmer, stirring, until fruit has plumped slightly, and most of the liquid has evaporated. Add to the lentil mixture, along with vinegar, sea salt, and pepper. Stir everything gently to combine. Taste, and adjust seasonings if necessary.

Serve the salad slightly warm or at room temperature, over handfuls of the cold, crisp greens.

Larb Kai

Makes 4 entrée or 6 appetizer servings

With its combination of hot, sour, salty, and sweet, this salad is quintessentially Thai. It's a Northeastern dish, but I remember tasting it for the first time in the southern province of Saraburi. If you visit the kingdom—or just a Thai restaurant—ask for "laab," and request it spicy. Not farang *(foreigner) spicy, Thai spicy.*

The salad seems a bit labor intensive but is well worth the effort.

Larb is traditionally served with glutinous (sticky) rice. For a dinner party featuring other Thai foods, serve it on a shallow platter over lettuce, with garnishes arranged around the sides. If you're serving cocktails or snacks, the salad is ideal wrapped in lettuce leaves as individual appetizers.

¼ cup brown or white rice

8 ounces tempeh, well steamed

1 tablespoon peanut or canola oil

3 cloves garlic, thinly sliced

2 tablespoons soy sauce

1 tablespoon agave nectar, or
   sweetener of your choice

½ cup fresh lime juice

1 tablespoon Thai or Serrano chiles,
   minced or 2 jalapeños, ½ habañero

2 tablespoons minced fresh lemongrass

½ small red onion, thinly sliced

½ cup loosely packed cilantro,
   coarsely chopped

½ cup loosely packed mint,
   coarsely chopped

1 medium head romaine or green leaf
   lettuce, washed and leaves separated

1 carrot, shredded

1 cucumber, peeled, seeded, and
   sliced into ½-inch slices

1 lime, thinly sliced

SALADS

Dry toast the rice in a skillet over medium heat. The grains will brown slightly, pop, and become fragrant. Don't allow them to scorch. Using a mortar and pestle, food processor, blender, or coffee grinder, pulverize the rice into a coarse powder. Set aside.

In a food processor, pulse the tofu or tempeh until ground fine. Heat the oil in a cast-iron skillet over high heat. Add garlic and tempeh, and cook, stirring, until slightly browned.

Transfer the mixture to a medium bowl, and add soy sauce, sweetener, lime juice, chili, reserved crushed rice, lemongrass, onions, cilantro, and mint. Stir well to combine. Allow the flavors to meld while you prepare the garnishes.

Arrange lettuce leaves on a shallow platter. Spoon larb mixture over lettuce. Place the carrot, cucumber, and sliced lime around the perimeter of the platter. Serve slightly warm, at room temperature, or cold, with rice (preferably glutinous) or cellophane noodles on the side.

For wheat-free substitute tamari for soy sauce

Fresh Kale Salad with Hazelnut Vinaigrette

Makes 4 entrée or 6 appetizer servings

A toss in this nutty vinaigrette makes raw kale surprisingly delicious. I use a combination of purple and curly kale, but any kind is fine.

8 ounces kale

3 apples, chopped into ¾-inch pieces

3 carrots, shredded

½ cup currants

½ cup raw sunflower seeds or chopped raw hazelnuts

½ cup Hazelnut Vinaigrette (page 63)

Chiffonade the kale into ¾-inch strips, then give it a few good crosswise hacks. Toss together with apples, carrots, currants, and sunflower seeds or hazelnuts. Add the vinaigrette and toss again. Allow the flavors to meld, at room temperature, for at least 10 minutes. Serve.

The salad keeps exceptionally well, and has great flavor the next day.

Cannelloni, Chickpea, and Green Bean Salad with Tomatoes and Fresh Thyme

Makes 4 entrée servings or 6 side-dish servings

I love the flavor of thyme and grow big bunches in my herb garden every year. It's excellent in this salad, where fresh ingredients, simply prepared, come together without pretense. If making it in advance, decide how you like your arugula. If you want it crisp, keep the elements separate until serving. If tender, just toss it all together and allow the arugula to melt into everything as it stands.

Fresh rosemary or sage substituted for the thyme would be just as nice.

½ pound fresh green beans, cut diagonally into 1-inch pieces

1 (16-ounce) can cannelloni, great northern, or other white beans, rinsed and drained

1 (16-ounce) can chickpeas, rinsed and drained

3 tablespoons white wine vinegar

1 tablespoon olive oil

2 cloves garlic, minced

1 tablespoon fresh thyme

1 teaspoon Dijon mustard

½ teaspoon sea salt

½ teaspoon ground black pepper

1½ cups grape or cherry tomatoes, halved

6 to 8 cups fresh arugula, for serving

fresh thyme sprigs, for garnish (optional)

Steam the green beans briefly in a steamer until crisp-tender, about 5 to 8 minutes. If you prefer, skip this step and keep the beans raw, simply marinating them in the vinaigrette. Transfer the green beans to a medium bowl and add the cannelloni and chickpeas. In a 2-cup measure or small bowl, whisk together the vinegar, oil, garlic, thyme, mustard, sea salt, and pepper. Pour the vinaigrette over the bean mixture, and toss everything together. Add tomatoes, and gently toss again.

To serve, loosely distribute arugula over a large, shallow platter. Heap salad over it, and garnish with additional thyme sprigs, if desired. Bring to the table at room temperature.

Frijoles Mezclados

Makes 8 to 10 servings

This fresh, fat-free combination of beans and seasonings is like optimism in a bowl. It's simple to toss together, excellent over salad greens or tucked into a burrito, and certain to make you grin on tasting it.

1 (25-ounce) can pinto beans, drained and rinsed, or 2½ cups dried cooked beans

1 (25-ounce) can black beans, drained and rinsed, or 2½ cups dried cooked beans

1 (25-ounce) can kidney beans, drained and rinsed, or 2½ cups dried cooked beans

2 ears corn, kernels cut

1 loosely packed cup cilantro, roughly chopped

1 red or white onion, diced

1 Jalapeño pepper, seeded and minced

2 cloves garlic, minced

Juice of half a lime

1 teaspoon sea salt

1 teaspoon freshly ground pepper

Mix everything together in a gigantic bowl. Cover and refrigerate, for up to 3 days, before serving.

Adzuki, Soybean, and Chinese Long Bean Salad

Makes 4 entrée or 6 side-dish servings

Chinese long beans can be found at Asian groceries. Regular green beans are a fine substitution, although the long sort add something special to this unusual, citrus-laced salad.

¼ cup orange marmalade

2 tablespoons soy sauce

1 tablespoon rice vinegar

3 green onions, thinly sliced

2 cloves garlic, minced

1½ cups frozen shelled edamame

½ pound Chinese long beans or green beans, ends trimmed, sliced into 2-inch bits on the diagonal

1 (16-ounce) can adzuki beans, rinsed and drained

4 medium radishes, very thinly sliced

In a medium bowl, whisk together the marmalade, vinegar, soy sauce, green onions, and garlic.

Cook the edamame according to package directions and add to the bowl of dressing. Steam the long beans until bright green and just tender, 1 to 2 minutes. Run them under cold water, drain, and add to the bowl. Add the adzuki beans and toss to combine.

For wheat-free substitute tamari for soy sauce

Mediterranean Couscous Salad

Makes 4 to 6 entrée servings

The amount of vegetables at the start will seem intimidating. Don't worry; it gets reduced by nearly half during the roasting process.

To serve as a side dish, simply omit the greens and serve warm.

Vegetables

1 pound eggplant (1 medium), chopped into 1-inch chunks

8 ounces mushrooms, halved

1 pound onions (2 medium), chopped into ½-inch thick half-moons

1 pound zucchini (2 to 3 medium), chopped into ½-inch thick half-moons

1 pound yellow squash (2 to 3 medium), chopped into ½-inch thick half-moons

1 pound tomatoes (3 medium), roughly chopped into ½-inch chunks

5 to 10 cloves garlic (depending on taste), minced

¼ cup capers, rinsed and drained

½ cup tightly packed basil, finely chopped

1 tablespoon sea salt

Couscous

1¼ cup couscous

1½ cups boiling water or vegetable stock

1 teaspoon olive oil

½ teaspoon sea salt

To Serve

6 ounces spring mix, or other baby lettuces

Balsamic vinegar, for serving (optional)

Heat the oven to 350° F. Toss together all the vegetable ingredients directly on a large rimmed baking sheet. Roast 30 to 40 minutes, stirring occasionally.

Meanwhile, place the couscous in a medium bowl. Add water or stock, oil, and sea salt. Cover it with a plate, and allow it to rest for 10 minutes. Fluff with a fork before using.

Remove the vegetables from the heat. Mound couscous on a shallow platter, and top with vegetables. Serve the greens in a separate bowl, allowing guests to take couscous, vegetables, and greens as it suits them.

Before storing as leftovers, combine the couscous and vegetables to insulate the grains and maintain a nice texture.

Curtice Street Salad

Makes 6 to 8 luncheon servings

This recipe is adapted from a tearoom where I worked, and it became a fast favorite. The tearoom sat on Curtice Street, next door to a small antique shop (shoppe, that is) whose owner graciously lent her family's chopped salad recipe, which had been passed down through several generations.

This is the vegan version. Serve with a muffin and cup of soup for a light lunch.

2 cups jicama, chopped into ½-inch cubes

2 cups celery, halved lengthwise down the ribs, then chopped into ¼-inch pieces

2 cups red grapes, halved

1 cup walnuts

¾ cup Lemon-Dill Dressing (page 72)

6 to 8 large romaine leaves, for serving

Toss together jicama, celery, grapes, walnuts, and dressing, stirring well to combine. Serve over romaine leaves.

If you plan to make this ahead, keep the walnuts separate until serving, since they'll get soggy as they sit.

Omega Protein Salad

Substitute 2 cups cooked cubed seitan for the jicama, and increase walnuts to 1½ cups. Continue as directed, and top with a spoonful of flax or hemp seeds, if desired.

Avocado-Quinoa Salad with Tamarind-Citrus Syrup

Makes 4 entrée salad servings

Here, cooling citrus, piquant onion and parsley, and toasted quinoa are nestled in buttery avocado halves and drizzled with a sharp and sweet tamarind-citrus syrup. Packed with calcium, protein, and healthy fat, the salad makes a filling addition to any meal.

For a lower-fat option, pile the salad over greens. Use only one avocado, and serve in thin slices over the quinoa mixture.

SALADS

Avocado-Quinoa Salad

1 cup quinoa

2 cups water

1 clove garlic, peeled and smashed
   once with the side of a knife

½ teaspoon sea salt

1 orange

1 grapefruit

2 cups firmly packed parsley,
   finely chopped

½ onion, diced

2 avocados

1 lime, cut into 8 wedges,
   for serving (optional)

Tamarind-Citrus Syrup

2 teaspoons tamarind paste

2 teaspoons orange-grapefruit juice
   (reserved from cut fruit)

1 teaspoon agave nectar

⅛ teaspoon cayenne pepper

Place the quinoa in a dry saucepan over medium-high heat, and shake the pan constantly until quinoa is tinged brown and fragrant, 3 to 5 minutes. Some of the grains will have begun to pop, and you'll smell a distinct nuttiness once it's sufficiently toasted. Add the water, garlic, and sea salt. Bring the mixture to a rapid boil, then reduce the heat to a simmer and cook until the liquid is absorbed. Remove from the heat, toss the garlic if you like, and shovel the quinoa into a medium bowl. For quicker cooling, mound up onto the sides in a thin layer. Transfer it to the refrigerator to cool.

Supreme the orange and grapefruit: using a sharp knife, slice off the ends and remove all skin and pith. Hold the fruit in one hand, and make deep cuts just next to the rind to release the jeweled slices (see the Pink Grapefruit Sorbet on page 210 for more details on supreming). Squeeze juice from the leftover pulp and skin into a small bowl, reserving it for use in the syrup. In a medium serving bowl, combine the cooled quinoa, orange, grapefruit, parsley, and onion. Don't worry about crushing the citrus; a good stir will muddle it, releasing just enough juice to flavor the salad. At this point, the mixture can be made up to 2 days in advance and refrigerated until ready to serve.

To make the syrup, whisk all ingredients together in a small bowl.

To serve: halve and seed the avocados. Using a very large spoon, scoop the fruit from its shells and place each half on a smallish plate. Mound an equal portion of the quinoa mixture over the avocado halves. Drizzle syrup attractively around plates, and place lime wedges alongside, if desired.

Tamarind Paste

When purchasing tamarind paste, look for the thick, seedless variety that contains no added sugar or spices. Most easily found at Indian or Middle Eastern groceries, it is referred to as both "paste" and "concentrate."

Caesar Salad

Makes 2 servings (double or triple as needed)

The well-known classic, tangy with lemon and garlic, and scattered with hearty croutons.

Any good bread will work for the croutons. Try sprouted grain or pumpernickel for a unique, earthy flavor.

2 slices bread, cut into 1-inch cubes
1 tablespoon olive oil
1 teaspoon minced flat-leaf parsley
½ teaspoon sea salt
1 clove garlic, halved
1 tablespoon mayonnaise
½ teaspoon Dijon mustard
¼ teaspoon sea salt

2 2-inch pieces of nori, clipped or
    shredded into very small pieces
2 teaspoons fresh lemon juice
1 teaspoon olive oil
⅛ teaspoon ground black pepper
1 head romaine lettuce, cut into
    2-inch pieces

Heat the oven to 350° F. On a baking sheet, toss together the bread, olive oil, and parsley. Sprinkle sea salt over, and toss again. Toast until golden-brown 10 to 15 minutes, then set aside to cool while you make the dressing.

In a salad bowl, mash together the garlic, salt, mayonnaise, and Dijon, using the back of a fork or wooden spoon. Add the nori and fresh lemon juice, and mash again. Slowly whisk in the olive oil; the consistency should have a runny creaminess. Add the romaine to the bowl, stirring to coat evenly. Top with croutons and serve immediately.

Ice Baths (see also Ice Bath Shortcut, page 100)

An ice bath is simply a bowl of ice water used for cooling cooked foods. While the insides of steamed or boiled ingredients will continue cooking if left at room temperature, an ice bath rapidly halts the process. It also restores the crispness of vegetables, and locks in their vibrant colors. Be sure to choose a bowl large enough to accommodate your ingredients, and drain thoroughly after a quick dunk to prevent foods from becoming soggy.

SALADS

Orzo, Asparagus, Pea, and Mint Salad

Makes 4 side-dish servings

Spring is a perfect time for salads, and this one makes use of the season's freshest: asparagus, peas, and mint. Brightened with lemon and not much else, these few ingredients combine quickly for a healthy and delicious meal.

1 cup orzo
1 teaspoon good-quality olive oil
1 teaspoon fresh lemon juice or
    apple cider vinegar
½ teaspoon lemon zest
¼ teaspoon sea salt

¼ teaspoon ground black pepper
½ pound asparagus
1 cup fresh or frozen peas
¼ cup lightly packed mint leaves
Mixed greens, for serving (optional)

Cook orzo in well-salted water according to package directions. Drain, rinse, and remove to a medium bowl. Stir in the olive oil, vinegar, sea salt, and pepper. Transfer it to the refrigerator and allow it to chill while you blanch the vegetables.

While the orzo cooks, in a medium saucepan, bring 4 cups water to boil. In another bowl, prepare an ice bath: fill halfway with ice water, and set aside.

Firmly grasp several asparagus spears, and bend until the ends snap off. Repeat with the remaining spears. Slice asparagus into 1-inch pieces on a diagonal. Plunge the asparagus and peas into the boiling water to blanch. They will cook very quickly, in about 1 minute. Remove the vegetables with a large slotted spoon the instant they turn bright green, transferring them to the ice bath. Drain and add them to the orzo mixture.

Chiffonade the mint: stack leaves, long side facing you, and roll into a tight bundle. Holding a sharp knife perpendicular to the roll, slice thinly to create shreds of green. Add to the salad, cover, and refrigerate for at least 20 minutes.

To serve, mound a handful of greens on each plate and top with a generous scoop of salad. The salad can also be made up to two days in advance, and is an ideal picnic offering.

Spinach and Strawberry Salad

Makes 4 servings

This bright salad is dusted with a savory topping of selenium-rich Brazil nuts.

⅓ cup Brazil nuts, coarsely chopped
¼ teaspoon toasted sesame oil
¼ teaspoon plus ¼ teaspoon sea salt
2 tablespoons olive oil
3 tablespoons apple cider vinegar
½ teaspoon Dijon mustard
1 teaspoon sugar, agave nectar, maple syrup, or other sweetener

¼ teaspoon ground black pepper
8 cups fresh baby spinach
½ medium red onion, halved and thinly sliced into moonish shapes
2 cups fresh strawberries, green tops removed, sliced

In a smallish bowl, combine the Brazil nuts, sesame oil, and the first ¼ teaspoon of the sea salt. Set aside.

In a medium skillet over high heat, combine the olive oil, vinegar, Dijon, sweetener, pepper, and the remaining ¼ teaspoon of salt. Taste, and adjust the salt and pepper if necessary. Bring to a boil, then remove from the heat. Off the heat, add the spinach and onion, tossing gently until spinach is slightly wilted. Add the strawberries and stir to combine.

Transfer the salad to a serving platter or individual serving plates. Scatter the reserved Brazil nut mixture over. Serve immediately.

Raw Spinach Salad

Substitute cold-pressed sesame oil for toasted oil and raw agave nectar for the sweetener. Whisk together the dressing off the heat, toss with the remaining ingredients, and allow it to sit at room temperature until wilted, about 15 minutes.

Sea Cucumber Salad

Makes 4 servings

Seaweed and crisp cucumber combine in this clean, bracing salad. Serve small quantities as a starter for an Asian meal.

2 cucumbers, peeled, halved,
   and seeded
1 tablespoon arame
¼ medium red onion

1 tablespoon rice vinegar
½ teaspoon sesame oil (not toasted)
½ teaspoon sea salt

Soak the seaweed in fresh water for 5 minutes to hydrate. Drain, and remove to a medium bowl.

   Slice cucumbers into ¼-inch half-moons, and add to bowl. Slice red onion into half-moons, as thin as possible, and add to bowl. Sprinkle with the vinegar, oil, and sea salt, and toss to combine. Serve immediately.

SALADS

Raspberry-Chèvre Salad with Champagne Vinaigrette

Makes 4 servings

Light, tangy dressing cuts an otherwise rich salad. Make the Chèvre and the vinaigrette up to a week in advance for easy assembly.

To make champagne vinegar from scratch, store leftover champagne in an open-mouthed jar at room temperature for several weeks. The natural sugars in the alcohol will ferment, and voila! Vinegar.

Champagne Vinaigrette

¼ cup champagne vinegar (white wine vinegar is a fine substitution)

¼ cup extra virgin olive oil

1 teaspoon Dijon mustard

½ teaspoon sea salt

¼ teaspoon ground black pepper

Raspberry-Chèvre Salad

8 cups (16-ounce bag) spring greens

1 cylinder Chèvre (page 64)

1 pint fresh raspberries

½ cup macadamia nuts, roughly chopped

Make the vinaigrette: whisk together the champagne vinegar, olive oil, mustard, sea salt, and pepper. Refrigerate until ready to use.

To assemble: arrange the greens on a largish, shallow platter. Crumble Chèvre over them and top with the raspberries and macadamia nuts. Drizzle a bit of vinaigrette over the salad, serving the rest on the side.

Baked Chèvre Salad

Heat the oven to 375° F. Slice the cylinder of Chèvre into 8 equal rounds. Coat the rounds in a mixture of 1 cup of dry bread crumbs (panko is ideal for this), ½ teaspoon of sea salt, and ¼ teaspoon of ground black pepper. Transfer the rounds to an ungreased baking sheet and bake until golden. Assemble salad as directed, topping with baked Chèvre rounds instead of crumbled bits.

Sunshine Slaw

Makes 4 servings

My parents tell me I knocked my brother down as he learned to walk, and poked him in the eyes as he learned to read. I remember none of this, except his years-later retaliation by hacking off my hair as I slept. Then suddenly, Jon was an adult, and one of my favorite people. He's the only person who consistently laughs at my jokes, and he always has something good to say about what I'm up to.

He's not much for cooking, so when he told me about a use for the profusion of kumquats in our mother's Los Angeles backyard, I listened. I'm glad I did.

This tasty salad features kumquats and sun-colored bell peppers, thinly sliced and tossed with green onions, grape tomatoes, and a rice Dijon vinaigrette. Fatty avocado and earthy greens offset the slaw's sweet acidity. Try it, and be inspired that even a nondomestic twenty-something single guy can dream up fantastic food.

SALADS

6 to 8 medium kumquats

1 red bell pepper, seeded and sliced into ⅛-inch strips

1 yellow bell pepper, seeded and sliced into ⅛-inch strips

2 green onions, white and green parts, thinly sliced

½ cup grape or cherry tomatoes

1 tablespoon rice vinegar

1 teaspoon neutral vegetable oil

1 teaspoon agave nectar

1 teaspoon Dijon mustard

¼ teaspoon sea salt

¼ teaspoon ground black pepper

8 cups greens, for serving

1 avocado for serving (optional)

Halve the kumquats lengthwise and seed. Slice lengthwise into the thinnest strips possible. Toss into a medium bowl, along with peppers, onions, and tomatoes.

In a small bowl, whisk together the vinegar, oil, agave nectar, mustard, sea salt, pepper, and any accumulated juices from kumquats. Pour the mixture over vegetables and gently toss to combine.

To serve, evenly divide the greens between 4 plates. Top with slaw. Slice avocado lengthwise and fan slices over each portion. The slaw can be served immediately, or kept separate from the greens and stored in the refrigerator up to overnight.

For raw substitute raw cider vinegar for rice vinegar,
and use raw agave nectar and cold-pressed oil

Simple Italian Salad

Makes 4 servings

Make this flavorful salad to accompany Grilled Pizza (page 142), and serve with a glass of good red wine.

Balsamic Marinated Mushrooms

1 cup halved mushrooms

1 tablespoon balsamic vinegar

1 clove garlic, minced

¼ teaspoon dried basil

¼ teaspoon crushed red pepper

¼ teaspoon sea salt

⅛ teaspoon ground black pepper

⅛ teaspoon dried oregano

Quick Pickled Red Onions

Half a large red onion, sliced into thin rings

1 tablespoon apple cider vinegar

¼ teaspoon sea salt

⅛ teaspoon agave nectar or other sweetener

Salad

8 cups fresh romaine lettuce

¼ to ½ cup fresh basil, torn into small pieces

3 to 4 Roma tomatoes, cut into ¾-inch chunks

1 large roasted red pepper (I use jarred), sliced into thin strips

½ cup black olives, halved

2 tablespoons pine nuts, toasted if you like

In two medium bowls toss together ingredients for the Balsamic Marinated Mushrooms and Quick Pickled Red Onions, and allow them to marinate at room temperature 15 to 30 minutes while assembling the salad.

In a large bowl, toss together the romaine and basil. Layer the remaining ingredients on top: first the tomatoes and roasted pepper, then the marinated mushrooms and pickled onions, and finally the olives and pine nuts.

Serve with Fresh Herb Vinaigrette (page 61), or whisk together reserved juices from mushrooms and red onions with several tablespoons olive oil for a quick dressing.

For raw leave pine nuts untoasted and use raw agave nectar in red onions

For low-fat omit oil in dressing

SALADS

Soups, Curries, and Stews

Every autumn, I eagerly anticipate Soup Season—the time of year that makes you wish everything were shrouded in broth, and hands ache to hold these warm, steaming bowls. But why wait? These soups, curries, and stews give ample reason to declare the start of this season now.

Tomato-Coconut Curry

Makes 4 servings

This quick and simple soup is inspired by my favorite local vegetarian restaurant, and it will convince you to change into pajamas and snuggle into your couch. Pair it with wedges of Broccoli and White Cheddar Panini (page 89), and transform a rainy afternoon into an indoor picnic. If you have leftover cooked vegetables like broccoli or carrots, chop finely and add with the tomatoes.

Fire-roasted tomatoes are excellent here. Be sure to purchase them crushed, rather than ground or diced, as this alters flavor and texture significantly.

1 teaspoon olive oil

½ medium onion, diced

2 cloves garlic, minced

1 (28-ounce) can crushed tomatoes, fire-roasted if available

1 cup water

½ cup coconut milk

½ teaspoon curry powder

½ teaspoon sugar

½ teaspoon sea salt

Dash of cayenne

In a medium saucepan over medium heat, combine the olive oil, onion, and garlic. Cook, stirring constantly, until soft and translucent, 5 to 7 minutes. Add the remaining ingredients and simmer 15 minutes, stirring occasionally.

Serve hot. The soup can be made several days ahead and easily reheated.

Tomato-Basil Bisque

Omit the curry. Add 1 tablespoon finely chopped fresh basil, or 1 teaspoon dried, before simmering.

Pineapple-Cucumber Gazpacho

Makes 4 luncheon or 6 first-course servings

This ingenious zesty and sweet soup was inspired by the excellent cookbook Raw Food, Real World. *The pared-down version takes only minutes to assemble and is ideal as a first course or light summer lunch.*

If made in advance, halve the amount of jalapeño and onion, as it will intensify significantly on sitting. And if you have an aversion to cilantro, just substitute mint leaves.

1 pineapple, skinned, cored, and roughly chopped

2 cucumbers, peeled and roughly chopped

2 tablespoons minced jalapeño pepper (about ½ a jalapeño), seeded

5 green onions, white parts only (reserve the green stalks for garnish)

Juice of two limes

1 cup water

1 teaspoon sea salt

½ cup packed cilantro leaves, roughly chopped

Cilantro or mint leaves, for garnish

Reserved chopped green onions, for garnish

In a blender or food processor, process half of the pineapple, half of the cucumber, jalapeño, and the green onion, lime juice, and water until fairly smooth. Taste, and adjust the seasonings, adding more salt, lime, or jalapeño if you prefer.

Add the remaining pineapple, cucumber, and cilantro, and process until just incorporated; the gazpacho should still be quite chunky.

Refrigerate for up to 2 days, or serve immediately, garnished with cilantro and green onions.

SOUPS, CURRIES, AND STEWS

Samosa Soup

Makes 6 servings

I think samosas are about the most comforting food in existence. The humble potato filling dotted with peas, mashed and perfectly spicy. The substantial, warm bundle, heavy in the hand. And few things have the consoling power of fried dough.

For that sort of comfort without the work of wrapping and working with hot oil, I make this soup of potatoes, peas, and spices. Served with a dollop of chutney, it's rest in a bowl.

8 medium potatoes, peeled and cut into ¾-inch pieces

¼ teaspoon fennel seeds

½ teaspoon cumin seeds

½ teaspoon black mustard seeds

¼ teaspoon coriander seeds

½ teaspoon fenugreek seeds

¼ teaspoon ground turmeric

¼ teaspoon garam masala

1 to 2 dried red chiles

½ teaspoon sea salt

2 tablespoons olive or vegetable oil

4 cloves garlic, minced

3 cups vegetable broth

1 tablespoon fresh lemon juice

1½ cups fresh or frozen and thawed peas

1 cup water

Chutney or tamarind paste, thinned with water to a drizzling consistency, for serving

Steam the potatoes until just beyond fork-tender, about 10 minutes. Drain and leave to rest in a strainer.

Meanwhile, coarsely grind the fennel, cumin, mustard, coriander, fenugreek, turmeric, and garam masala in a coffee grinder or with a mortar and pestle. Crumble in the chiles, add sea salt, and set aside.

In a large saucepan or stockpot, over medium-high heat, sauté the garlic in the oil for 1 minute. Add the spice mixture, and stir constantly for 1 minute more. Add the potatoes. Cook the mixture until the potatoes begin to brown slightly, smashing them against the saucepan with a sturdy spoon as you go. Leave a good amount of chunkiness.

Reduce the heat to medium-low. Add the vegetable broth and scrape up any browned bits. Simmer, uncovered, for 5 minutes. Stir in the lemon juice, peas, and water. Adjust salt to taste, remove from the heat, and ladle into deep bowls. Drizzle with thinned tamarind paste, if you like.

Harvest Pumpkin Stew

Makes 6 stew-filled pumpkins

This recipe sounds fairly involved, but all of the elements can be prepared up to 2 days in advance and refrigerated until ready to assemble. It's also got loads of ingredients, so if you don't have peas or hate oregano, it'll be fine without.

Stew

1 pound yams or sweet potatoes, peeled and cut into 1-inch pieces

1½ pounds red or russet potatoes, peeled and cut into 1-inch pieces

1 pound autumn squash (such as pumpkin, butternut, or delicata) peeled and cut into 1-inch pieces

2 tablespoons plus 2 tablespoons olive oil

2½ teaspoons plus ½ teaspoon sea salt

½ teaspoon plus ½ teaspoon ground black pepper

4 cloves garlic, minced

3 ribs celery, leaves included, sliced

2 carrots, sliced

1 onion, diced

8 ounces mushrooms, sliced

¼ cup flour

5 cups salt-free vegetable stock or water

1 (15-ounce) can cannelloni or great northern beans, drained and rinsed, or 1½ cups cooked

1 cup fresh or frozen peas

Fresh corn cut from 2 cobs, or 1½ cups frozen corn

½ teaspoon dried thyme, or 1 teaspoon fresh

½ teaspoon dried sage, or 1 teaspoon fresh

½ teaspoon oregano, or 1 teaspoon fresh

½ teaspoon rosemary, or 1 teaspoon fresh

¼ cup fresh parsley, roughly chopped

Pumpkins

6 small pumpkins (about 2 pounds each; pie pumpkins are ideal)

About 3 tablespoons olive oil

2 tablespoons sea or kosher salt

1 teaspoon ground black pepper

Buttermilk Biscuit dough (page 37)

Make the stew: directly on a baking sheet or roasting pan, toss together the sweet and red potatoes, squash, 2 tablespoons of the olive oil, and ½ teaspoon each sea salt and pepper. Roast at 350° F until tender, about 1 hour, stirring occasionally. Set aside. (If your oven is large enough or you're halving the recipe, the pumpkins can be baked alongside.)

In a large stockpot over medium heat, combine the remaining 2 tablespoons of olive oil, 2½ teaspoons of sea salt, and ½ teaspoon of the pepper, as well as the garlic, celery, carrots, onion, and mushrooms. Cook, stirring constantly, until the vegetables are tender and the onions go translucent, 6 to 8 minutes. Add the flour, and stir for 2 minutes; the vegetables should be well coated and will appear mushy.

Pour in 1 cup of the stock or water, and mix thoroughly, dislodging any bits stuck to the bottom of the pot. Add the remaining 3 cups of stock, and the beans, peas, corn, thyme, sage, oregano, and rosemary, and cook 15 to 20 minutes, stirring occasionally. The stew should be bubbling away and slightly thickened. Season with additional salt (another teaspoon or so) and pepper to taste, and stir in the parsley. Use immediately, or cover and refrigerate for up to 2 days.

Prepare the pumpkins: heat the oven to 350° F. Generously oil a large baking sheet (or 2), and set aside.

Using the tip of a good serrated knife, draw a circle around the top of a pumpkin as a guide. Cut out a 6-inch-diameter hole in the tops of the pumpkins. Scoop out the seeds, and thoroughly scrape out the stringy pulp with a largish spoon, being careful not to pierce the skin. Repeat with the remaining pumpkins. Rub the insides of the pumpkins with olive oil, and season with salt and pepper. If you like, toss the seeds with olive oil, balsamic vinegar, and sea salt, and roast alongside.

Bake the pumpkins, with tops alongside, on prepared baking sheet, 20 minutes. Transfer the tops to a wire rack, flip the pumpkins, and bake upside-down for another 20 minutes. The pumpkins should be fairly soft, but not collapsing. Set aside until ready to assemble.

To assemble: heat the oven to 425° F. If the parts were made ahead and refrigerated, bring everything except the biscuit dough to room temperature. Place pumpkins on a large baking sheet, reserving tops for garnish.

Return the stockpot of stew to low heat, and bring to a simmer. Evenly ladle the stew into each pumpkin.

Divide the biscuit dough into 6 equal pieces. Roll each into a ball, and pat into a ½-inch thick round. Place a round over each serving of stew.

Bake 15 to 20 minutes, until the biscuits have puffed and turned golden. The tops should be crisp, while the biscuit underneath has a sort of dumpling quality. Carefully transfer them to shallow plates. Lean a lid against each pumpkin, and serve immediately.

Serving

If you don't have pumpkins available, the cooked stew can be spooned into individual oven-safe bowls, topped with biscuit dough, and baked as directed. For a giant pumpkin worthy of a holiday celebration (particularly if you don't know how many guests to expect), substitute one large pumpkin for the mini pumpkins. Prepare the pumpkin as you would the small ones. Ladle in the finished stew, cover the top with biscuit dough, and bake as directed.

Tropical Fruit Consommé

Makes 4 servings

Consommé, a classic French soup base, is made by simmering stock for ages, then clarifying the mixture until completely transparent. This version is sweet rather than savory, and comes together in minutes rather than hours. Served cold, its clean flavor is perfect for dessert or a first course.

Use the smallest melon baller you have to make diminutive orbs of papaya and melon, or simply cut the fruit into ½-inch chunks. Banana, pineapple, guava, or sapote can also be substituted for any of the fruits listed.

Use a large Mexican papaya rather than a small Hawaiian one, as it will allow you to remove larger balls of fruit. To extract ginger juice, simply grate a small amount of ginger on a rasp, and squeeze the excess juice into the consommé.

Tropical Fruit Consommé

2 cups water

½ cup strained lime juice

⅓ cup agave nectar

Pinch of sea salt

2 to 4 drops ginger juice, or a few teaspoons rum (optional)

Fruits

1 cup papaya balls, cut into ½-inch chunks

1 cup melon balls (gallia, honeydew, and cantaloupe work well here)

1 cup strawberries, quartered lengthwise

2 kiwi fruits, peeled and cut into ¼-inch slices

1 mango, cut into ½-inch squares or diamonds

4 scoops Coconut Gelato (page 189), for serving (optional)

4 Coconut-Lime Tuiles (page 203), for serving (optional)

Divide the fruit evenly between four bowls, and ladle the broth evenly over. Serve cold.

For a more elegant presentation, top each serving with a small scoop of Coconut Gelato. Gently fix a Coconut-Lime Tuile (page 203) in each scoop, balancing it to avoid the liquid below. Serve immediately.

For raw, low-fat, and quick fix omit gelato and tuiles
For wheat-free omit tuiles

Wild Rice–Mushroom Soup with Vermouth

Makes 6 servings

This soup is incredibly sexy. Mushrooms are earthy and raw, which points to inhibition, while vermouth is evocative of martinis, the ultimate sexy drink. Together, these ingredients create a dark, steamy broth to be enjoyed with someone you love. Add a pinch of cayenne for extra heat.

1 tablespoon olive oil

½ medium onion, diced

5 cloves garlic, minced

2 pounds assorted mushrooms (I like a combination of cremini, button, and portabella), wiped clean and sliced

3 tablespoons vermouth (dry sherry is a fine substitution)

¾ cup wild rice

4 cups mushroom or vegetable broth

2 cups water

1 teaspoon sea salt

½ teaspoon dried thyme

½ teaspoon ground black pepper

In a large stockpot over medium-high heat, sauté the onion and garlic in olive oil until softened and the onions go translucent, 3 to 5 minutes. Add the mushrooms, along with a generous pinch of sea salt. The mushrooms will remain firm and dry for several minutes, then begin to sweat, and eventually soften and release their liquid. Stir gently throughout this process, which will take about 5 minutes. Once this happens, cook 5 minutes more. Drizzle in vermouth, and cook for another 3 minutes.

Add the wild rice to the mixture; it will still be full of dark liquid that hasn't yet evaporated. Cook, stirring constantly, for 3 to 5 minutes more. Add the stock, water, sea salt, thyme, and pepper. Bring to a simmer, then reduce the heat to low. Cover and simmer until rice is fully cooked, about 45 minutes.

Ladle into warmed bowls and serve with a hearty loaf of bread.

Spicy Butternut Squash Soup

Makes 6 servings

This recipe is very simple, and so lovely and warming. The color of the finished soup is a gorgeous deep orange. Perfect for an autumn dinner party, as it can be made several days in advance and reheated.

1 teaspoon olive oil

4 cloves garlic, minced

2 stalks celery, roughly chopped

1 largish butternut squash, peeled and
    cut into 1-inch chunks

2 apples (I like Gala), peeled and cut
    into 1-inch chunks

3 cups vegetable broth

1 teaspoon sea salt

1 teaspoon ground pepper, white if
    you can find it

½ teaspoon dried sage leaves

½ teaspoon chipotle pepper in adobo

Juice of one lime

¾ cup candied squash or pumpkin
    seeds, for garnish (optional)

In a stockpot or large saucepan over medium-high heat, sauté the garlic and celery in olive oil. Cook, stirring, until soft but not browned, 5 to 7 minutes. Toss in the squash and apples. Cook several minutes longer, then add the vegetable broth, sea salt, pepper, sage, and chipotle pepper.

Reduce the heat to low, cover, and cook for 15 to 20 minutes. The squash and apples should be very tender. Turn off the heat and allow them to cool slightly. Puree in batches in a blender or food processor. If you prefer a partially chunky soup, blend only half of the recipe. Return the pureed soup to saucepan and rewarm. Add the lime juice, and additional salt and pepper to taste.

Ladle into deep bowls, and top with candied squash or pumpkin seeds.

Chipotle Peppers

A chipotle pepper is a dried jalapeño with a deep, smoky flavor. It can be found dried or—as in this recipe—canned in flavorful adobo sauce. Add half a minced chile to vegetable dishes or soups for an intensely spicy bite.

Mung Bean Stew

Makes 6 servings

This humble meal is a variation on the ayurvedic kitcheree. Rice and mung beans provide nourishment and aid gentle detoxification, while spices regulate digestion. As part of a cleansing diet, use the stew to replace one or two daily meals and consume fresh fruits and vegetables for the remainder.

Enough austerity; this is a good, simple meal.

1 cup dried mung beans, soaked overnight
2 bay leaves
½ teaspoon turmeric
1 teaspoon coconut or other
    vegetable oil
1 onion, diced
4 to 6 cloves garlic, minced
1 teaspoon fresh minced ginger root
    (about ½ inch from a knob of ginger)
1 teaspoon ground cumin
1 teaspoon ground coriander

1 teaspoon ground black pepper
1 teaspoon garam masala
1 teaspoon whole mustard seeds
¼ cup water
2 tablespoons unsweetened shredded
    coconut (optional)
1½ teaspoons sea salt
6 cups cooked basmati rice, or 6
    Chapati (page 55), for serving
Fresh cilantro leaves, for serving

SOUPS, CURRIES, AND STEWS

Combine the beans, bay leaves, and turmeric in a medium saucepan with enough water to cover. Cover the pot and cook over low heat, stirring occasionally to prevent scorching. Simmer until beans are soft and beginning to split, about 1 hour. There should be a small amount of water left once the beans are done; add extra during the cooking process if the pot becomes too dry.

During the last 15 minutes of simmering the mung bean mixture, prepare the vegetables and spices. In a sauté pan over medium heat, sauté the oil, onion, garlic, and ginger. Cook, stirring, until soft but not browned, 5 to 7 minutes. Add the cumin, coriander, pepper, garam masala, and mustard seeds. Cook, stirring constantly, until the mustard seeds begin to pop, 2 to 3 minutes. Pour in water, and scrape the bottom to deglaze. Add sautéed mixture, coconut, and sea salt to mung bean mixture. Cook, stirring occasionally, for 15 minutes more. Stir in additional water as necessary to create a loose soup; it should be well combined and stew-like in consistency. Remove bay leaves, taste, and add more salt if necessary.

Serve topped with fresh cilantro leaves, with basmati rice or chapati.

For wheat-free serve with rice instead of chapati

Roasted Vegetable Soup

Makes nearly 1 gallon

This recipe makes oceans of soup, a worthwhile yield for chopping and slicing beyond what seems reasonable. Freeze half and eat the remainder for a week.

Be sure to clean the vegetables well—especially the leeks—prior to preparing them.

3 pounds potatoes, any variety, peeled (about 3 large)

1 pound parsnips, peeled (about 3 medium)

1 pound carrots (about 5 medium)

1 pound cabbage (half a large head)

1 pound celery

2 large leeks

2 medium onions

1 head garlic, minced

¼ cup olive oil

1 tablespoon sea salt

1 teaspoon ground black pepper

4 cups vegetable broth or water

1 teaspoon dried thyme

Heat the oven to 375° F.

Cut the potatoes, parsnips, carrots, and cabbage into ¾-inch chunks. Slice celery, leeks, and onions into ½-inch half-moons.

In the largest pan you have—or in several smaller pans—toss the prepared vegetables together with the garlic, olive oil, sea salt, and pepper. Everything should be in one layer, otherwise use additional pans to give the vegetables some space. Roast 40 to 45 minutes or until fork-tender, stirring every 10 minutes.

Transfer the roasted vegetables to a large stockpot. Add the stock or water and thyme, and bring to a boil over high heat. If any browned bits are stuck to the roasting pan, pour in a bit more water, scrape to deglaze, and add to the stockpot. Reduce the heat to low and simmer for 30 minutes, stirring occasionally.

Allow soup to cool slightly. Transfer half—vegetables and all—to a blender or food processor, and process until nearly smooth. Return to stockpot with the remaining soup, and heat through before serving.

Taste and adjusting seasonings if necessary. Ladle into deep bowls, and serve with a loaf of crusty bread alongside.

SOUPS, CURRIES, AND STEWS

Chocolate-Corn Chili

Makes 6 to 8 servings

Chocolate and cornmeal lend this stew a deep, earthy flavor. Serve with Pepita-Flax Cornbread (page 50) for a hearty meal.

1 teaspoon oil
2 medium carrots
2 stalks celery
1 medium onion
5 to 10 cloves garlic
1 chipotle pepper
1 jalapeño pepper, seeded
1 teaspoon sea salt
¼ cup cornmeal
2 cups water
1 (28-ounce) can diced or
    ground tomatoes
1 (14-ounce) can kidney beans, or
    1½ cups cooked

1 (14-ounce) can pinto beans, or
    1½ cups cooked
1 (14-ounce) can black beans, or
    1½ cups cooked
½ ounce semisweet or bittersweet
    chocolate
1 ear corn, kernels cut, or 1 cup
    frozen corn
Juice of half a lime
Garnishes: cilantro, green onions,
    avocado slices, fresh tomatoes, or
    Cashew Crema (page 65)

Heat the oil over medium-high heat in a large stockpot. Pulse the carrots, celery, onion, garlic, and peppers in batches in a food processor until very finely chopped, adding to the pot after each batch is completed. The texture should be closer to ground than diced. Alternatively, chop very fine by hand. Cook, stirring occasionally, until softened, 5 to 8 minutes.

Add the sea salt and cornmeal. Cook for 5 minutes more, stirring constantly. Pour in water to deglaze, scraping any browned bits from the bottom of the stockpot. Add the tomatoes, beans, and chocolate.

Let simmer uncovered for 45 minutes, until the chili has thickened slightly. Stir in the corn and lime juice. Turn off the heat and allow it to rest for 5 to 10 minutes. Ladle into deep bowls and serve with any or all of the listed garnishes.

Secrets to Rich, Substantial Vegan Soups

Add a fatty liquid, like coconut milk or cashew cream.

Reduce, reduce, reduce. Simmering liquids allows them to evaporate, and concentrates the flavors.

Blend half of the soup. When it's nearly finished, remove half to a blender (a food processor will leak), and process until smooth. Return the pureed soup to the pot, and stir well to combine.

Use legumes to add body: red or yellow lentils cook down to a thickening stew; cannelloni beans can be blended into a smooth puree. If you want to avoid nuts or coconut, beans are an excellent addition.

Joy Tienzo | Cook, Eat, Thrive

Entrées

Vegans think about things differently, and this is true of food, too. Entrées at the vegan table don't need to simply replicate common dishes or follow a typical protein-starch-vegetable formula. In these pages, you'll find a collection of dishes suitable for all sorts of occasions, from supper with the kids to elaborate dinner parties, and all events everyday to exotic.

Vegetable-Chickpea Tagine

Makes 8 generous servings

Tagine refers to the inverted conical clay vessel in which this Moroccan dish is made. Traditionally, it is cooked slowly over low heat, so condensation remains within and imparts a meltingly tender consistency.

Since the recipe will serve 8 people generously, assemble it for a North African-inspired dinner party. Serve the tagine over couscous, and eat with your hands, scooping up the flavorful juices with lavash. Pass a bowl of fiery Charmoula (page 71) alongside.

2 tablespoons olive oil

2 medium onions, thinly sliced

4 cloves garlic, minced

1 red pepper, cut into 1-inch pieces

2 medium zucchini, cut into ½-inch half-moons

1 eggplant, peeled and cut into ½-inch chunks

4 ounces kale (about ½ of a large bunch), cut into ½-inch chiffonade

2 (15-ounce) cans drained and rinsed canned chickpeas, or 3 cups cooked

1 (15-ounce) cans crushed tomatoes

5 apricots cut into quarters

¼ cup currants or raisins

⅛ cup pistachios (optional)

1 tablespoon plus 1 teaspoon Ras el Hanout (page 68)

2 teaspoons sea salt

Generous pinch of saffron

Charmoula (page 71), for serving

Moroccan Preserved Lemons (page 69), for serving

In a large tagine or large heavy stockpot over medium heat, combine the olive oil, onion, and garlic and cook until slightly softened, about 2 minutes. Add the red pepper, zucchini, eggplant, and kale. Cook, stirring constantly, for another 5 minutes. Stir in the chickpeas, tomatoes, apricots, currants, pistachios, Ras el Hanout, sea salt, and saffron. Bring to a boil, reduce to a simmer, and cover. Cook for 45 minutes to an hour, stirring occasionally.

For wheat-free serve with rice instead of lavash or couscous

Coriander "Honey"-Glazed Tofu with Bok Choy

Makes 4 servings

This unique combination of flavors melds to create a dish that's tasty and very low in fat. Follow with a bowl of fresh or canned lychees served over ice for a healthy meal full of clean flavors.

1 pound firm tofu

½ cup agave nectar

2 teaspoons orange flower water

1 teaspoon canola or olive oil

1 teaspoon white wine vinegar, rice vinegar, or any light colored vinegar

1½ teaspoons soy sauce

1 dried Thai chili (any whole, dried chili will do), crumbled

1 teaspoon fresh ground coriander

2 cloves garlic, thinly sliced

2 Asian pears, (or any firm variety) thinly sliced

⅓ cup cold water

1 teaspoon cornstarch

2 green onions, thinly sliced

6 to 8 heads baby bok choy, or 2 to 3 regular-sized heads

Brown rice or pearl barley, for serving

Drain the tofu, wrap tightly in a cloth towel or several paper towels, and weight with a heavy object for at least 15 minutes. While waiting for tofu, make the marinade. In a shallow casserole dish, stir together the agave nectar, orange flower water, oil, vinegar, soy sauce, chili, garlic, and coriander. When the tofu is pressed, pat it dry and slice crosswise into 8 pieces ½ inch thick. Place the tofu in the marinade, and allow them to rest at room temperature for 1 hour, or overnight in the refrigerator.

Heat the oven to 400° F. Place tofu on a nonstick or parchment-lined baking pan. Bake for 20 minutes, flip with kitchen tongs, and bake 15 to 20 minutes more. The tofu should be deep golden. Bake for an additional 5 minutes, if necessary.

Meanwhile, gently toss the sliced pears in marinade. Drain the marinade into a small saucepan, and set pears aside. Dissolve the cornstarch in ⅓ cup water. Add it to reserved marinade in the saucepan and bring to a simmer. Allow the mixture to become clear and thickened slightly, to about the consistency of thick maple syrup, 2 to 3 minutes. Remove from the heat. Stir in green onions and set aside.

Clean the bok choy and cut off the bottoms to separate the leaves. Steam until bright green and just tender, 3 to 5 minutes.

To serve, divide bok choy evenly among four plates. Mound the rice or barley next to it. Lean two slices of tofu against each pile. Heap the pears on top and drizzle a bit of sauce over them. Pass the remaining sauce on the side.

For wheat-free substitute tamari for soy sauce

ENTRÉES

Apricot-Glazed Seitan

Makes 4 servings

This is a simple one-dish dinner. Use an oven-safe saucepan (without any wooden or plastic handles), and transfer it directly to the oven.

1 tablespoon olive oil
1 medium onion, diced
½ cup apricot jam
2 small apricots, or 1 peach or
    nectarine, peeled and diced
1 tablespoon tomato paste
1 tablespoon molasses
1 tablespoon balsamic or apple
    cider vinegar

1 teaspoon sea salt
½ teaspoon freshly ground
    black pepper
Pinch dried red pepper flakes (optional)
16 ounces Basic Seitan (page 147),
    sliced into thin strips
3 green onions, thinly sliced, for serving
Rice, cooked, for serving

Heat the oven to 350° F.

In a medium saucepan over medium-high heat, combine the olive oil, onion, and a pinch of sea salt. Cook and stir until the onions are soft and slightly translucent, 3 to 5 minutes. Reduce the heat to medium, and add the jam, apricots (or other fruit), tomato paste, molasses, vinegar, sea salt, and pepper. Bring to a boil, then reduce the heat. Add seitan and stir briefly to combine. Transfer the saucepan to the oven and bake for about 30 minutes, stirring occasionally. The seitan should be colored a deep russet, and any excess liquid will have evaporated.

Remove from the oven and top with green onions. Serve over rice.

Asian-Style Glazed Seitan

Substitute 1 tablespoon maple syrup or agave nectar for the molasses, 1 tablespoon rice vinegar for the balsamic, and 1 tablespoon soy sauce for the teaspoon sea salt. Add 1 teaspoon grated ginger root and ½ teaspoon toasted sesame oil. If you like, omit the red pepper flakes, and toss in a dried, crumbled red Thai pepper. If you're really sick for heat, include half of a minced Thai bird chile (*prik chi fa*) or "mouse shit" chile (*prik kii nuu*). Continue as directed.

Apricot-Glazed Vegetables

Replace the seitan with 5 cups of whatever mixed veg you have on hand: mushrooms, zucchini, red peppers, sugar snap peas, green beans, precooked chunks of squash... Everything else goes as directed.

Stuffed Pasilla Chiles with Black Bean–Potato Filling and Cashew Crema

Makes 4 entrée servings

This dish is rich with the colors of the lands where it originated, full of pitch-dark soils and vibrant green canopies. Topped with runny, pale crema, the stuffed chiles bloom with intense and earthy flavors.

Several types of chiles can be used here; the key is that they be fresh, very large, and green. Double the number of chiles if using Anaheim or a smaller chile.

The relleno filling can be made up to 3 days in advance, as can the crema. Bring the filling to room temperature before using. If you like, serve with salsa instead of crema for a nearly fat-free dish. The filling can also be used as the sturdy interior of tamales or burritos, or thinned with water or stock to make black bean soup.

1 potato, peeled and halved (about ½ pound)
1 teaspoon vegetable oil
½ onion, diced
2 cloves garlic, minced
½ cup dried black beans
¼ teaspoon orange zest
⅛ teaspoon ground cumin

⅛ teaspoon ground black pepper
Generous pinch of sea salt
2 cups water
4 large pasilla chiles (ancho, poblano, or Anaheim chiles are a fine substitution)
1 recipe Cashew Crema (page 65)
Cilantro leaves, for garnish

Cook the potato in boiling salted water until fork-tender, 15 to 20 minutes. Drain and set aside.

In a medium saucepan over medium-high heat, combine the oil, onion, and garlic. Sauté until softened, about 5 minutes. Add the beans, zest, cumin, pepper, and sea salt, stirring thoroughly. Pour in the water. Bring to a boil, then reduce the heat and cook, covered, for 1 to 1½ hours, adding additional water if the pan begins to go dry. Set aside until ready to use.

To prepare the chiles, impale each on a long fork, or hold firmly with tongs. Hold it 1 to 2 inches over the flame of a gas burner on high heat until skin is charred and bubbly in spots. Repeat with the remaining chiles. Alternatively, place chiles on a baking sheet under a broiler until skin is blackened. Turn once to blister evenly. Quickly transfer the chiles to a bowl, cover with plastic wrap, and set aside for 10 to 15 minutes.

Keeping stems intact, peel the chiles. Make a lengthwise slit down each, and carefully remove the seeds and membranes. Place the chiles slit sides up on a lightly oiled baking sheet. Heat the oven to 375° F while you assemble the chiles.

To assemble, fill each chile with a quarter of the filling, gently spooning it in and allowing it to peek over the top slightly.

Bake the chiles for 15 minutes, then transfer to a shallow platter. Serve warm, garnished with cilantro and crema.

Supper Bowls

For simple, healthy dinners, build bowls of grains, legumes, and vegetables, topped with flavorful sauces. They're full of protein, and can be put together with little effort. Start with whatever leftovers you have, and layer them as you like, adding onions or garlic to the legumes or greens for extra flavor. Here are some guidelines to get you started:

Couscous, cannelloni beans, sautéed kale,
Lemon Olive Tofu, Tahini-Lemon Sauce

Pearl barley, fava beans, Pine Nut Brussels
Sprouts, Fresh Herb Vinaigrette

Quinoa, black beans, sautéed spinach,
Fried Plantains, Guacamole

White rice, black eyed peas, steamed collards,
Caribbean Sweet Potatoes, Ti Malice

Brown rice, pinto beans or Frijoles Mezclados, chopped
fresh romaine lettuce, salsa or Cashew Crema

Basmati rice, chickpeas, Fennel-Roasted Root
Vegetables, sautéed kale, Indian Carrots

White rice, tempeh or Asian Glazed Seitan, steamed
bok choy, Spicy Sesame Dressing

Tarte aux Poireaux et Pommes de Terre

Makes 6 luncheon or 8 breakfast servings

This is a combination of two classic French recipes: flamiche au poireau, a savory tart of leeks, cream, and cheese, and pommes Anna, a dense potato cake prepared with copious amounts of butter. Beginning with a base of pressed potatoes, the tarte is layered with creamy leek custard. Serve with a green salad for a casual lunch, or as part of a brunch buffet.

1 teaspoon olive oil

1 large leek, white and green parts, well cleaned and thinly sliced

2 tablespoons margarine, melted, or olive oil

3 large baking potatoes

1 teaspoon plus ½ teaspoon sea salt

1 (12.3-ounce) package silken tofu

¼ cup water

¼ cup all-purpose flour

¼ cup nutritional yeast

1 tablespoon fresh lemon juice

1 teaspoon baking powder

¼ teaspoon turmeric

¼ teaspoon paprika

¼ teaspoon ground black pepper

½ cup Chèvre, cut into small pieces (optional)

Heat the oven to 350° F.

In a large cast-iron skillet over medium heat, sauté the leek slices in 1 teaspoon olive oil until soft, 15 to 20 minutes. If they begin to stick or brown, add several tablespoons water.

While the leeks cook, prepare the potatoes. Peel and slice as thinly as possible. When the leeks are cooked, place them in a medium bowl and set aside.

Wipe the skillet and return it to the heat. Drizzle the margarine or olive oil over the bottom. Beginning with the outside, layer the potatoes in concentric circles. Evenly distribute the margarine or olive oil and 1 teaspoon of the sea salt throughout the potatoes, coating each layer with a bit of it. Weight the potatoes with another skillet filled with several cans, and cook them for 6 to 8 minutes. The potatoes will be sweating and fragrant.

While the potatoes cook, make the leek custard: in a blender or food processor, combine the silken tofu, flour, nutritional yeast, water, lemon juice, baking powder, turmeric, paprika, pepper, and the remaining ½ teaspoon sea salt. Process until completely smooth, scraping down the sides as necessary.

Transfer the custard to a medium bowl and fold in the leeks and Chèvre. Pour the custard over potatoes, without disturbing them, and smooth the top. Cook for 3 minutes more, then transfer the cake to the oven. Bake it for 15 to 20 minutes, until the top is golden and slightly puffed.

Joy Tienzo | Cook, Eat, Thrive

Lemon Olive Tofu

Makes 4 entrée servings, or about 6 cups

Serve hot as an entrée over cooked quinoa or barley, or chill and tuck it into a hummus-slathered pita. This is also an excellent pizza topping, as it closely mimics feta when cold.

Assemble and pop into the refrigerator before leaving for work, and you'll have a ready-to-bake dish when you arrive home in the evening.

1 (16 ounce) package firm or extra firm tofu

1 (14 ounce) can artichoke hearts, drained and quartered

¾ cup black olives

¾ cup green olives

2 tablespoons good-quality olive oil

Zest and juice from 1 lemon

4 to 6 cloves garlic, minced

½ to 1 teaspoon sea salt

½ teaspoon ground black pepper

Wrap the tofu in a clean kitchen towel and top with a quart-sized casserole dish, in which you'll assemble everything while the tofu presses.

In the casserole dish, briefly toss together all the ingredients except the tofu. Unwrap the tofu underneath and cut into ¾-inch cubes. Add the tofu and gently toss again. Allow it to marinate for at least 1 hour at room temperature, or overnight in the refrigerator.

Heat the oven to 375° F. Bake for 35 to 45 minutes, stirring occasionally, until the tofu is golden on the edges and nearly all of the liquid has been absorbed. Serve at any temperature.

Orange-Pepper Seitan with Quinoa Polenta, Black Bean Sauce, and Steamed Greens

Makes 4 servings

Packed with protein and calcium, this crisp, citrus-marinated seitan over mild polenta, black bean sauce, and greens makes for a low-fat, hearty meal.

The polenta and black bean sauce can be made ahead and reheated, while the seitan can be marinated up to a day in advance.

Seitan with Orange-Pepper Reduction

Juice of 1 orange

2 teaspoons ground black pepper

2 teaspoons orange zest

1 teaspoon vegetable oil

½ teaspoon sea salt

12 ounces Basic Seitan (page 147), thinly sliced

Quinoa Polenta

½ cup quinoa

3 cups water

2 cloves garlic, smashed

¼ teaspoon sea salt

Black Bean Sauce

1 (16-ounce) can black beans, drained and rinsed

Juice of 1 orange

2 cloves garlic

½ teaspoon sea salt

⅛ to ¼ teaspoon cayenne pepper, according to your preference

½ cup water

8 cups greens (spinach, chard, kale, and collards are all good), for serving

Marinate the seitan: stir together the orange juice, pepper, zest, oil, and sea salt. Add the seitan and toss to coat it. Let it marinate for 1 hour at room temperature, or up to overnight in the refrigerator.

Make the quinoa polenta: process the quinoa in a food processor or blender until it is the consistency of fine meal. Set it aside. In a medium saucepan, bring the water, garlic, and sea salt to a boil. Slowly pour in the quinoa, whisking constantly. Reduce the heat to low, cover, and gently simmer for 15 minutes, stirring occasionally (the black bean sauce can be prepared at this time). Remove from the heat, cover, and allow it to rest until serving time.

ENTRÉES

Joy Tienzo | Cook, Eat, Thrive

Make the black bean sauce: process the beans, orange juice, garlic, and cayenne in a food processor or blender until very smooth. Add water and blend again. Transfer to a small saucepan, and warm over low heat while you prepare the seitan.

Cook the seitan: heat the oven to 375° F with a baking sheet inside. Carefully add the seitan to preheated pan, reserving the marinade in a small saucepan. Sear seitan for 5 minutes, then flip with a thin spatula and cook 5 minutes more. Alternatively, sear the seitan in a cast-iron skillet over high heat until golden on both sides. Meanwhile, in a small saucepan or skillet, simmer the reserved marinade over medium heat until reduced by half; you should have about 2 tablespoons of reduction. Set aside.

To serve: steam the greens until tender and bright green, 3 to 5 minutes. Set aside.

Divide the black bean sauce evenly among 4 plates. Spoon polenta alongside in pools next to the bean sauce, marbleizing the two if you like. Distribute the greens evenly, mounding them onto the sauce and polenta. Place the seitan slices against the steamed greens, leaning them at a slant. Drizzle the orange-pepper reduction around the perimeter of the plate, and serve immediately.

Grilled Pizza

Makes 4 individual pizzas, or 1 large

Grilled pizza is excellent party food, as it allows guests to make their own choices and encourages mingling. Offer as many toppings as you like.

1 recipe Pizza Dough (page 45)
About ½ cup Garlic-Infused Olive Oil
    (page 77)

One of the topping combinations below

Divide the dough into quarters. For an even crust, roll to ¼ to ⅓-inch thickness with a rolling pin. For bubbles of soft dough interspersed with crisp, thin areas, pull and stretch and toss by hand. If you make a hole, it's okay; just don't put toppings there.

Lay the dough on the grill and cover for a minute or so until the dough puffs a bit and becomes slightly stiff. Brush the top with infused olive oil.

Using tongs, two metal spatulas, or your fingers (if you're particularly tough), flip the dough over. The pizza should be marked slightly. To avoid a soggy crust, brush the top with more olive oil.

Work fast: add one of the topping combinations below, being careful not to overload the pizza. Cover and cook another 1 to 2 minutes, or until the thicker edges of the pizza are no longer doughy.

Drizzle with a bit more olive oil, if desired, and serve.

After brushing generously with the infused olive oil, top with one of the following combinations

Thinly sliced cooked potatoes with Italian-Style Ground Seitan (page 70)
    and sprigs of fresh rosemary;

Muffaletta Spread (page 73) with Chèvre (page 64);

Lemon Olive Tofu (page 139), with or without tomato sauce;

Marinara with sliced red onions, capers, arugula, and coarsely ground pine nuts

Roasted Garlic (roasted according to instructions on page 88), fresh spinach,
    and green olives;

Caramelized onions, grilled zucchini, and fresh thyme;

Edamame Pesto (page 74), asparagus, and sautéed mushrooms;

Roasted vegetables (winter squash, zucchini, broccoli) drizzled with Cashew
Crema (page 65);

Grilled eggplant, fresh basil, and dollops of hummus (page 78);

Sliced heirloom tomatoes, avocado, and fresh basil;

Peppercorn Ranch (page 63), Seitan Bacon (page 41), fresh corn, and
chopped green onions

Oven-Baked Pizza

To bake pizza off the grill, heat an oven to 450° F, with an overturned baking sheet
inside as you heat it. Roll out the dough, and have toppings ready. When ready to
make the pizza, scatter a handful of cornmeal over the pan, then slap the rolled
out dough onto the pan. Brush the top with olive oil and add the toppings. For a
crisper crust, toss a few ice cubes onto the bottom of the oven to add humidity.
Quickly close the door.

Bake until dough is slightly puffed and the center is heated through. Depending
on the thickness of your dough, this should take anywhere from 15 to 25 minutes.
Remove, drizzle with additional oil, and serve hot.

Menus for Occasions

These menus will allow you to entertain with ease and confidence. Many of the elements can be prepared several days in advance, so you can enjoy your guests instead of focusing only on food.

New Year's Eve Gala

Savory Sticks, page 52

Mushroom Pâté en Croûte, page 84

Assorted store-bought dips and vegetables

Whipped Truffle Mousse, page 181, with fresh fruits

Chocolate-Dipped Strawberries, page 204

Champagne

Romantic Dinner for Two

Spinach and Strawberry Salad, page 112, or Raspberry-Chèvre Salad, page 114

Wild Rice–Mushroom Soup with Vermouth, page 125

Ras el Hanout–Roasted Beets, page 171

Sundae of Hazelnut Cherry Brownies with Port Glaze, page 200, Vanilla Bean Frozen Custard, page 212, or store-bought nondairy ice cream, and chopped hazelnuts

Caribbean-Inspired Garden Party

Mofongo, page 154, made in hors d' oeuvres sizes

Bannann Peze (Fried Plantains), page 164, topped with mounds of Riz et Pois Rouges, page 146, and Ti Malice, page 74

Caribbean Sweet Potatoes, page 167, in phyllo cups

Crêpes Fanon, page 216, or fresh fruit spears of pineapple, mango, banana, and papaya

Kid-Friendly Dinner

Barbecue Ranch Salad, page 99

Cayenne-Crumb Baked Macaroni, page 150, topped with steamed broccoli "trees"

Graham Crackers, page 214, and fresh fruit

French Bistro Supper

Salade Niçoise, page 100

Creamy Saffron Asparagus, page 161

Tarte aux Poireaux et Pommes de Terre, page 138

Lavender–Rice Pudding Brûlée with Blueberries, page 190

Crisp white wine and baguette

South American Dinner Party

Palm Heart Ceviche, page 83

Avocado-Quinoa Salad with Tamarind Syrup, page 177

Stuffed Pasilla Chiles with Black Bean–Potato Filling, page 136, and Cashew Crema, page 65

Venezuelan Hot Chocolate, page 26

East Asia Fusion Lunchbox

Larb Kai Salad, page 102

Adobong Gulay, page 156

Wedges of Sweet Rice Cake, page 220

Thermos of Thai iced tea prepared with coconut milk

ENTRÉES

Sunday Brunch

Peach-Almond Pain Ressuscité, page 38

Red Pepper–Chèvre Frittata, page 42

Perfect Potatoes, page 34

Fresh fruit platter

Coffee, tea, and Bloody Marys, page 21

Poker Night

Buttermilk Onion Rings with Spicy Dipping Sauce, page 94, or Peppercorn Ranch Dressing, page 63

Hot and Sweet Popcorn, page 90

Chocolate Chip Cookies, page 199

Dirty Martinis, page 25, and assorted vegan beers

Moroccan Meal

Oranges sprinkled with orange flower water

Moroccan Mint Tea, page 25

Vegetable-Chickpea Tagine, page 133

Couscous or lavash

Cardamom Crêpes with Coconut Gelato, Pistachios, and Orange Blossom "Honey," page 188

Late-Afternoon Italian Supper

Risotto Dorato, page 152

Simple Italian Salad, page 116

Pine Nut Brussels Sprouts, page 172

Italian Cornmeal Cake, page 194, with fresh fruit

Afternoon Tea

Tea-Smoked Tofu Sandwiches, page 96

Curtice Street Salad, page 108, or Raspberry-Chèvre Salad, page 114

Sandwiches of Carrot Bread, page 51, spread with Chèvre, page 64, or nondairy cream cheese and lime zest

Chocolate-Dipped Strawberries, page 204

Cream Scones, page 53, with Lemon Curd, page 178, and jam

Assorted hot teas with nondairy milk and sugar

Thanksgiving

Greens au Gratin, page 166

Caramelized Onion and Lentil Salad, page 101

Harvest Pumpkin Stew, page 122

Gingered Pear Trifle, page 193

Easter Dinner

Orzo, Asparagus, Pea, and Mint Salad, page 111

Roasted Vegetable Soup, page 128

Seitan Roast with Agave Apples, page 151, over cooked grains

Pink Grapefruit Sorbet, page 210, and Marzipan Cookies, page 201

Vegan Wedding Fare

Cannelloni, Chickpea, and Green Bean Salad with Tomatoes and Fresh Thyme, page 104

Lemon Olive Tofu, page 139, or Grilled Pizza Bar (see Grilled Pizza, page 142)

Pilaf of mixed grains

Greens au Gratin, page 166, or Creamy Saffron Asparagus, page 161

At every table, a Roasted Garlic Bowl, page 88, and loaf of good bread

Italian Cornmeal Celebration Cake, page 194

White Peach Sangria, page 24, or champagne

Riz et Pois Rouges

Makes 4 servings

After being part of a medical outreach to Haiti, I have remembered two things very clearly. First, how to inquire in Creole if someone is experiencing burning during urination ("Boule kou pipi?"). And second, that the country is home to some of the best cooking anywhere.

With its French, African, and Arabic influences, Haitian cuisine makes abundant use of legumes (peanuts, pigeon peas, and other beans), and rice. Riz et pois rouges, or rice and red beans, is a national dish, prepared in different ways across the country. This version is traditionally flavored with oregano and served with spicy sos (sauce) Ti Malice. Make it even heartier by substituting brown rice for white and increasing the amount of water to 2¾ cups.

2 tablespoons olive oil or other vegetable oil

1 large onion, chopped

4 cloves garlic, minced

2 to 3 slices tempeh or seitan bacon, coarsely chopped (optional)

1 cup uncooked white rice

½ teaspoon oregano

Pinch of cayenne pepper or ¼ teaspoon crushed red pepper

1 (25-ounce) can kidney beans, drained and rinsed, or 3 cups cooked kidney beans

2 bay leaves

½ teaspoon sea salt

2½ cups water

4 plantains, fried according to Bannann Peze recipe (page 164)

Ti Malice, for serving (page 74)

In a large saucepan over medium-high heat, combine the onion, garlic, and tempeh or seitan bacon in the olive oil. Sauté until the onions go translucent, about 2 to 3 minutes. Add the oregano, cayenne, rice, kidney beans, bay leaves, sea salt, and water, and stir well to combine. Allow the mixture to come to a boil, then reduce the heat to medium-low. Cover, and simmer until all liquid is absorbed and the rice is tender, about 30 minutes.

Remove the bay leaves and give the rice a final stir. To serve, mound onto a plate with a stack of plantains. Pass a bowl of Ti Malice alongside.

For soy-free use seitan bacon
For wheat-free use tempeh bacon

Basic Seitan

Makes 2 pounds, or about 8 servings

This recipe is fairly bland, allowing for customization and use in any recipe requiring it. For a more distinct flavor, mix one of the spice rubs on page 70 into the dough. You can also prepare it as usual, coat with a spice rub, and bake at 350° F for 30 to 40 minutes. This makes the most delicious seitan roast, it can be thinly sliced into filling for sandwiches.

Seitan is like a koi fish; it grows to fit its body of water. For spongier seitan, place just a few pieces in a large pot. For firmer stuff, pack several pieces into a smaller one.

2¼ cups vital wheat gluten

¼ cup nutritional yeast

1¼ cup water

¼ cup soy sauce

2 cloves garlic, grated or pressed

Several dashes liquid smoke (optional)

1 teaspoon coarsely ground fresh pepper (optional)

8 to 10 cups water

⅓ cup soy sauce, or 2 teaspoons sea salt

In a large bowl, combine the wheat gluten and nutritional yeast. In a 2-cup measure or medium bowl, stir together the water, soy sauce, garlic, liquid smoke, and pepper. Make a well in the dry ingredients, and pour in the liquid. Mix with a spoon or spatula until the mixture firms up, then knead with your hands for 1 to 2 minutes. Set aside for a moment while making the broth.

In a large stockpot off the stove, combine water and soy sauce or sea salt.

Shape the gluten mixture into a log and cut it into 6 to 8 pieces. Gently place in the broth and bring to a low simmer on the stovetop. Partially cover and simmer for 1 to 1½ hours, turning over at least once. The seitan will expand significantly and may look very spongy; it will firm as it cooks.

Allow it to cool completely in the broth. The seitan can be refrigerated in its liquid for up to 10 days, or frozen for several months.

ENTRÉES

Sage-Ricotta Gnocchi with Spicy Squash Mash

Makes 4 entrée servings

Over 20 years ago, Judy Rodgers of Zuni Café popularized the idea of gnocchi made with ricotta cheese instead of potatoes. This version uses a tofu ricotta mixture, which yields light, tender gnocchi that hold together without fail. Having tried both, I can honestly say the vegan version is comparably good, if not better than its dairy counterpart.

Beyond all the roasting and shaping and chilling is a really delicious meal that really isn't very difficult to put together. Start the gnocchi the evening before, and roast the squash in advance, if you like.

Gnocchi

1 (16 ounce) package extra firm tofu

2 tablespoons fresh lemon juice

1 teaspoon lemon zest

2 cloves garlic

1 teaspoon sea salt

1 tablespoon nutritional yeast

2 teaspoons extra virgin olive oil

½ cup all-purpose flour

2 tablespoons finely chopped fresh sage leaves (about ¼ cup whole leaves)

Additional flour, for dredging

Mash

2 pounds hard winter squash (butternut, delicata, and kabocha are good choices)

1 tablespoon plus 1 tablespoon extra virgin olive oil

½ teaspoon plus ¼ teaspoon sea salt

¼ teaspoon ground black pepper

4 cloves garlic, minced

½ teaspoon crushed red pepper flakes

To Serve

1 tablespoon olive oil

Fresh sage leaves

Ground black pepper

Make the gnocchi: in a food processor, combine the tofu, lemon juice, zest, garlic, sea salt, nutritional yeast, and oil until fairly smooth. Transfer to a medium bowl and fold in the flour and sage. Cover the dough and chill for at least 2 hours.

When ready to shape the dough, line a baking sheet with waxed paper, or dust liberally with flour. Pinch off thumb-sized bits of ricotta dough and gently roll each into a ball between the palms. Using your thumb and forefinger, roll the dumpling over the tines of a fork, pressing to make an indentation. Then drop it onto the prepared baking sheet below and flick it gently to turn and coat with a bit more flour. Repeat with the remaining dough; you'll have 40 to 50 gnocchi. Transfer the baking sheet to the refrigerator and chill for at least an hour, up to a day.

Make the mash: heat the oven to 400° F. Halve the squash, and scoop seeds from the center, reserving them for garnish. Cut the halves coarsely into a few large pieces and toss with 1 tablespoon oil, ½ teaspoon sea salt, and black pepper. Place them cut side up on a baking sheet and bake for 40 to 45 minutes, turning several times for even roasting. Allow them to rest until cool enough to handle, then scrape the flesh into a medium bowl. Decrease the heat of the oven to 350° F to roast the squash seeds.

Meanwhile, rinse the seeds and pat them dry. Toss with a generous pinch of sea salt and a few drops of olive oil to coat. Roast in the 350° F oven until lightly golden, 12 to 15 minutes. Set aside.

Bring a very large pot of salted water to a boil. Your water should be quite salty, like the ocean. Have the gnocchi at hand, along with a colander in which to drain it. Leave it all to wait for a moment while you finish the squash.

Heat the remaining tablespoon of oil in a medium saucepan over medium heat, and sauté the garlic for 1 minute. Add the reserved squash, the remaining ¼ teaspoon of sea salt, and red pepper flakes. Cook, mashing with the back of a spoon, until most of the liquid has evaporated and the squash has the consistency of thick mashed potatoes. Remove from the heat and cover until ready to serve. The mash can be prepared up to a day in advance and reheated over low heat before serving.

To cook the gnocchi, gently drop the dumplings into the boiling pot. Cook until they begin to float, 3 to 5 minutes, then cook for 1 minute more. Drain and leave them in the strainer while you get on with assembling the dish.

To serve: heat 1 tablespoon olive oil in a large skillet. Toss in whole sage leaves and cook until crisp, about 2 minutes. Remove with a slotted spoon and set aside on a paper towel-lined plate. Add drained gnocchi to the skillet and gently toss to coat with oil.

Divide gnocchi evenly among the plates. Place a large dollop of mashed squash over each portion and top with reserved toasted squash seeds, fried sage, and ground black pepper. Serve immediately.

Making Gnocci en Masse

The gnocchi can also be made en masse and stored for meals whenever you like. Simply freeze the uncooked dumplings in a single layer on a parchment-lined baking sheet, then transfer them to a freezer-safe plastic bag. To prepare, boil as directed straight from the freezer. Follow the directions above for cooking: wait for the gnocchi to float—this may take an additional 2 minutes or so—then cook 1 minute more. Continue as directed.

ENTRÉES

Cayenne-Crumb Baked Macaroni

Makes 8 entrée or 12 side-dish servings

You will not be disappointed by this, I promise: spicy crumbs concealing dense pasta saturated with a creamy cheese sauce. Serve with a feisty sangiovese or shiraz, the perfect balance to this rich supper.

I prefer to use celentani (also called cavatappi), the whimsical corkscrew-shaped pasta, for the macaroni. It holds just the right amount of sauce, and can be found in most supermarkets.

If making the macaroni for children, arrange steamed broccoli florets in the crumbs: macaroni and trees!

Macaroni

1 pound uncooked celentani or macaroni

2 cups raw cashews, soaked in boiling water for at least an hour and drained

2 cup water

2 cloves garlic

3 tablespoons tahini, preferably raw

3 tablespoons nutritional yeast

1 teaspoon ground flaxseed

¼ cup fresh lemon juice

2 teaspoons sea salt

¼ teaspoon ground black pepper

¼ teaspoon ground fresh nutmeg

Cayenne Crumbs

4 slices wholegrain bread, old or lightly toasted

¼ teaspoon cayenne

2 tablespoons margarine

Make the macaroni: heat the oven to 350° F. Generously grease a 5-quart or 9 by 13-inch baking dish, and set aside.

Cook pasta al dente according to package directions. It should have a slight bite, but be completely cooked. Drain and transfer to prepared baking dish.

Meanwhile, make the sauce: in a blender or food processor, combine the remaining ingredients and blend until completely smooth. Pour the mixture over the cooked macaroni, stirring thoroughly. The macaroni should be saturated with sauce. The best way to do this is to agitate it, allow it to rest a moment, and agitate it again. Repeat this a few times and set aside.

Melt together the margarine and cayenne in a medium bowl, and set aside. Pulse the bread in a food processor or blender until coarse crumbs form. Add to margarine mixture and toss to combine. Distribute the cayenne crumbs evenly over macaroni. Bake it for 30 to 35 minutes, covering the top with foil if it browns too quickly. The top will be golden and crisp, while the interior is a creamy, molten muddle. Serve hot.

For soy-free substitute olive oil for margarine in cayenne crumbs

Seitan Roast with Agave Apples

Makes 6 to 8 servings

Like a traditional roast, the seitan is trussed to create a tidy package, then browned to add flavor. Serve it at your next holiday gathering, and slice leftovers thin for sandwiches.

2 pounds Basic Seitan (page 147), with several drops liquid smoke added to cooking liquid
¼ cup (½ stick) margarine
1 tablespoon olive oil
3 tablespoons agave nectar

¼ teaspoon sea salt
¼ teaspoon ground black pepper
¼ cup water
4 apples, peeled and cut into ¼-inch slices

Pull and squeeze the seitan "dough" into a log about 12 inches long. If the seitan shrinks back while shaping, allow it to rest for several minutes before proceeding. Tie a 60-inch length of kitchen twine or (preferably unwaxed) dental floss around the width of one end, about 1½ inches from the top. Pull the long end of the floss down 1½ inches more, and again tie around the width. Repeat the spacing and tying every 1½ inches. You should have about 6 ties around the circumference, connected by a length of twine. Trim the excess, and place the seitan in the cold seitan broth.

Transfer it to the stovetop and simmer over low heat 1 to 1½ hours. Allow it to cool completely in the broth. This can be done several days in advance of cooking the roast.

When ready to cook, heat the oven to 375° F. Wrap seitan with a clean kitchen towel and squeeze to remove excess liquid. Remove twine or floss.

In a cast-iron skillet over medium heat, melt together margarine, olive oil, agave nectar, sea salt, and pepper. Once it begins to bubble slightly, add seitan and cook until lightly browned, 3 to 5 minutes. Turn and cook 3 to 5 minutes more, repeating until all sides are golden.

Transfer skillet to the hot oven, and roast 10 to 12 minutes, until the seitan is deep golden. Remove the roast seitan to a serving platter and allow it to rest while you prepare the apples. Return the skillet to the stove, pour in the water, and scrape up any browned bits with a metal spatula. The mixture will bubble gloriously. Continue cooking until the liquid has reduced and thickened slightly, 3 to 5 minutes.

Add the apples to the pan and cook, without stirring, about 3 minutes. Once the apples have gone golden on the bottoms, flip them and continue cooking until uniformly colored.

Slice the roast into ¼-inch slices on a diagonal. Mound caramelized apples over it, allowing the juices to cascade over the side, and serve.

ENTRÉES

Risotto Dorato

Makes 6 servings

Despite its humble ingredients—rice, wine, and stock—devotion to a stovetop and at least 30 minutes of patience allows risotto to command ridiculous prices in restaurants. This golden, homemade version is just as rich, gleaming with roasted white asparagus and oyster mushrooms. If you have it, drizzle with a bit of white truffle oil for a gilded finish.

Asparagus-Mushroom Topping

1 bunch (about 1 pound) white asparagus

1 tablespoon plus 1 tablespoon olive oil

½ teaspoon sea salt

1 pound oyster mushrooms, brushed clean

Risotto

3 tablespoons olive oil

1 onion, diced

2 cloves garlic, minced

2 cups arborio rice

1 cup dry white wine

1½ teaspoons sea salt

6 cups mushroom or vegetable stock

2 tablespoons margarine

¼ cup chopped flat-leaf parsley

½ teaspoon ground black pepper

¼ cup chopped flat-leaf parsley, for serving (optional)

Heat the oven to 375° F. Toss together the asparagus, 1 tablespoon of the olive oil, and ½ teaspoon sea salt. Roast, stirring occasionally, while you make the risotto. After 20 minutes, remove and set aside.

In a sauté pan or large pot, heat the 3 tablespoons olive oil over medium heat. Add the onion and garlic, and cook for 3 minutes, stirring constantly. Pour in the rice and stir to coat it with a thin film of oil. When the rice begins to make small pings, like glass beads bumping together, add the wine and 1½ teaspoons sea salt.

Increase the heat to medium-high and cook until the wine has nearly evaporated, about 2 minutes. Add ¾ cup of the stock at a time, stirring in a slow "S" until it evaporates. Repeat this process of stirring until evaporation every few minutes until all stock has been used. This will take anywhere from 25 to 35 minutes.

When the risotto has been simmering for 15 or so minutes, cook the mushrooms. Heat 1 tablespoon of the oil in a cast-iron skillet over high heat. Add the mushrooms, along with a generous pinch of sea salt. Sauté until golden brown on one side, about 3 minutes, then turn and brown the other side, 1 to 2 minutes more. The mushrooms should remain relatively dry, without releasing their juices. Remove from the heat, add the reserved asparagus, and toss to warm through.

ENTRÉES

When the risotto has absorbed all of the stock, try a taste. The grains of rice should be separate, very slightly al dente, and veiled in their sauce. Remove from the heat, and stir in the margarine, parsley, and pepper. Taste again, and adjust the seasonings if necessary.

To serve, mound risotto into 6 deep bowls. Top with the asparagus-mushroom mixture, and sprinkle with parsley.

Risotto Cakes

Since risotto does not keep well and becomes gluey on reheating, risotto cakes are a simple way to make use of the day-old dish.

Heat 2 teaspoons of oil in a cast-iron skillet over medium-high heat. Drop risotto in ¼-cup mounds about ½-inch high onto the hot skillet. Cook until golden brown, about 3 minutes. Flip with a metal spatula and continue cooking for 3 minutes more. After the first flip, use the spatula to gently flatten the cakes and press any errant pieces of rice toward the center. If the cakes still don't hold together, flip once more and press again. Transfer to a wire rack to cool slightly.

Eat as is, or over a salad of mixed greens, avocado, grapefruit supremes, and Agave, Mustard, and Poppy Seed Dressing (page 72).

Mofongo with Cilantro-Lime Gremolata

Makes 4 entrée servings

Mofongo, a Puerto Rican specialty, is made of green plantains that are fried, then mashed and stuffed with assorted fillings...which are also fried. This version is slightly healthier, mounded high with roasted vegetables and dotted with garlicky gremolata. The vegetables, plantains, and gremolata can all be made up to a day in advance and then brought to temperature before serving.

Chayote is a pale green gourd that tastes mildly of cucumber. One end is narrow, while the other is larger and gathers like a puckered mouth. Small fruits are preferable, as they have thin skin and don't require peeling before use.

While traditional Mofongo is fried, the roasted variation below yields equally good results.

Serve the accompanying gremolata mounded atop a spoon on each plate, allowing your guests to use as much or as little of the piquant sauce as they like.

2 zucchini, sliced into ½-inch
half-moons

2 large tomatoes (or 4 small Romas),
diced into ½-inch pieces

2 chayote, pattypan, or sunburst
squash, seeded and diced into
½-inch pieces

1 onion, thinly sliced

1 teaspoon sea salt

1 tablespoon olive oil or other
vegetable oil

4 green plantains

Several cups vegetable oil, for frying

½ teaspoon sea salt

½ teaspoon ground black pepper

Cilantro-Lime Gremolata
(page 77)

Heat the oven to 375° F. In a large casserole dish or cake pan, toss together the zucchini, onion, tomato, chayote or squash, oil, sea salt, and pepper. Roast for about an hour, while you prepare the rest of the meal.

Make the gremolata according to recipe directions and set aside.

Prepare and fry plantains according to Bannann Peze recipe directions (page 164). Remove them from the hot oil using a slotted spoon, and transfer plantains directly to a large bowl, and sprinkle in sea salt and pepper. Don't be tempted to drain the plantains; you'll need the residual oil to get the texture right.

Using a heavy pestle, the end of a rolling pin, or the bottom of a glass jar (anything solid and similarly shaped will work), bash the plantains into pieces. They should be mostly in chunks, and far from smoothly mashed, but they should hold together when pressed against the side of the bowl.

Line 4 ramekins with foil, and spoon in the smashed plantains, distributing evenly. Use the back of a spoon to spread the plantains over the bottom and sides, creating a hollow in the center. The top edges don't need to be smooth and can remain nicely jagged. At this point, the plantains can be prepared in the ramekins up to a few hours in advance. Rewarm for 5 to 7 minutes with the roasting vegetables just prior to serving.

At this point, the vegetables should be near finished. When done, they will be soft and tipped with brown. Set aside.

When ready to serve, lift the Mofongo from the ramekins, and gently peel off the foil exterior. Unmold onto plates, open side up, and fill with roasted vegetables, mounding them over the top. If you have more vegetables than will fit, allow them to spill over and onto the plate. Serve with a spoonful of gremolata on each plate, and pass any leftovers alongside. Serve immediately.

Oven-Fried Mofongo

For a nontraditional but comparably good Mofongo, cut the plantains into ½-inch pieces. Toss with 2 tablespoons of oil, ½ teaspoon of sea salt, and ½ teaspoon of ground black pepper. Roast them according to the method on page 34 (Perfect Potatoes): heat the oven to 450 with a large pan inside. Once very hot, add the plantain mixture. Cook for 15 to 20 minutes, stirring every 5 minutes.

Adobong Gulay
(Vegetable Adobo)

Makes 4 servings

Adobo, Spanish for "seasoning," takes various forms depending on the culture that adopts it. In the Philippines, where it is a national dish, adobo refers to a medley of ingredients first browned, then slow-cooked in soy sauce, vinegar, garlic, bay leaves, and black peppercorns. Filipinos serve it with white rice, which best highlights its sharp flavors.

Adobo can be made with nearly any vegetable. Zucchini, bamboo shoots (labong), carrots, or tomatoes are all good substitutions for the eggplant, okra, and string beans.

The greens commonly used in adobo are called kankong, *or swamp cabbage; use this if you can find it. Here, spinach or mustard greens are used, but any variety intended for cooking—collards, kale, and so on—will work.*

2 tablespoons plus 2 tablespoons vegetable oil

8 ounces seitan, torn or cut into ½-inch pieces

6 cloves garlic, thinly sliced

1 onion, thinly sliced

2 Thai eggplants, cut into ½-inch half-moons

½ pound okra, left whole

½ pound string beans, halved crosswise

4 cups spinach or mustard greens

⅓ cup soy sauce

⅓ cup white vinegar

2 bay leaves

½ teaspoon whole black peppercorns

White rice, cooked, for serving

Heat the first 2 tablespoons of the oil in a large, heavy sauté pan or stockpot over medium heat. Sauté the seitan until golden, turning once, about 5 to 7 minutes. Crispy bits will form, and the seitan will absorb nearly all of the oil. Remove the seitan and set aside. Heat the remaining 2 tablespoons oil, add the garlic and onion, and cook for 2 minutes. Once the onions go translucent, add the okra, eggplant, and beans, stirring to coat. Cook, stirring occasionally, until vegetables are soft and most of the liquid has evaporated, about 10 minutes. Reduce the heat to medium-low and add the greens and reserved seitan. Stir in soy sauce, vinegar, bay leaves, and peppercorns.

Continue cooking until the liquid forms a sauce and thickens slightly. This should take about 30 minutes, after which the vegetables will absorb the sauce and take on a glossy sheen. Taste the Adobo; it should be really piquant, with a balance of tang and saltiness. If the flavor is too acidic for your taste, add a generous pinch of sugar. Turn off the heat, remove bay leaves, and allow it to rest until ready to serve.

Mound it over the rice and serve hot. Leftovers are also delicious cold or at room temperature, and will keep for up to a week.

Sides

Garlicky greens, crisp potatoes, perfectly cooked summer squash... Side dishes are the faithful, understated champions of the dinner table. What else could be so dutifully present and yet so uncelebrated? Bring your sides to the center with these unique dishes that pay tribute to their fresh, nutritious ingredients. They're sure to be noticed at your next meal.

To transform a side dish into a complete meal, simply add crumbled seitan, tempeh, or tofu prepared with a spice rub, or a few cups of legumes, and serve over cooked grains.

Fennel-Roasted Root Vegetables

Makes about 6 cups

The combination of grounding root vegetables and warming spices is incredibly comforting when the chill of autumn sets in. Use other tubers or squashes if you like; the recipe is very flexible.

Garam masala, a combination of spices including cinnamon, nutmeg, and cloves, can be purchased at Indian or Middle Eastern groceries.

1 pound potatoes (any variety, about 3 medium), cut into ¾-inch chunks

1 pound sweet potatoes or yams, cut into ¾-inch chunks

1 pound winter squash (butternut or delicata are great), peeled and cut into ¾-inch chunks

1 pound carrots, cut into ¾-inch-wide slices

2 onions, thinly sliced

5 cloves garlic, minced

2 tablespoons olive oil

2 tablespoons maple syrup

1 tablespoon fennel seeds

2 teaspoons sea or kosher salt

1 teaspoon garam masala

½ teaspoon ground black pepper

Generous pinch of dried red pepper flakes (optional)

Heat the oven to 375° F. Thoroughly oil a rimmed baking sheet. Set aside.

In a large bowl, combine all ingredients, tossing well to coat. Spread evenly on prepared baking sheet and bake for 50 to 65 minutes, stirring every 15 minutes or so. The vegetables should be tender when pierced with a fork: spotted with a bit of brown, the onions roasted to caramelized softness. And taste them; the texture should be like something you'd really want to eat. Remove from the oven and serve hot.

The leftovers are excellent (served cold or at room temperature) over fresh greens, sprinkled with a bit of balsamic vinegar.

Citrus Almond Kale

Makes 4 side-dish servings

Served raw, kale is cruel and unpalatable, and requires valiant convincing to believe it's edible. Quickly cooked, it gets infused with flavor and goes from harsh to satiny in an instant.

Any citrus zest can be substituted for the lemon: orange, tangerine, lime, kumquat, whatever you have. Just promise me if you come across a citron, in all its crinkly-fingered glory, you'll save it for something more unusual than this.

1 tablespoon olive oil
1 pound kale, stems intact, roughly
  chopped into ¾-inch pieces
3 cloves garlic, minced

¼ cup sliced or slivered almonds
½ teaspoon lemon or other citrus
  zest (about ½ lemon)
½ teaspoon sea salt

Heat a cast-iron skillet over high heat. Add the oil, garlic, and almonds, and sauté for 1 minute. Toss in the kale, zest, and sea salt. Continue to cook, stirring constantly. The kale will wilt slightly right away, but keep stirring until its grey-green cast completely turns a deep emerald, about 4 minutes. Serve hot, over brown rice or other cooked grains.

SIDES

Creamy Saffron Asparagus

Makes 4 side-dish servings

Asparagus handily snaps at the exact place when tender bud turns to tough stem. To take advantage of this natural convenience, grasp several stalks at both ends and bend until they break.

The asparagus can also be steamed, then tossed with the saffron sauce and warmed before serving. Cold leftovers are excellent in salad.

1 shallot, minced

2 tablespoons fresh orange juice

1 tablespoon white wine or
  sherry vinegar

Generous pinch of saffron

¼ teaspoon paprika

½ cup mayonnaise

1½ pounds asparagus, tough
  ends removed

1 tablespoon olive oil

Make the saffron sauce: in a small bowl, whisk together the shallot, orange juice, vinegar, saffron, and paprika. Allow it to sit at least 10 minutes to allow the flavors to meld (cook the asparagus while you wait). Whisk in the mayonnaise.

Sauté the asparagus in olive oil in a large skillet over medium-high heat. Toss and cook until just tender, 5 to 7 minutes.

Pour saffron sauce over the asparagus, tossing gently to warm through, about 1 minute. Serve immediately.

A Guide to Grains

The listing below serves as a general guideline. Keep the following in mind when cooking grains:

Rinsing grains removes excess starch and allows you to remove any unnecessary bits.

Combining grains can create a wonderfully varied dish. Be sure to choose grains with approximately the same cooking time, or add them to the pot progressively.

Toasting improves the flavor of most grains, and is easily done in a heavy saucepan over medium heat. Cook until fragrant, and shake or stir regularly to prevent scorching. Toasting also slightly reduces cooking time, so be mindful of this to avoid overcooking.

Adding oil before cooking lends fluffiness, as the fat insulates the grains.

Replacing some of the cooking water with a flavorful liquid such as stock, nondairy milk, or fruit juice will enhance and deepen the taste of the finished grains.

Adding salt rounds out the flavors. For quick cooking grains (such as couscous, oatmeal, or polenta), toss in a generous pinch prior to cooking. For longer-cooking stuff (such as wild rice or barley), add it at the end.

Cook 1 cup of the following with the listed amount of liquid for the listed time. Yields are approximate. Cover the grains and cook over low heat, unless indicated otherwise. Check for doneness during the last 5 minutes, and add some extra liquid if necessary. To skip using a pan altogether, simply combine grains and liquid in the amounts below in a rice cooker.

Amaranth

2 cups liquid (or 3 cups for porridge)

20 to 25 minutes

Yield: 4 cups

Barley

3 cups liquid (or 4 cups for porridge)

40 to 45 minutes

Yield: 4 cups

Buckwheat

2 cups liquid

15 minutes

Yield: 3 cups

Cornmeal

4 cups liquid

25 to 30 minutes

Yield: 4 cups

Couscous (quick-cooking)

1¼ cups liquid

5 minutes at low heat, then let stand covered 10 minutes

Yield: 3 cups

Fonio

4 cups liquid

20 minutes

Yield: 4 cups

Joy Tienzo | Cook, Eat, Thrive

Grits

5 cups liquid

25 to 30 minutes

Yield: 4 cups

Kamut

4 cups liquid, or more

1½ to 2 hours, drain after cooking

Yield: 1½ cups

Millet

2½ cups liquid

25 to 30 minutes

Yield: 4 cups

Oats (rolled)

2 cups liquid

5 to 10 minutes

Yield: 2 cups

Polenta

3 cups liquid

15 minutes

Yield: 4 cups

Quinoa

2 cups liquid

15 minutes

Yield: 3 cups

Rice (brown)

2 to 2¼ for short-grain, 2¼
to 2½ for long-grain

35 to 45 minutes, very low heat

Yield: 3½ cups

Rice (white)

1¾ to 2 cups liquid

15 to 18 minutes, very low heat

Yield: 3 cups

Rye

3 cups liquid

50 to 60 minutes, low heat,
drain after cooking

Yield: 3 cups

Spelt

4 cups liquid, or more

1½ to 2 hours, drain after cooking

Yield: 1½ cups

Steel-cut oats

4 cups liquid

25 to 30 minutes, uncovered

Yield: 4 cups

Teff

2½ to 3 cups liquid

15 minutes

Yield: 4 cups

Triticale

4 cups liquid, or more

1½ to 2 hours, drain after cooking

Yield: 1½ cups

Wheat berries

4 cups liquid, or more

1½ to 2 hours, drain after cooking

Yield: 1½ cups

Wild rice

3 cups liquid

40 to 55 minutes

Yield: 3½ cups

Caramelized Broccoli

Makes 4 side-dish servings

Cooking broccoli slowly over low heat allows its natural sweetness to develop, and draws out a layered earthiness. It takes ages, requires copious amounts of oil, and is the best preparation for this cruciferous vegetable I know.

Frozen broccoli also gives a comparable result, although it will take longer for the liquid to evaporate and the finished texture will be slightly mushier.

4 cups fresh broccoli, cut into florets (about 1 pound)	1 medium onion, thinly sliced
2 tablespoons olive oil	3 cloves garlic, coarsely chopped
1 teaspoon sea salt	½ teaspoon freshly ground pepper
	Pinch of Italian red pepper

Combine all ingredients in a large skillet, preferably cast-iron, over low heat. Allow them to cook, stirring every 10 minutes or so, for about an hour. If the broccoli begins to brown, add a few tablespoons water or an additional slosh of oil. When done, the broccoli should have a nutty flavor and deep olive color.

Serve as a side, over cooked grains, or in Broccoli-Cheese Bruschetta (page 89).

Caramelized Broccoli-Cheese Soup

For a quick broccoli-cheese soup, simply combine finely chopped Caramelized Broccoli with Sharp White Cheddar Sauce (page 75). Thin with water to the desired consistency and heat through before serving.

Bannann Peze (Fried Plantains)

Makes 4 servings

Green plantains ooze a sap that sticks to your fingers in spite of any amount of washing. To prevent this, rub your hands lightly with cooking oil before handling the plantains. If the substance does stick, remove it by scrubbing with a bit of salt.

Before you begin working, have ready a slotted spoon, a cutting board that can handle heat, a rolling pin, and a plate lined with paper towels.

SIDES

4 green plantains

Vegetable oil, for frying

1 teaspoon sea salt or coarse kosher salt

½ teaspoon freshly ground black pepper

Heat about 1 inch oil over medium heat in a heavy, high-sided medium saucepan.

Cut off the ends of each plantain. Make a slit lengthwise through the peel, and pull the plantain open to remove. Slice the plantains into ½-inch slices on a slight diagonal.

Check the oil: it should register 365° F on a food thermometer. If a plantain slice dropped into the oil sizzles rapidly, it's ready. Gently add about a quarter of the plantain slices to the hot oil. Allow them to cook 3 to 4 minutes, repositioning as necessary to avoid sticking.

Using the slotted spoon, lift a slice out. It should appear gloriously golden and crispy. If not, cook a few minutes more. Remove the cooked plantains from the oil, and transfer to the paper-lined plate. Sprinkle with salt and fresh pepper. Repeat with the remaining plantains.

Deep-Frying

Deep-frying may seem intimidating, but there's really not much to it. These tips will ensure a crisp, golden exterior on your favorite foods with minimal work.

The best oils for frying are neutral in flavor, with a high smoking point. Canola, corn, sunflower, and safflower are all good choices.

Use plenty of fat (enough to cover the food), but do not fill your pot more than ⅔ full. Always heat the oil uncovered.

Keep moisture away from the fat, as it will result in sizzling, which can cause burns.

The oil should register 365° F on a frying thermometer. Some recipes may call for hotter or cooler oil, but this temperature suits most foods.

Fry in small batches to prevent overcrowding and uneven browning.

After frying a batch, remove any residual bits with a strainer or slotted spoon, and allow the fat to return to its proper temperature.

Used oil can be strained into a glass jar and kept, at room temperature, to be re-used several times. Each use lowers the smoking point slightly, so the oil's quality lessens with each batch.

Fried fare is best served immediately, but you can keep already-fried foods warm on a towel-lined plate in an oven set to very low heat.

SIDES

Greens au Gratin

Makes 6 side-dish servings

With some help from an underrated tuber, unassuming greens are transformed into a creamy, soothing side dish. This simple side uses sunchokes, also called Jerusalem artichokes, to bind everything together. Sprouted breadcrumbs, baked until golden, create a hearty crust.

Peel the sunchoke as you would fresh ginger, using a spoon to scrape the brown skin from the white interior flesh. To make the cup of bread crumbs called for, just toast and blend 2 pieces of bread. If using greens with a high sodium content (such as chard), reduce the salt by ¼ teaspoon.

1 pound sunchokes, peeled and cut into 1-inch chunks
¾ cup unsweetened nondairy milk
1 tablespoon flour
2 cloves garlic
1 teaspoon sea salt
½ teaspoon ground black pepper
½ teaspoon sea salt

½ teaspoon ground nutmeg (freshly ground if possible)
1 tablespoon plus 1 teaspoon olive oil
16 ounces mixed greens (such as spinach, chard, kale, and broccoli raab)
1 cup wholegrain bread crumbs (from 2 slices of bread)

Heat the oven to 350° F. Oil a 2-quart gratin or casserole dish and set it aside.

Steam the sunchoke chunks until fork-tender. Transfer to a blender or food processor, along with nondairy milk, flour, garlic, sea salt, pepper, nutmeg, and 1 tablespoon of the olive oil. Blend until very smooth and set aside.

Steam the greens until very bright green and slightly tender, about 5 minutes. Shake them briefly to drain, and transfer to the prepared dish. Pour the sunchoke mixture over the greens, prodding at them a bit to evenly distribute the sauce.

In a small bowl, toss the bread crumbs with the sea salt, pepper, and the remaining 1 teaspoon olive oil. Scatter the crumb mixture over the top and cover with foil. Bake 15 minutes. Uncover and bake 15 minutes more, until the gratin is bubbly and golden.

Remove from the oven and allow it to rest for 15 minutes before serving. This dish is lovely mounded over grains and topped with crispy sliced seitan—be sure everyone gets a generous sprinkling of crumb topping! It's also delicious alone, eaten in a big bowl while curled up on the sofa.

Sunchokes

Sunchokes, or Jerusalem Artichokes, are a knobby root in the sunflower family that taste faintly of artichokes. Look for plump chokes free of any sunken or moist spots. Although this recipe requires cooked sunchokes, they are crisp and sweet when raw, and make a great addition to salads.

Caribbean Sweet Potatoes

Makes 4 side-dish servings

Serve this flavorful dish instead of Fried Plantains to accompany Riz et Pois Rouges (page 146), or chill and spoon over fresh greens. You might want to make a double batch; the sweet potatoes tend to disappear quickly.

2 pounds sweet potatoes (2 to 3 medium), cut into 1-inch chunks
½ cup coconut milk
Juice of 1 lime
½ medium red onion, thinly sliced
¼ cup cilantro, roughly chopped
¼ cup chopped peanuts

½ teaspoon sea salt
½ teaspoon fresh black pepper
⅛ teaspoon allspice
2 tablespoons unsweetened flaked coconut, for serving (optional)
2 tablespoons whole peanuts, for serving (optional)

Steam the sweet potatoes until fork-tender. Set aside for a moment to cool slightly.

Meanwhile, in a large bowl, whisk together the coconut milk, lime juice, onion, cilantro, peanuts, sea salt, pepper, and allspice. Add the still-warm sweet potatoes and toss gently to combine. Allow the mixture to sit for at least 15 minutes for sweet potatoes to absorb the dressing.

Serve hot, cold, or at room temperature, sprinkled with the coconut and peanuts.

SIDES

Raw Zucchini Noodles

Makes 2 servings

If you prefer to avoid starchy pastas, these noodles are an excellent complement to any raw or cooked sauce. To serve hot, the strands can be quickly stir-fried in a wok or cast-iron skillet until just steaming.

1 clove garlic, minced
½ teaspoon sea salt
½ teaspoon ground black pepper

¼ teaspoon cold-pressed olive oil
2 medium zucchini

Combine the garlic, sea salt, pepper, and olive oil in a small bowl, and set aside.

Using a vegetable peeler, remove slices of zucchini. They should be wide and long, with a bit of green skin edging every noodle. When you reach the seeded center and all the skin is gone, discard or reserve the zucchini for another use. Add to garlic mixture, toss gently to combine, and marinate at room temperature for at least 15 minutes and up to an hour. On sitting, the noodles will soften and release a bit of liquid.

Pour off any accumulated liquid. Serve with Raw White Cheddar Sauce (page 75), Cilantro-Lime Gremolata (page 77), or any raw or cooked marinara.

SIDES

Hot Basil Eggplant

Makes 2 generous side-dish servings

This is my favorite way to eat eggplant: in burnished sections tossed with hot chiles, ginger, and basil in a flavorful sauce. Use Thai basil if you can find it, and pinch off sections that each have several leaves, with a bit of stem included.

Have all ingredients close at hand. Things go very quickly after frying the eggplant.

2 tablespoons hoisin sauce

2 tablespoons soy sauce

2 teaspoons agave nectar

2 teaspoons rice vinegar

4 Chinese eggplants

3 tablespoons vegetable oil

3 cloves garlic, minced

1 inch ginger root, peeled and thinly sliced

1 jalapeño pepper, thinly sliced into rings

½ cup packed whole basil leaves

2 cups cooked rice or grains, for serving (optional)

In a small bowl, stir together the hoisin sauce, soy sauce, agave nectar, and vinegar. Line a plate with paper towels and set aside.

Halve the eggplants lengthwise, then cut into 2-inch pieces on a diagonal. Heat oil in a cast-iron skillet or wok over medium-high heat. Add eggplant and fry until browned on one side, about 2 minutes. Flip and cook, stirring as necessary, until cut sides are a deep russet color, 2 to 4 minutes more. With a slotted spoon or kitchen tongs, transfer to the towel-lined plate.

Pour off all but ½ teaspoon of oil from the skillet and return to heat. Add the garlic, ginger, and jalapeño, stirring quickly. Pour in sauce, and remove skillet from stove; the residual heat will cook everything through. Add the eggplants and basil, and toss once more to coat.

Serve immediately over grains, if desired, avoiding the pieces of ginger and jalapeño unless you're particularly brave.

For wheat-free substitute tamari for soy sauce

SIDES

Indian Carrots

Makes 4 to 6 side-dish servings, or 1 dozen servings as a garnish

While in the south of India, I once went exploring. A fellow traveler followed, and we stumbled onto an expansive green field, shrouded in mist. I knew that tea wasn't grown at this altitude, but the leaves were too intense to be anything ordinary. We ran through rows of soil, breathing in the deeply fragranced earth.

Our wistfulness stopped abruptly when we realized that several farmers had spotted us. After considering a quick escape, we were surprised by incredible graciousness. The farmers called to us and beckoned to a clearing in the middle of the rows. They welcomed us toward a tiny corrugated metal cabin, out of which an entire family emerged. They brought chai, and asked us to stay for dinner. Reaching into the earth, a man uprooted a handful of his crop—carrots!—and thrust it into our arms. We talked, laughed, and made balloon animals with the children. Carrots swung from my hands, their tops still attached, as I walked out of the mist and back into the everyday.

Years later, I've made a life with that friend who joined me on that adventure. We always remember the field as the place that brought us together.

If I could return to that moment, I would have prepared the carrots simply that evening: left raw, and spiced with fennel and cumin. This variation on carrot pickle (gajar ka achaar) is my celebration of India, and to the beautiful and generous family who shared their field of carrots.

½ teaspoon whole coriander

½ teaspoon whole cumin

½ teaspoon fennel seeds

½ teaspoon mustard seeds

¼ cup apple cider vinegar

¼ teaspoon olive, coconut, or other vegetable oil

Juice of half a lemon

1 medium onion, diced

1 tablespoon sea salt

2 teaspoons minced fresh ginger

½ teaspoon lemon zest

2 dried red chiles, crumbled

2 pounds carrots (about 10 large)

Coarsely crush the coriander, cumin, fennel, and mustard in a coffee grinder or mortar and pestle. Transfer to a large bowl and add the vinegar, oil, fresh lemon juice, onion, sea salt, ginger, zest, and chiles. Set aside while preparing the carrots.

Divide carrots into 2-inch segments, and halve each segment lengthwise. Place cut side down on a surface and slice vertically, making long, very thin strips. Add carrots to liquid and toss to combine. Allow the flavors to meld for an hour at room temperature, or overnight in the refrigerator.

Serve cold or at room temperature, as an accompaniment to a raw meal or garnish for Indian dishes. Served over fresh greens, the accumulated liquid also makes a hot and tangy salad dressing.

Ras el Hanout–Roasted Beets

Makes 4 side-dish servings

Ras el Hanout fragrances these tender and tangy beets.

1 pound beets (greens not included), peeled

1 tablespoon fresh lemon juice or vinegar

1 tablespoon olive oil or vegetable oil

2 cloves garlic, thinly sliced

1 teaspoon sea salt

½ teaspoon Ras el Hanout (page 68)

Cashew Crema (page 65), for serving (optional)

Heat the oven to 375° F.

Steam beets until fork tender. Allow them to rest until cool enough to handle, and cut each beet into 8 wedges.

In a 2-quart baking dish, toss together all the ingredients. Transfer to the oven and roast 20 to 25 minutes, stirring occasionally. When done, the beets will be fragrant and deep burgundy in color.

Drizzle with Cashew Crema and serve.

Ras el Hanout Beet Puree

Allow the roasted beets to cool slightly, and transfer to a food processor. Add ½ cup vegetable broth or water and process until smooth. Drizzle in additional liquid as needed to achieve a velvety texture. Use as a base for entrées, marbleizing with streaks of Crema, if you like.

SIDES

Pine Nut Brussels Sprouts

Makes 4 side-dish servings

Before these cruciferous gems were in Brussels, their predecessors grew in ancient Rome. Centuries later, the buds sprang up in Belgium, and have been enjoyed (or detested) ever since. This unusual preparation with olive oil, pine nuts, and grapes gives a nod to their early heritage.

1 pound Brussels sprouts (about 20), bases trimmed, and halved
1 cup red grapes, halved
3 tablespoons pine nuts
2 cloves garlic, minced

1 tablespoon olive oil
1 teaspoon sea salt
½ teaspoon ground black pepper
½ teaspoon red pepper flakes (optional)

Heat the oven to 375° F.

Steam the Brussels sprouts 5 to 7 minutes, until just tender.

While the sprouts steam, toss the remaining ingredients together in a large baking dish or pan. Once steamed, shake the sprouts dry, and allow excess moisture to evaporate for a moment. Add to the pan, tossing well to combine (hands are an ideal tool here).

Roast 20 to 22 minutes, stirring every 10 minutes, until sprouts are golden and grapes are puckered slightly. Serve hot.

Gomen (Ethiopian Cabbage)

Makes 4 side-dish servings

In Ethiopia, cabbage is cooked with generous amounts of oil and seasoned with African birds-eye peppers. If you cannot find these particular chiles, which are red and thin, substitute a jalapeño or small Thai chili.

Ethiopian dishes are meant to be scooped up with tangy injera, *the bubbly soft flatbread made from fermented teff flour. It can also be served with pita, lavash, or over any cooked grains.*

1 (15-ounce) can diced, crushed, or whole tomatoes

1 large head cabbage

1 red onion, diced

¼ cup plus 2 tablespoons vegetable oil (such as canola or safflower)

2 cloves garlic, minced

1 fresh hot pepper, halved, seeded, and very thinly sliced

1½ teaspoons sea salt

Puree the tomatoes in a blender or food processor. Remove the hard core from the cabbage and slice into pieces approximately 2½ inches thick.

In a large pot, dry cook the onion over medium-high heat, stirring constantly. When the onion goes translucent, add ¼ cup of the oil, and continue cooking. Add the tomatoes, garlic, and pepper. Cook and stir for 3 minutes.

Add the cabbage and 1 teaspoon of the sea salt, and cover without disturbing. Allow it to cook for 3 minutes, then stir well. Cover again and cook 20 to 25 minutes over medium-high heat. Halfway through, add the remaining 2 tablespoons oil and ½ teaspoon sea salt. When done, the cabbage will be silky and translucent.

Serve hot, cold, or at room temperature.

Roasted Garlic and Cannelloni Bean Smashed Potatoes

Makes 6 generous side-dish servings

These smashed potatoes are swathed in a velvety puree of roasted garlic and white beans. Serve topped with sautéed bitter greens and a roasted portabella mushroom.

1 head garlic

1 (15-ounce) can cannelloni beans, drained and rinsed, or 1½ cups cooked

1½ pounds red potatoes (about 3 medium)

1 tablespoon olive oil

½ teaspoon dried thyme

1 teaspoon sea salt

¼ teaspoon freshly ground pepper, white if you have it

⅓ to ½ cup nondairy milk, vegetable broth, or water

Fresh thyme leaves, for garnish (Italian parsley is a fine substitution)

Roast the garlic according to instructions on page 88.

While the garlic gets toasty, prepare the potatoes: peel half of them and cut them into 1-inch chunks. Submerge them in boiling, salted water and cook until very tender, 10 to 15 minutes. Drain and set aside in a large bowl.

When the garlic is done, allow it to cool a bit, then squeeze the soft cloves into a food processor. Add the beans, olive oil, thyme, salt, and pepper, and puree until smooth. Alternately, mash with a fork until very well combined.

Dollop the bean mixture onto potatoes, smashing roughly with a fork. Add nondairy milk, broth, or water, several tablespoons at a time, continuing to smash as you go. The end consistency should be fairly creamy, with chunks of potato throughout. Taste, and adjust the seasonings if necessary.

Return the mixture to a saucepan to warm through, stirring gently over low heat.

Sprinkle with thyme and serve warm, preferably dripping with the inky-dark juices of a roasted and sliced portabella.

Desserts

Whether you're biting into a simple piece of fruit or an elaborate multilayered confection, a sweet finish lends a sense of closure and satisfaction to any meal.

This is the largest section of the book, and that's no accident.

Basic Sweet Crêpes

Makes 12 6-inch or 8 9-inch crêpes

These crêpes are perfect for impromptu desserts: prepare them in advance, and fill with Whipped Coconut Cream and pineapple chunks, Chèvre and Lemon Curd, or Whipped Truffle Mousse and fresh raspberries. The trick in creating excellent crêpes lies primarily in the handling, rather than the actual recipe. This batter is very runny, and creates delicate, liqueur-scented rounds.

I prefer not to grease the pan, and if it is hot enough, you probably won't need additional fat. Use a small spatula or two teaspoons to execute a skillful flip. I use my fingers, which have developed an alarmingly high pain tolerance after thousands of crêpes.

1 cup all-purpose flour	2 tablespoons sugar
¾ cup nondairy milk	1 tablespoon rum, Grand Marnier, or
¾ cup water	other liqueur
¼ cup margarine or	1 teaspoon vanilla extract
shortening, melted	Generous pinch of sea salt

Combine all ingredients in a blender or food processor for 30 seconds. Scrape down the sides, and blend again for 2 minutes. Refrigerate for 1 hour or overnight.

Heat a small or medium pan, or a crêpe pan, over medium heat. Pour in several tablespoons of batter, quickly swirling to coat the pan. Use just enough batter to coat the pan; the crêpes should be quite thin. When the edges begin to brown, slide a small spatula ½ inch under a corner. If the pan is hot enough, the crêpe should release easily. Flip over, and cook the second side until spotty brown.

Remove to a plate, and cover with a clean dish towel until all crêpes are finished. Serve as directed in recipes.

To freeze finished crêpes for later use, place squares of waxed paper or parchment in between the crêpes as they finish cooking. Allow them to cool completely, and wrap well in plastic, then foil. The crêpes will keep for up to 3 months.

Coconut Caramel

Makes about 1 cup

With essentially two ingredients, this gooey sauce is the perfect finish for all sorts of desserts. If you've never made caramel before, start with this recipe. Its satiny texture will woo you, and soon you'll be pouring it over everything.

¼ cup cold water
Pinch of cream of tartar (preferred),
    or a few drops of lemon juice
    or vinegar

1 cup sugar
¾ cups coconut milk (full-fat, not
    light), at room temperature

In a medium, heavy-bottomed saucepan, combine the cold water, cream of tartar, and sugar. Avoid Teflon, as the coating can be damaged by extreme temperatures. Stir the mixture briefly with a clean finger to dissolve any lumps.

Cover and cook over medium heat, swirling to dissolve, 3 to 7 minutes. When the syrup is completely clear and all crystals have dissolved, uncover and increase heat to medium-high. Cook until deep brown. Be patient; this can take around 10 minutes.

Immediately remove from the heat and pour in half of the coconut milk. Do this with great caution; it will bubble up intensely. Brave the heat on your hands and whisk until smooth. Whisk in the remaining coconut milk. Allow it to cool slightly before serving or storing. Keep in the refrigerator in a glass jar for up to a month.

Lemon Curd

Makes about ¾ cup

Some people like lemon, and some people love lemon. This is for the latter.

Use the puckery-sweet spread on scones, slices of Italian Cornmeal Cake (page 194), or folded into Vanilla Bean Frozen Custard (page 212).

½ cup sugar
¼ cup cold water
3 tablespoons cornstarch

⅓ cup fresh lemon juice
2 teaspoons lemon zest
½ teaspoon margarine

In a small saucepan off the heat, whisk together sugar, water, and cornstarch until dissolved completely. Bring to a simmer over medium heat. Once bubbles begin to form, stir in fresh lemon juice and zest.

Stir constantly in a smooth figure-8 pattern. The best tool for this is a heatproof spatula, as it allows you to reach into the corners. The mixture will begin to thicken at the corners and sides. Stir quickly, or employ a whisk to smooth it out. The thickening process will take 5 to 8 minutes overall. Once the curd thickens almost uniformly, reduce the heat to low and cook 1 minute more.

Remove the curd from the heat and press through a strainer into a small bowl. Stir in margarine. Allow it to cool 5 to 10 minutes, then press a sheet of plastic directly onto the curd to prevent a skin from forming. Refrigerate until well chilled.

Use immediately, or transfer to a glass jar to serve later. The curd will keep, refrigerated, for several weeks.

Caramel

Although this recipe is fairly simple, it does require some understanding of the caramelization process. When sugar is heated to the point of melting (with or without water), it begins to color and caramelize. If left as is, it will solidify into a hard mass. If water is added, it becomes a thin sauce. If water and fat are added, the caramel develops body and a satiny texture.

Since crystallization is the enemy of a good caramel, preventing it is important. There are several ways to do this:

Incorporate an acid into the sugar/water mixture (cream of tartar, lemon juice, or vinegar). This keeps the sugar crystals from joining together. Cream of tartar is the best choice because it does not impart a flavor.

Once heated, do not stir the sugar mixture, and don't touch it with anything (like a candy thermometer).

Cover the pan until the sugar mixture is completely dissolved; the steam will wash any crystals into the pan.

Keep the temperature high enough. Simmering the sugar mixture for too long over low heat gives time for crystallization to occur.

Caramel can burn very quickly, but for a proper sauce, take the sugar to the darkest point before it actually does. It should be the color of an older penny, and should smell a bit sharp. It might take a few tries to muster the courage, but it's worth it. The color can be tested by carefully dipping strips of white paper into the bubbling sugar.

Adding coconut milk will make the caramel bubble up—use a pan with high sides and stand back. Caramel is extremely hot and can do serious damage, so you might consider wearing plastic gloves while making it.

Vanilla Custard

Makes about 2 cups

Serve this creamy and versatile dessert as a pudding, tartlet filling, or sandwiched between split Cream Scones (page 53) with fresh strawberries for shortcake.

⅓ cup sugar

2 tablespoons plus 1½ teaspoons cornstarch, sifted

Generous pinch sea salt

1 cup nondairy milk

1 cup coconut milk (soy creamer is a fine substitution)

Seeds scraped from 1 inch of vanilla bean, or 1½ teaspoons vanilla extract

In a heavy medium saucepan off the heat, combine sugar, cornstarch, and sea salt. Whisk in ¼ cup of the coconut milk to make a slurry. Slowly pour in the remaining coconut milk and nondairy milk, whisking vigorously as you go. If using the vanilla bean, add it now.

Place the saucepan over medium heat, and stir constantly until the custard begins to thicken. I prefer a flexible spatula for this, as it reaches into the corners thoroughly. Before the mixture thickens, you'll have cooked it 4 to 6 minutes, and then steam will begin to rise across the surface. Suddenly, the custard will appear creamy and will cut a swath (see note below). Cook 1 to 2 minutes longer at a simmer, lowering the heat if necessary.

Remove from the heat and stir in vanilla extract, if using it. Transfer it to a medium bowl and allow it to cool, uncovered, for 15 minutes. Stir occasionally to redistribute the heat, then press a sheet of plastic wrap directly onto the custard to prevent a skin from forming.

Chill until completely cold, at least 2 hours and up to a day, before serving.

Lemon Custard

Reduce vanilla to 1 teaspoon. Add 1 tablespoon fresh lemon juice, 1 teaspoon lemon zest, and an extra pinch of sea salt with the vanilla.

"Cutting a Swath"

To determine if it "cuts a swath," dip the back of a spoon into the mixture, and lift it out. Run your finger down the back of the spoon, and if the remaining stuff stays put and doesn't run into the "swath," you're set.

Whipped Truffle Mousse

Makes 2 cups

This basic cream can be used as a mousse, frosting, pudding, dip, or filling for Chocolate Truffle Cake (page 222). It's incredibly simple to make, and keeps wonderfully in the refrigerator. Be sure to use a good-quality chocolate, as its flavor is very pronounced here.

1 (12.3-ounce) package silken tofu, at room temperature

1 tablespoon maple syrup or agave nectar

6 ounces semisweet chocolate, coarsely chopped

Blend the silken tofu in a food processor until completely smooth, scraping down the sides to incorporate all of the tofu.

Melt the chocolate according to instructions below.

With the food processor running, pour the melted chocolate down the feed tube. Run a spatula along the bottom and sides of the processor, add the maple syrup, and blend again.

Refrigerate for at least 20 minutes prior to serving, or store, covered and refrigerated, for up to a week.

Mexican Chocolate Pudding

Add ½ teaspoon cinnamon and a small pinch of cayenne with the maple syrup or agave nectar. Serve dusted with additional cinnamon.

Mint Chocolate Pudding

Add ¼ teaspoon mint extract or mint schnapps (Bacchus Brand Mint Schnapps is vegan) with the maple syrup or agave nectar.

Fudgsicles

Add 1 cup water with the maple syrup or agave nectar. Divide the mixture evenly between 6 to 8 popsicle molds, depending on size. Freeze until solid.

> ### Melting Chocolate
>
> To melt small pieces of chocolate in the microwave, place in a glass bowl and heat on high. Stir at 15-second intervals with a clean, dry spoon or spatula. Be sure no water comes into contact with the chocolate, as this will cause it to seize and become grainy, ruining the batch.
>
> Alternatively, melt chocolate in a saucepan over very low heat, stirring slowly and constantly. Remove from the heat when nearly smooth, and stir until any lumps are completely melted.

White Chocolate Buttercream

Makes about 4 cups

This buttercream is something I won't say about most foods: it is exquisite. It has the flavor of real cocoa butter, and the rich airiness of a mousseline buttercream. Use it to frost cupcakes, fill napoleons, and spread over cookies.

2 tablespoons cocoa butter

1 cup shortening, at room temperature

½ cup (1 stick) margarine, cold

4 cups powdered sugar

1 tablespoon nondairy milk or water

1 teaspoon vanilla extract

1 teaspoon fresh lemon juice

Melt the cocoa butter in the microwave or on a stovetop over low heat until liquid (a few solid bits are okay). Set aside to cool slightly.

In a large bowl, beat the shortening and margarine with an electric hand mixer, or in the bowl of a stand mixer, until smooth. Add 1 cup of the powdered sugar, and beat until combined. Add the remaining powdered sugar and beat until smooth. Add nondairy milk or water, vanilla, and fresh lemon juice, beating after each addition. With the mixer still running, slowly drizzle in cocoa butter, beating and scraping down the sides as necessary until completely incorporated.

Use it immediately or cover and transfer to the refrigerator for up to 3 days. Allow it to come to cool room temperature, and briefly beat with an electric mixer or whisk before using.

Purchasing Cocoa Butter

I shouldn't advise you to purchase nonfood items and use them as food. If I follow this advice strictly, I'll recommend ordering cocoa butter online from a confectioner, which you can do with relative ease.

But, if clutched by a momentary lapse in judgment, I might tell you to just purchase cocoa butter from a drugstore, the same stuff pregnant women rub on their bellies (be sure the label specifies that it's not processed with hexane). It's very inexpensive and simple to find, and works excellently here.

Orange Blossom "Honey"

Makes about ½ cup

Orange flower water can be found at most Middle Eastern groceries.

½ cup agave nectar

2 teaspoons orange flower water

Stir together the agave nectar and orange flower water. Store in a jar at room temperature, or in the refrigerator.

For raw use raw agave nectar

Spiced Balsamic Syrup

Makes about ¾ cup

Drizzled over ice cream or fresh fruit, this syrup has a unique and layered bite. Refrigerated or not, it will keep for upwards of 6 months.

1 cup white wine
⅓ cup balsamic vinegar
¼ teaspoon ground cinnamon, or
    1 stick cinnamon

4 whole black peppercorns
¼ teaspoon ground, or 3 whole cloves
Juice and zest of ½ lemon
½ cup sugar

Combine all ingredients in a medium saucepan and bring to a boil. Reduce the heat to low, and simmer for 40 to 45 minutes, until reduced by at least half. Remove the syrup from the heat and let it sit for 10 minutes. Pluck out the cinnamon stick, if using, and strain the syrup into a glass jar. Allow it to cool slightly before using.

Other Suggested Uses

Drizzle over a baked sweet potato
Use in Rosemary-Fig Focaccia (page 58)
Whisk together with Dijon mustard and
    olive oil for a distinctive salad dressing

Swirl into Vanilla Bean Frozen
    Custard (page 212) along with
    figs, peaches, or sautéed apples

Ganache

Makes about 2½ cups

Ganache is one of those things that seem terrifying, and then you try it once and wonder why you haven't eaten it for supper every night.

This concoction is incredibly versatile, and can cost very little per batch, depending on the quality of chocolate you choose.

Use it to create a flawless finish on Chocolate Truffle Cake (page 222). Dip strawberries, banana chunks, and vegan marshmallows into warm ganache for a decadent fondue. Or whisk in hot almond milk for rich, smooth hot chocolate.

1 pound good-quality semisweet chocolate, coarsely chopped or semisweet chocolate chips

¾ cup coconut milk (full-fat, not light)

1 teaspoon vanilla extract or other flavoring (optional)

Pinch of sea salt (optional)

Place the chocolate in a medium bowl and set aside.

In a small saucepan, heat the coconut milk and sea salt over medium heat until bubbles form at the edges. Pour it over the chocolate and allow it to rest for 5 minutes. Add any extracts or flavorings at this point, but do not stir.

Using a flexible spatula or spoon, make small circles in the center of the mixture. The chocolate will slowly begin to combine. Continue mixing gently until it all comes together. Try not to incorporate too much air into the mixture, as this will create small bubbles that mar the finish of poured ganache.

Allow the ganache to rest again, about 10 to 15 minutes. It is ready for use when a spoonful dropped into itself smoothes out and its warmth is about that of body temperature.

Why Add Salt to Sweets?

A small amount of salt rounds out a dessert's subtle flavors and lends balance to its sweetness. Don't hesitate to add a pinch to your favorite desserts and baked goods.

Understanding Ganache

Classic ganache is made with a 1:1 ratio of heavy cream and bittersweet or semi-sweet chocolate. Heavy cream is about 36 percent fat, while coconut milk contains approximately 25 percent. While a good ganache can be made with equal parts chocolate and coconut milk, reducing the latter allows it to set more easily.

Although this recipe calls for pouring the liquid over the chocolate, some cooks add the chocolate to the liquid; this is simply a matter of personal preference.

Flavoring Ganache

Ganache can be flavored easily and quickly with extracts (such as vanilla, almond, peppermint), or liqueurs (amaretto, port, rum).

To add complexity of flavor to ganache beyond simple vanilla, infuse it with one or more flavorings. Citrus zest, loose tea, whole spices, herbs, and edible flowers are excellent choices.

There are two methods for imparting these flavors:

In *hot infusion*, the liquid is scalded, then ingredients are added. After 30 to 60 minutes, the flavored liquid is strained, reheated if necessary, and poured over the chocolate. This is the best choice if time is a consideration.

In *cold infusion*, flavorings are added to cold liquid and refrigerated overnight, then strained, heated, and poured over the chocolate. The advantage here is that because the flavor extraction doesn't involve heat, the nuances remain very pure, with no harsh overtones. If you have the time, or want a tea infusion without wicked tannins, this is an excellent choice.

Simple Syrup

Makes 1 cup

Use this basic recipe to sweeten liquids, or try one of the flavored variations in desserts and drinks. Try keeping a small jar in your bar area—the syrup dissolves immediately to create any mixed drinks in an instant.

1 cup sugar   1 cup water

Combine sugar and water in a medium heavy-bottomed saucepan, stirring briefly to dissolve. Bring to a boil, then reduce the heat and simmer for 5 minutes. Remove from the heat, cover, and cool 30 minutes. Pour into a glass jar and store, tightly covered, in the refrigerator for up to a month.

Citrus Syrup

Add zest of one lemon, lime, orange, or half a grapefruit with sugar and water. Continue as directed and strain into a jar to store. For a more intense citrus flavor, allow the zest to steep in the syrup, straining just before use.

Fresh Berry Syrup

Add 12 ounces roughly chopped fresh or frozen fruit (such as blueberries, raspberries, cranberries) with sugar and water. Continue as directed, straining it several times through a strainer or once through multiple layers of cheesecloth. Press the fruit gently with a spatula to extract liquid, and store

Dried Herb Syrup

Add 1 tablespoon dried crushed herbs (such as lavender, coriander, basil) with sugar and water. Continue as directed, and strain the syrup into a glass jar to store.

Fresh Herb Syrup

Add ½ cup roughly chopped fresh herbs (such as cilantro, mint, lemongrass, rosemary) with sugar and water. Continue as directed, and strain into a glass jar to store.

Liqueur Syrup

Stir in 2 tablespoons liqueur (such as Grand Marnier, Frangelico, rum) after removing syrup from the heat. Continue and store as directed.

Spiced Syrup

Add 5 whole peppercorns or allspice berries, 3 whole cloves, 1 stick cinnamon, and a strip orange or lemon peel with sugar and water. Continue as directed, and strain into a glass jar to store.

Whipped Coconut Cream

Makes about 2 cups

Think vegans can't have whipped cream? Not so. The cream skimmed from coconut milk transforms into rich fluff, perfect for dolloping onto your favorite desserts. This recipe yields a lightly sweetened topping; add a teaspoon more sugar if you prefer a sweeter version. Be sure to use full-fat coconut milk.

1 (14-ounce) can coconut milk
1 tablespoon sugar

½ teaspoon vanilla extract, rum extract, or other flavoring

Place a medium bowl (glass, metal, or ceramic are all fine) and the beaters of an electric hand mixer in the freezer to chill.

Refrigerate the unopened can of coconut milk for 1 hour or freeze for 20 to 30 minutes. The fattier "cream" will rise to the top, leaving thinner coconut liquid underneath.

Remove the can from the refrigerator, being careful not to shake or overturn it, and open it. Using a small spoon or spatula, slowly begin to skim the cream from the top, and transfer to the chilled bowl. You should get about 1 cup before the thin liquid appears underneath; try not to include any of this. Reserve the remaining coconut milk for another use.

Add sugar and vanilla or flavoring, and begin whisking with the chilled beaters of an electric hand mixer. The cream is done when it thickens and soft peaks form when a beater is lifted. Stiff peaks may be achieved if the coconut milk is particularly high-fat, but don't whip the cream so long that it warms and begins to liquefy.

Cover and refrigerate for up to 2 hours before serving, whisking briefly before using.

Cardamom Crêpes with Coconut Gelato, Pistachios, and Orange Blossom "Honey"

Makes 4 servings

Turkey is a country of political and religious complexities, dance clubs, and historic ruins. But what I love best are its dogs.

I woke in Antalya one morning, determined to reach the city's nearby mountains. They looked to be a mile away, so I set off for a 20-minute jog. I ran past luxurious hotels and along sandy shorelines. I passed a large industrial area and a shipyard. Five miles later, the mountains looked as far as when I'd started, and I realized my estimate had been really flawed! I ran a mile further, then turned back.

On the way, I picked up a caravan of dogs. A lanky pup with a long nose, a short, shaggy sort, and one with the largest paws I had ever seen. With each mile, another dog, until I had collected five of them! They ran with me for some time, all of them, and I was disappointed to find myself back where I'd started. I said goodbye as they panted and stared with large, damp eyes. Those lovely Turkish dogs.

This dessert celebrates the richness of that country. Coconut Gelato is heaped over Crêpes, then drizzled with Orange Blossom "Honey," and sprinkled with pistachios. The addition of orange flower water to agave nectar creates an amber syrup with a surprising likeness to honey, while pistachios round out an otherwise cloying combination of flavors.

In the spirit of many Middle Eastern desserts, it's also quite sugary. Serve it with a strong cup of black coffee, preferably the Turkish variety.

Crêpes (page 177), with ½ teaspoon ground cardamom added to the batter
2 cups Coconut Gelato (recipe follows)

½ cup Orange Blossom "Honey" (page 183)
½ cup coarsely chopped pistachios

For each serving, mound 3 crêpes on a plate. Top with a scoop of gelato and a drizzle of "honey." Sprinkle pistachios over them and serve immediately.

Coconut Gelato

Makes about 1 quart

This gelato is made luxuriously creamy with the addition of agar flakes and coconut oil. Add mint extract, chocolate chips, or peanut butter to vary the flavors.

2 (14-ounce) cans coconut milk
(full-fat, not light)
1 tablespoon agar flakes
½ cup water
⅔ cup sugar or agave nectar

1 teaspoon vanilla extract
¼ teaspoon sea salt
1 tablespoon coconut oil (optional, for
a creamier gelato)

In a small saucepan off the heat, combine the agar flakes and ½ cup water, and allow them to soften for 1 hour. Simmer the mixture until nearly dissolved, and set aside.

In a blender, combine the coconut milk, sugar or agave nectar, vanilla, and sea salt. Pass the agar mixture through a sieve into the blender and blend again. Refrigerate until completely cool, about 1 hour. Blend again, drizzling in the coconut oil while the machine is running.

Freeze in an ice cream maker according to manufacturer's directions. Without an ice cream maker, you can freeze the mixture in a shallow dish, whisking every 15 minutes, to make a coconut slush.

Lavender Rice Pudding Brûlée with Blueberries

Makes 6 dessert or breakfast servings

This dessert is evocative of glorious summers, when blueberries are abundant and ask to be eaten by the handful. A slow walk around the neighborhood means running your fingers through lavender bushes, too tempting not to yield pockets full. And while the air hangs thick outside, you escape the heat by slipping into the cool stillness of a museum or café.

Brûléed lavender pudding captures this balance of hot and cold, crisp and creamy.

The sugar topping must be caramelized just before serving; it softens on sitting. And to brûlée the pudding, you'll need a torch. Skip the puny kitchen things, and just borrow or buy a decent blowtorch. They're surprisingly easy to operate, and make you feel rad like Jennifer Beals in Flashdance.

The pudding, unbrûléed, is also divine for breakfast.

2½ cups nondairy milk

1 teaspoon dried lavender

2½ cups cooked white rice

½ cup coconut milk or additional
    nondairy milk

½ cup sugar

Generous pinch of sea salt

½ teaspoon vanilla extract

1 pint blueberries, rinsed and
    patted dry

About ¼ cup sugar, for brûléeing

Additional blueberries, for serving

In a small saucepan, heat the nondairy milk until just boiling. Remove it from the heat and stir in lavender. Cover and allow it to infuse for 15 minutes. Strain the infused milk into a medium saucepan, pressing firmly with the back of a spoon to extract the lavender essence. Add the rice, coconut milk, sugar, and sea salt. Bring to a simmer over medium-low heat and cook until creamy and thick, 30 to 35 minutes. Go through the pudding with a wire whisk occasionally to break up any lumps of rice and to prevent a skin from forming on top.

Remove the pudding from the heat, and stir in vanilla. Divide blueberries evenly among 6 ramekins. Pour pudding over blueberries, smoothing the tops; a ½-cup measure is ideal for this. Press a sheet of plastic directly onto the surface of the puddings, and refrigerate until thoroughly chilled, at least 4 hours or overnight.

To serve, sprinkle each pudding evenly with 1½ teaspoons sugar. Heat the torch to medium heat, and hold the torch about one inch from the pudding. Making small circles, caramelize the sugar. It will bubble, melt, and go golden. Don't allow the sugar to burn past a medium brown color, but do be sure it's completely melted.

Place the ramekins on plates and sprinkle each pudding with additional blueberries. Serve immediately, encouraging your guests to enjoy a satisfying *crack* as they fracture the burnt sugar topping.

Strawberry-Lemon Rice Pudding

Omit the lavender and skip the infusion steps. Add the zest of 1 lemon along with nondairy milk. Substitute 1 pint strawberries, cut into ¼-inch slices, for the blueberries. Allow the pudding to cool for 15 to 20 minutes before pouring into ramekins. Refrigerate and brûlée as directed, or top with sliced strawberries and fresh mint.

On Brûléeing

If you don't have a blowtorch, you can brûlée the pudding under a broiler. Remove the puddings from the refrigerator to warm slightly. Cold ramekins can shatter when heated rapidly, so be mindful of this.

Sprinkle the puddings with sugar as directed. Place ramekins on a baking sheet, and slide under the hot broiler. Watch carefully, as the sugar can go from perfectly caramelized to burnt in a flash. Caramelizing will take between 1 and 4 minutes, depending on the heat of your broiler. Carefully remove and serve immediately.

Gingerbread

Makes 9 servings

This is at once richly spicy and gossamer-light. Use as part of the Gingered Pear Trifle (page 193) or simply dust with powdered sugar and serve warm.

½ cup coconut or vegetable oil
½ cup sugar
½ cup molasses
¼ cup applesauce
1½ cups all-purpose flour
½ teaspoon baking powder
¼ teaspoon baking soda

½ teaspoon sea salt
1 teaspoon ground ginger
¼ teaspoon cinnamon
¼ teaspoon cloves
¼ teaspoon nutmeg
½ cup boiling water

Heat the oven to 350° F. Oil and flour a 9 by 9-inch square or 9-inch round baking pan, and set aside.

In a medium bowl, stir together the oil, sugar, molasses, and applesauce. In a separate bowl, whisk together the flour, baking powder, baking soda, sea salt, and spices. Add the dry mixture and boiling water alternately in several batches, beginning and ending with the dry. Pour the batter into prepared pan, smoothing the top.

Bake for 35 to 40 minutes, until the top springs back when pressed, or a knife inserted near the center comes out clean. Transfer it to a wire rack and allow it to cool completely in the pan.

The gingerbread will keep well in an airtight container, at room temperature or refrigerated, for several days.

Gingered Pear Trifle

Makes 4 servings

Spicy gingerbread and cool lemon cream make for a splendid English-style dessert. This is the perfect end to a dinner party, as all of the elements can be made up to a day in advance and assembled quickly.

The gingered pears are delicious over Vanilla Bean Frozen Custard (page 212), drizzled with melted ganache, or as an addition to any salad. The sour lemon cream can be poured over fresh fruit for a simple breakfast, or used as a tartlet filling.

Gingered Pears

2 ripe but firm pears, peeled and
    thinly sliced
2 tablespoons agave nectar
1 tablespoon sweet dessert wine or
    white wine (optional)

⅛ teaspoon freshly grated ginger
1 teaspoon fresh lemon juice
Pinch of sea salt

Sour Lemon Cream

1 (12.3-ounce) package firm or extra
    firm silken tofu
½ cup powdered sugar

Juice and zest of 1 large lemon
½ teaspoon vanilla extract
Pinch of sea salt

½ recipe Gingerbread (page 192) cut into 4 pieces, each split crosswise
Crystallized ginger, for garnish

Make the pears: gently toss together all ingredients. Set aside to macerate for at least 15 minutes while you make the sour lemon cream.

Make the sour lemon cream: in a food processor, process the silken tofu until completely smooth, scraping down the sides as necessary. Add powdered the sugar, lemon juice, zest, vanilla, and sea salt. Blend again. Taste the cream; it should be nicely tart without an overt soy flavor. Add a bit more fresh lemon juice or zest if necessary to adjust the flavor. Chill in the refrigerator until ready to use.

To assemble: in 4 parfait or wine glasses, layer half the Gingerbread, half the pears, and half the cream, in that order. Repeat with the remaining ingredients. Top with crystallized ginger, and serve immediately.

Italian Cornmeal Cake with Roasted Apricots and Coriander Crème Anglaise

Makes 4 servings

When I think of dessert, this is exactly what I want: golden, spongy slices of cornmeal-flecked cake, heaped with roasted summer apricots, blushy as baby bottoms. All in a pool of thin, cool custard infused with lemony coriander. It's complex, yet simple, and impressive without pretension.

Crème Anglaise, or "English custard," is a thin, pourable cream that can be served over virtually any dessert. This recipe makes just enough for drizzling, so double the recipe if you want extra. Spoonfuls of lemon curd would also make an excellent adornment for the cake.

All the elements can be made in advance. When serving, the cake should be room temperature, the apricots warm, and the Anglaise very cold.

Italian Cornmeal Cake

1¼ cups nondairy milk

¾ cup sugar

⅓ cup oil

½ teaspoon lemon zest

1 tablespoon plus 1 teaspoon fresh
   lemon juice

1 teaspoon vanilla extract

1 cup flour

½ cup cornmeal

1 teaspoon baking powder

½ teaspoon baking soda

¼ teaspoon sea salt

Roasted Apricots

6 ripe but firm apricots

1 tablespoon brown sugar or other
   granulated sweetener

½ tablespoon margarine, cut into
   small bits

1 teaspoon fresh lemon juice

Coriander Crème Anglaise

½ cup nondairy milk

1 teaspoon coriander seeds, crushed
   into coarse bits

2 tablespoons sugar

2 teaspoons cornstarch, sifted

Pinch of sea salt

½ cup coconut milk

Make the cornmeal cake: heat the oven to 350° F. Oil and flour a loaf pan (9 by 4-inch) and line the bottom with parchment or waxed paper. Set aside.

In a medium bowl or 2-cup measure, whisk together nondairy milk, sugar, oil, zest, fresh lemon juice, and vanilla.

In a largish bowl, whisk together flour, cornmeal, baking powder, baking soda, and sea salt. Fold wet ingredients into dry, whisking to combine.

Pour batter into prepared pan and bake until gold and springy on top, 50 to 55 minutes. While the cake bakes, prepare the roasted apricots.

Roast the apricots: halve and pit apricots, then prick the skins with a fork. In a well-oiled baking dish (9 by 9-inch is ideal), gently toss together fruit, sweetener, margarine, and fresh lemon juice. Place apricots cut-side down, and transfer to the hot oven where your cake is already baking. Roast until fork-tender and juicy, 10 to 15 minutes, turning once. Remove, and set aside to cool slightly.

When the cake is done, allow it to cool 5 minutes in the pan. Then transfer it to a wire rack, top-side up, to cool while you get on with the Anglaise.

Make the crème Anglaise: prepare an ice bath (see page 110), and set aside.

In a small saucepan, or in the microwave, scald the nondairy milk. Stir in coriander seeds, cover (a small plate works well for this), and steep 20 minutes or in the refrigerator overnight.

In a heavy medium saucepan off the heat, combine the sugar, cornstarch, and sea salt. Whisk in the coconut milk to make a slurry. Place a strainer over the saucepan, and slowly pour in the coriander-infused nondairy milk, whisking vigorously as you go.

Place the saucepan over medium heat and stir constantly with a flexible spatula until the mixture thickens just slightly. It should be about the consistency of coconut milk. This will take about 5 minutes.

Remove it from the heat and transfer to a small bowl or 2-cup measure. Gently place in the ice bath, stirring occasionally while finishing the rest of dessert.

To serve: slice pound cake into eighths. Set aside 4 slices to eat later, and plate the remaining 4. Mound 3 apricot halves over each slice, along with any accumulated juices. Pour crème Anglaise around each serving, and bring to the table immediately. The dessert is lovely with a cup of apricot-infused black tea.

Italian Cornmeal Celebration Cake

This method will yield 16 birthday or 20 wedding cake servings.

Bake 2 recipes Italian Cornmeal Cake in 2 8-inch round cake pans. Split layers, and fill with Lemon Curd (page 178) or Whipped Truffle Mousse (page 181), using the same technique as with Chocolate Truffle Cake (page 222). Frost and decorate with White Chocolate Buttercream (page 182). Accompany the cake with fresh berries or miniature scoops of sorbet.

Selecting Fruit

If you don't have apricots available, try substituting other stone fruits such as peaches, nectarines, or even cherries. If no fresh stone fruits are on hand, use frozen and thawed instead. Frozen fruits are usually picked and processed at the peak of the season, so you should have a good result. If tinned is the only thing available, try to use the stuff in fruit juice, rather than syrup. Halve the roasting time (check frequently; it may require even less), and increase the temperature to 400° F.

Vanilla Bean Cheesecake

Makes 15 to 20 servings

The very best cheesecake is made simply—not with dairy or soy cream cheeses, but with raw cashews. Once soaked, the nuts blend into a luxuriously smooth cream, which meets with lemon juice, zest, agave nectar, coconut oil, and flecks of vanilla bean. This mousseline mixture tops a date nut crust, which tastes of caramel and graham crackers.

The amount of fat in this cheesecake is indefensible; I'm not even going to address it.

Crust

¾ cup raw pecans
¾ cup raw almonds
½ cup dried flaked coconut

½ cup dates (6 to 8 medjool)
¼ teaspoon cinnamon

Filling

3 cups raw cashews, soaked for at
    least 3 hours
¾ cup fresh lemon juice
¾ cup raw agave nectar
⅓ cup virgin coconut oil (any
    consistency is fine)

¼ cup water
½ teaspoon sea salt
Zest of 1 lemon
Seeds scraped from 3 inches of
    vanilla bean

Fresh fruit or fruit sauce, for serving (optional)

Make the crust: line a 9-inch round pan with plastic wrap, and set aside.

In a food processor, process the pecans, almonds, and coconut until fine but not oily. Add the dates and cinnamon, and process again, scraping down the sides as necessary. The crust is ready when it holds together when pressed against the side. Tumble the mixture into the prepared pan and use the bottom of a glass to press the crust firmly into the pan. Set aside.

Make the filling: combine all filling ingredients in a blender and process until completely smooth, scraping down the sides as necessary. This may take several minutes. Be patient and keep blending until all graininess is gone.

Pour the filling onto prepared crust. To release any bubbles, tap the bottom against a counter several times, then run a knife through the mixture in a figure-8 pattern. Smooth the top. Transfer it to the freezer, and chill until firm and thoroughly cold. This may take several hours.

To serve: gently lift the plastic overhang and transfer it to a platter. Ease the plastic out from underneath. Using a small offset spatula, smooth the creases from the sides. Cut with a sharp knife, rinsing it with hot water between servings to ensure perfect slices.

Serve with fresh berries or seasonal fruits, and a fizzy or tannic drink to cut the cheesecake's richness.

The cheesecake is perfect for variations

Strawberry Cheesecake—swirl with strawberry puree;

Caramel Apple—top chilled cheesecake with apples soaked in date caramel;

Cacao or Cacao Chip—add ¼ cup raw cacao powder or 3 tablespoons raw cacao nibs;

Key Lime—substitute limes for lemons and add a double measure of lime zest;

Pumpkin—substitute ½ cup carrot juice for ¼ cup water, and decrease lemon juice to ½ cup. Add 1 teaspoon cinnamon, ½ teaspoon nutmeg, ½ teaspoon ginger, and ¼ teaspoon allspice or cloves to filling.

Brown Sugar Pecan Bars

Makes 24 bars

Gooey pecan topping over a tender shortbread crust creates a decadent bar cookie perfect for passing at holiday gatherings.

Crust

1¼ cups all-purpose flour
½ cup (1 stick) margarine
¼ cup sugar

¼ teaspoon sea salt
1 to 2 tablespoons ice water

Filling

½ cup (1 stick) margarine
¾ cup brown sugar
¼ cup brown rice syrup or corn syrup
¼ cup coconut milk

¼ teaspoons sea salt
8 ounces (about 2 cups) pecan pieces or halves

Heat the oven to 375° F. Lightly oil a 9 by 9-inch square baking pan, line with parchment, and set aside.

In a food processor, pulse the flour, margarine, sugar, and sea salt until the mixture looks like coarse meal. Add 1 tablespoon water and pulse until the mixture comes together, adding another drizzle of water if necessary. Alternatively, whisk together the flour, sugar, and sea salt, and cut in the margarine. Add a bit of water, and press the dough against the sides several times.

Press dough into prepared pan, creating an even surface. An offset spatula really works best for this, but use your fingers if necessary. Transfer to the freezer until firm, 10 to 15 minutes.

Once chilled, prick the dough with the tines of a fork. Bake until edges are golden, 22 to 25 minutes. Set aside to cool while you make the filling.

In a large saucepan over high heat, combine the margarine, sugar, and brown rice syrup or corn syrup, whisking constantly. The syrup will darken a bit and should be completely smooth; this will take 2 to 3 minutes. Remove from the heat, and whisk in coconut milk and sea salt. Stir in pecans.

Spoon the warm filling over the crust, smoothing the top slightly. Bake until the bars are bubbling away and your kitchen is fragrant with toasting pecans, 20 to 22 minutes. Transfer to a wire rack to cool 5 to 10 minutes, until still pliable but not gooey. Cut into 6 pieces one way and 4 another to create 24 bars.

The bars can be stored at room temperature, tightly covered, for up to a week.

Chocolate Chip Cookies

Makes about 3 dozen cookies

Crisp around the edges, chewy in the center, these are chocolate chip cookies at their very best.

To make the oat flour called for in the recipe, process a heaping cup of oatmeal in a food processor or blender until very fine. Measure as you would regular flour.

1 cup all-purpose flour	1 cup brown sugar
1½ cups oat flour	½ cup (granulated) sugar
1 teaspoon baking soda	¼ cup nondairy milk
½ teaspoon sea salt	1 teaspoon vanilla
8 tablespoons (1 stick) margarine, or ½ cup vegetable oil plus a generous pinch of sea salt	1 cup chocolate chips

Heat the oven to 350° F. Lightly oil a baking sheet, and set aside.

In a medium bowl, whisk together the flours, baking soda, and sea salt. Set aside.

In another medium bowl using a hand held mixer, blend the margarine and sugars until well combined. Add the milk and vanilla and blend again. Add the flour and blend. Stir in the chocolate chips.

Drop by scant tablespoons onto the prepared baking sheet. Bake exactly 11 minutes. The cookies will appear slightly undone, but this ensures a crisp exterior and chewy center. Allow cookies to rest 5 minutes on the baking sheet; they will crinkle as they cool. Transfer to a wire rack, and devour with a cup of cold almond milk.

For soy-free use oil variation

Nut Butter Cookies

For the best peanut or cashew butter cookies, simply decrease the margarine or oil to 6 tablespoons, and add ⅓ cup peanut butter with the fat. Omit the chocolate chips, and proceed as directed.

Hazelnut Cherry Brownies
with Port Glaze

Makes 16 small brownies

If you can't find fresh or frozen cherries, use ½ cup dried. Soak in hot water for 5 minutes, and leave whole.

The port glaze also makes a divine chocolate sauce for sundaes or fresh fruit; heat it briefly until it reaches a pourable consistency.

¾ cup (1½ sticks) margarine
1½ cups sugar
1 teaspoon vanilla extract
¾ cup nondairy yogurt, or a scant
    ¾ cup nondairy milk plus 2
    teaspoons vinegar

¾ cup unsweetened cocoa
1 cup all-purpose flour
1 teaspoon baking powder
½ cup hazelnuts, coarsely chopped
¾ cup fresh or frozen and thawed
    cherries, pitted and halved

Port Glaze

½ cup port
¼ cup coconut milk or soy creamer

6 ounces semisweet chocolate,
    coarsely chopped, or semisweet
    chocolate chips

Heat the oven 350° F. Oil a 9 by 9-inch square baking pan. Melt the margarine in a large bowl in the microwave. Stir in the sugar, vanilla, and nondairy yogurt. Whisk in the cocoa, flour, and baking powder until batter is smooth and even. Fold in the hazelnuts and cherries. Pour batter into the prepared pan, smoothing the top.

Bake for 35 to 40 minutes, or until brownies just begin to slink away from the sides of the pan and the center is no longer sticky. Allow them to cool completely in the pan while you make the glaze.

When glaze is the proper temperature (see below), spread it over the brownies. It will take ages to set completely, so just wait until it's no longer runny (about 30 minutes) before cutting into 16 pieces.

Make the port glaze: in a microwave-safe container with high sides (a Pyrex 2-cup measure is ideal), reduce the port by half. This will take 3 to 5 minutes on high power. Add the coconut milk or soy creamer to the port, stirring as you pour. Return it to the microwave and heat until the mixture just begins to bubble, 1 to 2 minutes. Alternatively, reduce the port by half in a small saucepan on the stovetop; this should take 5 to 7 minutes. Add the coconut milk or soy creamer, and simmer for 2 to 3 minutes more.

Add the chopped chocolate to the port mixture and allow it to sit undisturbed for 3 minutes. Stir gently with a spatula until the mixture is smooth and the chocolate completely melted. Cool slightly before using. To test for proper spreading temperature, touch a bit of the glaze to your chin or just above your top lip; it should feel about the same temperature as your skin. Use as directed.

Marzipan Cookies

Makes about 2 dozen

These are my version of pastelitas de boda, *or Mexican wedding cake cookies. Instead of the conventional chopped pecans, they're dappled with bits of marzipan that melt and caramelize when baked.*

The cookies are fairly sweet, so pair them with strong coffee, tea, or unsweetened almond milk.

6 ounces prepared marzipan
2 cups all-purpose flour
1 teaspoon baking powder
¼ teaspoon sea salt
½ cup (1 stick) margarine

½ cup brown sugar
½ cup sugar
½ cup almond milk
½ teaspoon almond extract
½ cup powdered sugar, for rolling

Using a very sharp knife, chop the marzipan into ¼-inch pieces, and set aside. Line a baking sheet with parchment and set aside.

Whisk together the flour, baking powder, and sea salt. In a large bowl, beat margarine with a handheld electric mixer until creamy, about 1 minute. Add the sugars and beat again to combine. Add the almond milk and extract, and beat again briefly. The mixture will look curdled, but it's no problem. Beat in the flour. Stir in marzipan pieces.

Wrap the dough in plastic, and chill in the refrigerator for at least 30 minutes. The dough can be refrigerated for up to 3 days, or frozen for up to a month.

When ready to bake, heat the oven to 325° F. Roll the cookies into 1-inch balls, and place 2 inches apart on the prepared baking sheet.

Bake for 12 to 15 minutes, until cookies are firm to the touch and very slightly golden. Allow them to cool 5 minutes on baking sheets, then transfer them to a wire rack. When completely cool, roll in powdered sugar. Store at room temperature in an airtight container.

Chocolate Chai Cookies

Makes about 2 dozen

When the weather cools, it's time for richer, more warming foods, and here they are. These tea-spiced gems always have a place in my holiday cooking, and I really think you'll like their unusual flavor and sugary crunch. Steep some black tea just before whisking them together, and you can sip it while baking and have enough for the ¼ cup called for in the recipe.

6 ounces good-quality semisweet
    chocolate
1 cup whole wheat flour
¾ cups all-purpose flour
1 tablespoon cocoa powder
1 teaspoon ground ginger
½ teaspoon cinnamon
¼ teaspoon ground cloves
¼ teaspoon grated fresh nutmeg

⅛ teaspoon ground cardamom
Pinch of sea salt
½ cup vegetable oil or coconut oil
½ cup brown sugar
¼ cup hot, strong black tea
¼ cup molasses
1 teaspoon baking soda
Crystal or turbinado sugar, for
    rolling cookies

Chop the chocolate into ¼-inch chunks. Set aside.

Sift or whisk together the flour, cocoa, ginger, cinnamon, cloves, nutmeg, cardamom, and sea salt.

In a medium bowl, whisk together the oil, brown sugar, tea, molasses, and baking soda. The mixture will bubble up and appear to thicken slightly; continue whisking until no lumps remain. Add flour mixture to the liquid, mixing well to combine. Stir in chocolate chunks. At this point, the dough can be wrapped in plastic and refrigerated for up to 3 days or frozen for up to a month.

When ready to bake, heat the oven to 325° F. Lightly grease one large or two smaller baking sheets, or line them with parchment. Form dough into 1-inch balls. Roll in crystal or turbinado sugar and place on the prepared baking sheet 2 inches apart.

Bake 10 to 12 minutes. The cookies will puff, spread slightly, then crackle, revealing fissures of darker chocolate. Allow them to cool for a moment on the baking sheet, then transfer to a wire rack to cool completely. Alternatively, eat them warm, with a cup of tea or strong coffee.

Cashew Crisps

Makes about 4 dozen

These brittle rounds shatter into euphoric sweetness in the mouth.

½ cup cashew pieces

4 tablespoons (½ stick) margarine

3 tablespoons coconut milk

¼ cup oats (not quick-cooking)

½ cup sugar

1 tablespoon all-purpose flour

½ teaspoon orange zest

Toast the cashews in a 350° F oven until golden and fragrant, 6 to 8 minutes for raw cashews or 4 to 6 minutes for roasted. Transfer them to a food processor or blender, add oats, and process until finely ground. The mixture should be ground to the point that it resembles coarse crumbs, but not so much that the cashews have become oily.

Increase the heat to 375° F. Line a baking sheet with parchment, and set aside.

In a small saucepan over medium heat, combine the margarine and coconut milk until melted and bubbly. Stir in the cashew-oat mixture, sugar, flour, and zest.

Drop by half-teaspoonfuls 2 inches apart on the prepared baking sheet. Bake until golden, about 7 minutes. Allow cookies to cool 1 to 2 minutes on the baking sheet, then transfer to a wire rack with a thin spatula. Repeat with the remaining batter.

Store the cookies in an airtight container for up to a week.

Cashew Cones

Make only 4 cookies at once. After removing from the oven, wait until cookies are just cool enough to handle, about 30 to 60 seconds. Shape them around a cone mold or roll by hand into a cone shape, and allow them to cool, wide side down.

Coconut-Lime Tuiles

Substitute lime zest for orange, and continue as directed.

Chocolate-Dipped Strawberries

Makes 1 pound dipped berries

Deceptively simple, this technique can also be used to dip bananas, berries and dried fruits.

1 pound strawberries, preferably long-stemmed

8 ounces good-quality semisweet chocolate, or 1 cup chocolate chips

1 teaspoon nonhydrogenated shortening

Rinse the strawberries, pat dry, and set on a kitchen towel to dry completely; any hint of moisture will keep the chocolate from adhering properly.

Line a baking sheet with parchment and set aside.

In a 2-cup glass measure or medium bowl, melt chocolate and shortening in the microwave, stirring at 15-second intervals. The chocolate should be completely smooth, with no odd bits of solid chocolate.

Pinching the leaves and stem, dip each strawberry in the chocolate, covering it to within ½ inch of the leaves. Run the tip of the strawberry up the side of the measure, allowing any excess chocolate to drip off. Place each strawberry on prepared baking sheet. Once finished, transfer the sheet to the refrigerator for the chocolate to cool and firm, about 30 minutes.

The strawberries will keep, refrigerated, for up to 2 days.

Individual Sticky Toffee Puddings

Makes 6 puddings

Serve this classic British dessert with a strong cuppa tea.

If you don't have ramekins, the puddings can be baked in muffin tins, yielding 9 smaller servings. Oil and flour the tins, or line with baking cups. Fill 9 with batter, and decrease the baking time by 5 to 7 minutes.

Puddings

4 ounces pitted dates, coarsely chopped (10 to 12 large medjool)

¼ cup boiling water

½ teaspoon vanilla extract

¾ cups all-purpose flour

1 teaspoon baking powder

¼ teaspoon sea salt

¼ cup (½ stick) margarine

½ cup sugar

⅓ cup applesauce

Sticky Toffee Sauce

¼ cup (½ stick) margarine

½ cup coconut milk

¾ cups brown sugar

Heat the oven to 350° F. Oil and flour 6 ramekins, and set aside.

In a small bowl, pour the boiling water over the dates. Allow them to rest for at least 10 minutes, then transfer to a food processor or blender and process until nearly smooth. Stir in the vanilla and set aside to cool slightly.

In a medium bowl, sift or whisk together the flour, baking powder, and sea salt.

In a large bowl, beat together the margarine and sugar until light and fluffy, 1 to 2 minutes. Add the applesauce and beat again. Fold in the flour and date mixtures in 3 batches, beginning and ending with the flour.

Spoon the batter into prepared ramekins. Bake 20 to 25 minutes, until the tops spring back slightly when pressed or a knife inserted into the center comes out clean.

While the puddings bake, make the toffee sauce. In a small saucepan over low heat, combine margarine, coconut milk, and brown sugar. Cook, stirring constantly, until the mixture is completely smooth. Don't allow the toffee to boil, as it can curdle. The toffee will be runny, satiny, and delicious.

Transfer the puddings to a rack to cool for 10 minutes. Gently run a small, flexible spatula or paring knife around the edge of each pudding, then invert onto a plate to remove. Pour toffee over the puddings, turning a bit to coat completely, and allow puddings to absorb the sauce for at least 15 minutes. Serve, or cover and store overnight. If serving the next day, gently rewarm the puddings in a 250° F oven for 10 to 15 minutes, and drizzle with additional sauce before plating.

Caramel-Almond Bread Pudding

Makes 9 servings

This is ridiculous drizzled with Coconut Caramel (page 178) and coconut milk, and respectable scattered with fresh raspberries and sliced ripe pears.

Unbaked, the pudding freezes excellently, perfect for an easy breakfast or unexpected houseguest. Prepare the pudding to the resting stage, then cover well and freeze. Thaw completely before baking.

Pudding

½ pound stale white bread (I use a good French loaf), torn into 1-inch pieces

¾ cup plain nondairy yogurt, pureed silken tofu, or a scant ¾ cup coconut milk plus 1 teaspoon vinegar

¼ cup brown or dark turbinado sugar

¾ cup sugar

1¼ cups nondairy milk

1 cup coconut milk or soy creamer

1 teaspoon vanilla extract

¼ teaspoon almond extract

Caramel Topping

¾ cup slivered almonds

¾ cup brown sugar

3 tablespoons margarine

3 tablespoons coconut milk or soy creamer

Heat the oven to 350° F. Place the bread in an even layer in a well-greased 9 by 9-inch baking pan.

Assemble the pudding: whisk together the nondairy yogurt or silken tofu and white and dark sugars. Pour in the nondairy milk, coconut milk or soy creamer, and extracts. Pour the custard over the bread, saturating it completely. Allow the bread to absorb it while you make the caramel topping.

Prepare the caramel: in a microwave-safe bowl or on the stovetop, melt the brown sugar, margarine, and coconut milk or soy creamer together. Allow the mixture to bubble for about 1 minute in the microwave, or 3 on the stovetop, until the sugar is well dissolved. Scatter slivered almonds evenly over the pudding and drizzle with caramel. At this point, the pudding can be refrigerated up to a day before baking. Allow it to rest for at least 1 hour to absorb the liquid.

Bake 30 to 40 minutes or until slightly puffed and golden brown. Serve warm.

Chocolate-Cinnamon Bread Pudding

Add ½ cup cocoa powder and ½ teaspoon cinnamon when combining yogurt or tofu and sugars, whisking thoroughly to combine. In the microwave or on a stovetop, scald the coconut milk or soy creamer. Add 6 ounces roughly chopped semisweet chocolate and stir to melt. When melted, continue as directed. Omit the caramel mixture and almonds, instead dousing the pudding with about 1 cup ganache (page 184). If desired, sprinkle with ¼ cup chopped hazelnuts. Bake as directed. Serve with additional melted ganache on the side.

Persian Chia Pudding

Makes 4 proper or 2 generous servings

A raw twist on classic Persian rice pudding, this chia-based dessert is flavored with rosewater, cardamom, and pistachios. It's much quicker than cooked rice pudding, and you wouldn't even suspect it's raw. Rosewater is available at Middle Eastern grocery shops.

¼ cup chia seeds
¾ cup water, for soaking
½ cup water
¼ cup raw cashews (up to half can be substituted with hempseeds)
4 large medjool dates

¼ teaspoon rosewater
⅛ teaspoon ground cardamom
Generous pinch of sea salt
¼ cup unsweetened shredded coconut, for serving
¼ cup raw pistachios, for serving

In a medium bowl, stir together chia seeds and ¾ cup water. Set aside to soak; the seeds will begin to absorb the liquid, swell slightly, and appear translucent.

In a blender, combine the ½ cup water, cashews, dates, rosewater, cardamom, and sea salt, and process until completely smooth. Pour the cashew mixture over soaked chia seeds, and stir well to combine. Allow it to rest for about 5 minutes and stir again. The chia seeds will absorb more liquid on resting. Transfer to the refrigerator, and repeat the resting and stirring twice more. When it has reached the right texture, the pudding should appear thick and creamy.

Divide the pudding between 4 small dessert bowls. Divide coconut and pistachios evenly among them, sprinkling it over the top, and serve. The pudding will keep, covered and refrigerated, for several days (I'm not sure how many; it never lasts past evening at my house).

Chia Seeds

Chia seeds, also called salba, are an ancient crop grown by Mayans and Aztecs. The seeds are rich in essential fatty acids and several other nutrients. They're a raw food staple, and can be found at most health food stores.

When soaked, the seeds absorb liquid and take on a translucent appearance and chewy texture, similar to tapioca. Store presoaked chia in the refrigerator for use in drinks (⅓ cup chia seeds to 2 cups water is a good ratio), and dry seeds in the pantry for raw crackers and desserts.

Peanut Butter Shortbread with Concord Grape Sorbet

Makes 18 to 20 small cookies

This is the lovely, nostalgia-infused afterschool snack. Except the peanut butter is rich, sandy shortbread, and the jelly is grape sorbet, fragrant with red wine. Serve simply mounded into a bowl, or smashed together, sandwich style, and you won't mind being a grownup, not one bit.

½ cup nonhydrogenated shortening
½ cup creamy peanut butter
¾ cup sugar (try it with brown sugar for a richer character)

½ teaspoon vanilla
¼ teaspoon sea salt
2 cups all-purpose flour

Concord Grape Sorbet (page 209), for serving

In the bowl of a stand mixer, or in a medium bowl using a hand mixer, beat together the shortening, peanut butter, and sugar until pale and creamy, about 2 minutes. Add vanilla and sea salt, and beat again.

Slowly add the flour, beating at low speed until combined. The dough will appear crumbly and separated, but should hold together when pressed. If it remains crumbly, add water by the teaspoon until it becomes sufficiently clumpy.

On a lightly floured surface, pat, then roll the dough ⅓ inch thick. Cut shapes with cutters, or simply cut into wedges. Using a thin metal spatula, gently lift and place 1 inch apart on an ungreased cookie sheet. Refrigerate for 15 to 20 minutes, which will ensure crisp, defined shapes.

When ready to bake, Heat the oven to 325° F. Bake 20 to 25 minutes, until the shortbread is very lightly browned on top, but not at all dark. Transfer to a wire rack, and allow it to cool completely. Serve with Concord Grape Sorbet.

The shortbread will keep, at room temperature in an airtight container, for up to a month.

Concord Grape Sorbet

Makes 1 pint

A few years ago, I had the good fortune to live in a tiny apartment inside of a large mansion. The estate housed several acres of sprawling gardens, designed in the English style. Most afternoons were spent walking through them, across paths lined with dahlias and cosmos, and through a lane shaded by apple and cherry trees, and into a circular rose garden punctuated with flamboyant peonies (I love peonies!). My favorite part was a labyrinth of sturdy pergolas, dripping with age-old grape vines.

In autumn, the vines sagged with fragrant concord grapes, demanding to be picked. So I picked them, pounds and pounds of grapes, which were transformed into sorbets and glazes, and dehydrated into raisins. Concords have a rich, spicy flavor and spectacular purple color, so juicing them is an excellent way to preserve their jammy goodness. The juice can be frozen for use in later months, too. Of course, if you don't have grape arbors in your backyard, bottled concord grape juice is a good approximation of fresh, and you can make this sorbet year round. Look for a brand with 100 percent of the concord variety, rather than a blend of other juices.

2 cups concord grape juice

2 tablespoons cabernet sauvignon or other jammy red wine

2 tablespoons agave nectar

Generous pinch of sea salt

Stir together all ingredients and refrigerate until thoroughly chilled. Freeze in an ice cream maker according to manufacturer's instructions.

For raw use fresh juice

Pink Grapefruit Sorbet with Fresh Grapefruit and Hemp Seeds

Makes 1 pint sorbet, 4 dessert servings

Serve small scoops of this clean tasting sorbet as a palate cleanser or light dessert.
The wonderfully fatty quality of hempseed contrasts with the pale citrus sorbet and jewel-bright, succulent grapefruit sections.

5 pink grapefruits (you may only need 4, depending on juiciness)

3 to 4 tablespoons Simple Syrup (page 186) or agave nectar

Pinch of sea salt

2 tablespoons shelled hemp seeds

Remove ½ teaspoon zest from a grapefruit and place in a medium bowl. Juice 3 to 4 of the grapefruits (3 may give you enough juice), pressing juice through a strainer to remove seeds and pulp. Measure 2 cups juice into the bowl with the zest. Add 3 tablespoons syrup or agave nectar, along with the sea salt. Taste the mixture, adding more sweetener to suit your taste. It should be slightly sweeter than usually preferable, as this will lessen on freezing. Refrigerate the mixture until thoroughly chilled.

Pour the mixture through a strainer directly into an ice cream maker, and freeze according to manufacturer's instructions.

When ready to serve, supreme the remaining grapefruit: cut a round of skin from the top and bottom of the grapefruit, deep enough to just reveal the inside. Position it firmly on a cutting board, and slice down the sides, removing the skin and pith with a sharp knife. Hold the skinned fruit in one hand, and slice into it along the membranes, releasing the delicate sections from the grapefruit (these are *supremes*).

Place a scoop of sorbet in each of four chilled bowls. Divide the grapefruit sections evenly over the sorbet. Sprinkle evenly with hemp seeds, and serve immediately.

For raw use raw agave nectar

Frozen Desserts

Any beverage can be transformed into ice cream, sherbet, or sorbet. A few minor adjustments ensure a delicious and complication-free time of it:

Don't be fussy when selecting an ice cream maker. Except for very high-end machines for industrial and restaurant use, most models do essentially the same thing. Good machines under $50 abound, and you can usually find one for under $10 at a thrift store. Even the hand-crank versions make fine desserts, and friends can be coerced into sharing the labor with the promise of fresh-churned bliss.

Use a concentrated base liquid. For intense, flavorful desserts, choose liquids that aren't too weak or watery. Brew coffee a shade stronger, blend in additional fruit, add an extra bit of fat, and so on.

Sweeten beyond your taste. Freezing tempers our ability to experience sweetness, so a liquid should be a bit more cloying than you're comfortable with. Start with a liquid that seems perfect when cold, then add small amounts of agave nectar, maple syrup, simple syrup, or even stevia (all will dissolve immediately, allowing you to distinguish the actual flavor right away). Alternatively taste and add until it's slightly sweeter than you generally prefer.

Add a softening agent. Salt and liquor lower the freezing temperature of liquids, creating a more supple finished product. For every 2 cups of liquid, stir in 1 tablespoon liquor or a generous pinch of salt, or both. Agave nectar and corn syrup also lend frozen desserts a "chewier" texture, so consider using them as sweeteners.

Thoroughly chill the liquid before freezing in an ice cream maker. Don't skip this step in the interest of saving time; it makes the machine's work much easier and will prevent a mid churning meltdown.

Stir in additions at the right time. Chunks of chocolate or fruit can be added to the chilled mixture before freezing. For a distinct swirl, fold in purees to the finished product, or carefully pour in during the final churns of the ice cream maker; stop the machine before the ingredient is fully incorporated.

Taste, and taste again. Sample the liquid mixture before chilling, after chilling, and again in the ice cream maker. You can add more sweetness or acid even while churning, and this will give you the most accurate indication of the dessert's flavors.

Space is the enemy. To avoid infusing your frozen desserts with the flavors of frozen leftovers, do not leave them in the ice cream maker. Instead, transfer to a chilled glass container. Press a piece of plastic firmly against the dessert, and replace the lid. It may lose some of the initial velvety texture, but should keep for at least a month.

Vanilla Bean Frozen Custard

Makes 1 pint

Richer than ice cream and fragrant with vanilla bean, this decadent custard can easily be customized with a variety of flavorings and you can easily make a raw version.

The addition of alcohol lowers the freezing temperature of the custard, making the finished dessert softer and creamier. The taste of vodka is nearly undetectable; use a flavored liqueur to impart subtle essences of dark rum, amaretto, Grand Marnier, or brandy.

1 cup raw cashews
About 4 cups water, boiling
½ vanilla bean (about 3 inches)
1 cup water

½ cup agave nectar or simple syrup
Generous pinch of sea salt
1 tablespoon vodka or other liquor (optional)

Pour 2 cups boiling water over the cashews and allow them to sit for 1 minute. Drain, cover with boiling water again, and soak for 2 hours or overnight.

Meanwhile, split the vanilla bean lengthwise and scrape out the seeds with the edge of a knife. In a small saucepan, whisk together the water, agave nectar, and vanilla bean seeds, and bring just to a simmer. The vanilla seeds might remain in clumps, and that's fine; they'll separate later. Remove from the heat, cover, and steep for at least 10 minutes.

Drain cashews, rinse, and drain again. In a blender on high speed, combine the soaked cashews, half the vanilla syrup, and sea salt. Process until completely smooth, scraping down the sides as necessary. This may take up to 5 minutes of continuous blending. Pour in the remaining syrup and vodka, and blend again.

Transfer to the refrigerator and chill until completely cold, 1 to 2 hours. Freeze in an ice cream maker according to manufacturer's instructions. For a simple, elegant dessert, serve small scoops with cookies or fresh fruit.

For raw substitute warm water for boiling, use raw agave nectar,
and do not heat the syrup mixture

Chocolate Ice Cream

Sift 2 tablespoons cocoa powder into the vanilla syrup. Simmer and steep as directed.

Joy Tienzo | Cook, Eat, Thrive

Jasmine Ice Cream

Instead of the vanilla syrup, whisk together 1 cup cooled jasmine (or other flavored) tea, ½ cup agave nectar, ½ teaspoon vanilla extract, and a pinch sea salt. Do not heat or steep, and continue as directed.

Stracciatella

Meaning "little shreds" in Italian, stracciatella is simply vanilla ice cream with chocolate bits. To the firm but still-churning ice cream, stir in ½ cup finely chopped good-quality dark chocolate. Chocolate chips are also a fine substitution.

Banana Caramel Pecan Ice Cream

Makes about 1 pint

The idea of banana ice cream originated with raw-foodists, who, having exhausted the many virtues of the mighty banana, finally resorted to hacking it to pieces in a food processor. Thus, the simplest ice cream was born.

But there's always something more to be done with it: add pecans, salty like classic butter pecan ice cream. And dates, with their dark chewy bite, for the perfect caramel pecan flavor. Try your own additions of pineapples and cherries, cacao nibs and coconut and brazil nuts, or tumble it into an almond-date crust and top with fresh strawberries for a raw ice cream pie...

4 medium frozen bananas, broken into chunks

1 teaspoon vanilla extract, or seeds scraped from 1 inch of vanilla bean

½ teaspoon sea salt

½ cup raw pecans

2 dates, halved and pitted

In a food processor, combine the bananas, vanilla, and sea salt. The bananas will be pulverized into tiny bits, then the bottom layer will begin to come together as a big soft mass. Scrape down the sides and continue processing until the mixture is smooth and free of lumps; it should appear whipped and airy. Add pecans and dates, and pulse until just mixed in. Serve immediately. The ice cream does not keep well but can be frozen for a few hours.

Graham Cracker

**Makes 1 10-inch tart shell, 4 6-inch shells, approximately 20 2-inch shells,
or 2 dozen graham crackers**

*Finding graham crackers that don't contain honey can be a challenge. These healthy
crisps will satisfy your childhood cravings in a bee-friendly way.*

¾ cups all-purpose flour
½ cup whole wheat flour
2 tablespoons wheat germ
¼ teaspoon cinnamon

½ cup (1 stick) margarine
¼ cup brown sugar
2 tablespoons agave nectar

Have ready a baking sheet, and a 10-inch tart pan, 4 6-inch tartlet pans, or about 20 2-inch mini tartlet pans.

In a medium bowl, whisk together the flours, wheat germ, sea salt, and cinnamon. Set aside.

Beat together the margarine and brown sugar in a large bowl with a handheld electric mixer until smooth, about 1 minute. Add the agave nectar and beat again. Slowly add the flour mixture, beating on low speed, until well combined.

Form the dough into a rough disk and wrap in plastic. Chill for at least 20 minutes, up to 3 days.

When ready to bake the dough, heat the oven to 325° F. If using tiny tartlet pans, simply press bits of dough into them to a ⅛-inch thickness. If using the 6-inch or 10-inch size, roll the dough out on a piece of plastic to a ⅛-inch thickness. Loosely roll the pastry around your rolling pin, and drape gently over the tart pan. Prick the bottoms with the tines of a fork, and chill in the freezer for 10 minutes. Any scraps can be baked along with the tart.

Place the pan(s) on a baking sheet and bake 25 to 30 minutes, until deep golden brown. Rotate after 10 minutes, spearing any puffed bits with a fork.

Transfer to a wire rack to cool in the pans. To protect the sharp edges, keep in the tart pans until just before using.

Graham Cracker Cookies

To make shapes, roll out as directed and cut out using a cookie cutter. Chill in the freezer for 10 minutes. Bake for 16 to 20 minutes.

Alternatively, roll out the dough, and cut into 1 by 2-inch pieces. Separate, and chill in the freezer 10 minutes. Lightly mark with a fork, pressing the tines across the width of the cookie four times. Bake as directed for shaped cookies.

Fruit and Cream Tart

Makes 8 to 12 servings

What could be lovelier than vanilla-scented custard in a homemade graham cracker shell, adorned with glazed fresh fruits?

Vary the toppings according to what produce is in season and the liqueurs you prefer.

2 cups Vanilla Custard (page 180), thoroughly chilled

½ recipe Graham Cracker (page 214), baked in a 10 inch tart pan and cooled

2 to 3 cups fresh fruit, cut or whole (see ideas below)

½ cup fruit jelly

1 tablespoon liqueur or water

Spoon the Vanilla Custard into the prepared tart shell, smoothing the top. Arrange the fruit on top in a pretty pattern.

In a small saucepan, heat jelly and liqueur or water over very low heat until melted. Brush gently over fruit with a pastry brush, careful not to disturb the arranged fruit. Refrigerate for at least 15 minutes. Although best when just assembled, the tart can also be made several hours in advance and chilled in the refrigerator before serving.

Fruits

Blueberries, blackberries, and sliced strawberries with Limoncello glaze

Sectioned navel and blood oranges, sliced kiwi fruit, and sliced bananas with brandy glaze

Fresh pears and halved concord grapes with Grappa glaze

Mango slices and large coconut flakes with dark rum glaze

Sliced apricots, plums, and nectarines with Amaretto glaze

Crêpes Fanon

Makes 4 servings

The dessert on which this is based contains brandy, Grand Marnier, and orange juice. It was said to have the ability to "reform a cannibal into a civilized gentleman." This version, which fuses French and Caribbean flavors, has the ability to reform omnivores into civilized vegans.

Do not—as I have learned firsthand—attempt to light the rum with a candle if you are without a long match. You'll drip wax all over the crêpes, and it probably won't light, anyway. Use a lighter or regular match instead.

The crêpes are named for Frantz Fanon, the Caribbean-born author, psychiatrist, and liberationist.

½ pineapple, cut into ¾-inch chunks
⅓ cup pineapple juice (reserved from cutting pineapple)
½ teaspoon orange zest
2 tablespoons margarine

1 tablespoon plus 1 teaspoon sugar
2 tablespoons plus 1 tablespoon rum (I use dark, but any will do)
1 recipe Crêpes (page 177)

In a medium saucepan over medium heat, combine the pineapple juice, zest, margarine, sugar, and 1 tablespoon of the rum. Bring to a simmer, whisking until well-combined. Add pineapple chunks, stir to coat, and remove from the heat.

To serve, fold each crêpe into quarters, and layer attractively on a shallow platter. Spoon pineapple mixture over the top. Heat the remaining 2 tablespoons rum in a small saucepan until just barely warm. Drizzle over everything, quickly bring the platter to the table, and use a long match or lighter to ignite. Let the flames die down, and eat immediately.

Kitchen Safety

I am constantly setting things on fire. Accidentally, that is. A stray kitchen towel. A recipe I've placed too close to a lit burner...Be prepared for this to happen—it probably will, at some point.

Once while at brunch, my Mr. leaned against the dial of a gas range, activating the burner. Oblivious to the fire at his back, he went on chatting and eating. As flames leapt up the back of his shirt, he calmly set down his plate and laid on the floor. Still on fire, he began rolling from side to side. We onlookers were utterly confused—it isn't often you see someone catch fire! The flames extinguished, he stood to his feet, completely composed. "Hmm," he announced jauntily, "stop, drop, and roll really does work."

While my kitchen accidents tend to feature screaming and attempts to run somewhere, I've learned to manage them well. Keep a bowl of water nearby when frying or cooking foods that spatter so you can plunge a burnt hand in quickly, if necessary. Remember to breathe. Be mindful when using knives, and remember that a dull knife is more likely to cause injuries than a sharp one. As someone who has cut off the tip of her index finger—twice—I can attest to this. If possible, keep a first aid kit and fire extinguisher on hand.

When the odd scrape or burn does occur, being prepared can really decrease the severity of the situation, ensuring that the only thing left from your accident is a good story.

Raw Carrot Cake with Lemon-Cashew Buttercream

Makes 12 servings

Blending golden raisins into the batter yields a mildly sweet cake. If you prefer a sweeter dessert, substitute dark raisins or add 2 to 3 dates to the mixture.

Raw food recipes aren't always precise, because unlike flour, sugar, and liquids in regular baked goods, the consistency of ingredients can vary significantly; some dates are moister than others, carrot pulp has different moisture levels, and so on. Get comfortable tinkering a bit.

This recipe makes plenty for frosting and decorating. Use any leftovers as a dip for fresh fruit.

Cake

1½ pounds carrots (6 to 8 large), trimmed and scrubbed well or peeled

1½ cups almonds, soaked for 1 hour and drained

1 cup shredded dried coconut

1½ cup golden raisins, soaked for 15 minutes and drained

1 teaspoon fresh grated ginger

1 teaspoon cinnamon

¼ teaspoon ground nutmeg

Pinch of ground cardamom

¾ cup dark or golden raisins

½ cup walnuts or pecans (optional)

Buttercream

3 cups raw cashews, soaked for 1 hour or overnight, and drained

2 cups (about 20) pitted Medjool dates, soaked for 15 minutes and drained

1 cup fresh lemon juice

2 teaspoons lemon zest

1¼ cup water

To Assemble and Decorate

1 carrot, peeled

1 tablespoon raw agave nectar

Spirulina powder

¼ cup reserved buttercream

Make the cake: in a food processor or blender, process the carrots until they reach a fine, pulpy consistency. This will require several rounds of scraping down the sides and blending to get the texture right. Gather them into a kitchen towel or cheesecloth and squeeze over a bowl to remove excess juice. Try to get the pulp as dry as possible (use the remaining juice in soups or smoothies). Measure 3 cups pulp into a large bowl, and set aside.

Process the almonds, dried coconut, golden raisins, and spices until the texture is paste-like and homogenous. This might take a while, scraping down the sides and redistributing the mixture as necessary. The dough will form a ball in your food

Cake Pans

If you don't have a 6-inch round pan, simply pat the batter into a round. It won't be perfect, but you've got plenty of license with the shape, as it stays malleable for as long as you need.

processor when well blended. Add half the carrot pulp and process again. Transfer to the bowl of remaining carrot pulp and use your hands to thoroughly combine the mixture. It should hold together when pressed between two fingers, while still feeling fairly light. If the consistency is too dry, add a few tablespoons of reserved carrot juice. If it is too moist, add a bit of shredded coconut. Stir in raisins and walnuts and pecans.

Divide the carrot mixture into thirds, and line a 6-inch cake pan with plastic wrap (see note below). Using a spatula, press a third of the cake mixture firmly into the pan. Smooth the top to create an even surface, and dab the spatula into the corners to create sharp edges. Fold plastic wrap over the batter, and invert onto a plate. Repeat with the remaining carrot mixture; you will have 3 layers of carrot cake. Refrigerate until ready to assemble.

Make the buttercream: in a blender, process the cashews, dates, fresh lemon juice, zest, and about half the water until very smooth. A high-speed blender is the very best tool for this. Add the remaining water and blend again. The consistency should be just softer than a conventional buttercream; it will thicken slightly when refrigerated. Cover and refrigerate at least 20 minutes or until ready to use.

Assemble the cake: using an offset spatula, spread a dab of buttercream over a cake plate or cardboard round. Flip the first layer of cake onto the plate, nudging it into the center. Spread about ¾ cup of buttercream evenly over the first layer, extending slightly beyond the edge. Repeat with the remaining cake layers until you have 3 layers of cake with 2 layers of buttercream sandwiched inside.

Dollop about ½ cup of frosting over the top, and spread over the whole cake, catching any loose bits to create a smooth surface. Rotate the cake plate as you smooth the sides with an offset spatula, sealing any gaps between layers, or where the cake meets the plate. Refrigerate for at least 20 minutes.

If you plan to decorate the cake, fill a pastry bag fitted with a star tip with 1 cup of buttercream, and set aside. Spread the remaining frosting over the cake, starting with the top, then working your way down the sides. Make swoops and swirls, or aim for a smooth refined look—your choice. If using reserved buttercream, pipe borders around the bottom and/or top of the cake with the star tip. Return the cake to the refrigerator, then squeeze any remaining buttercream into a bowl; you'll tint this with spirulina, if you like.

With a vegetable peeler or mandoline, make long, wide strips of carrot. Toss them with agave nectar to coat and allow them to sit until softened slightly, about 15 minutes. Meanwhile, mix the last bit of buttercream with ½ teaspoon of spirulina, and fill a pastry bag fitted with a leaf tip.

Roll the carrot strips from one end to another, into rosettes, and place them decoratively on the cake. Pipe leaves around the rosettes, and down the sides of the cake, if you like. Refrigerate until ready to serve.

Sweet Rice Cake with Mango and Salt-Lime Sorbet

Makes 8 to 12 servings

My mother-in-law is from the Philippines and makes this traditional cake on many occasions.

Serve it with cups of hot, strong coffee. The rice cake tastes very sweet to most western palates and requires a bitter or sour contrast to temper it.

Cake

2½ cups glutinous (sweet) rice, soaked for 1 hour

½ cup brown sugar

1½ cups water

1 (14-ounce) can coconut milk

Topping

1 cup coconut milk

1 cup brown sugar

To Serve

Salt Lime Sorbet, for serving (recipe follows)

2 fresh mangos, peeled and sliced

Heat the oven to 335° F. Generously oil a 9-inch round baking pan, and set aside.

Thoroughly drain the soaked rice, then add ½ cup brown sugar, stirring to remove any lumps. Add water and 1 can coconut milk and stir again. Pour into prepared pan, cover with foil, and transfer to oven. The cake may appear dangerously close to overflowing but will not rise any further. Bake 40 minutes, until the cake is fragrant.

After about 30 minutes, make the topping: in a small saucepan over medium heat, whisk together 1 cup coconut milk and 1 cup brown sugar. Continue cooking until the mixture is bubbling and slightly darker, 5 to 7 minutes. Uncover the cake, and pour the topping over it. Cover again and return it to the oven for 30 minutes more.

Transfer to a wire rack to cool completely. The cake can be made several days in advance and refrigerated (or not—it keeps surprisingly well at room temperature) before serving.

Serve topped with fresh mango slices and small scoops of Salt Lime Sorbet.

Salt Lime Sorbet

Makes 1 pint

The perfect compliment to Sweet Rice Cake is a sharp sorbet that cuts through its gooey coconut richness. Full of fresh lime flavor, the sorbet shines in all its raw, briny glory.

If you'd like to serve it without the rice cake, accompany small scoops with equally sized scoops of fresh watermelon. The salty acidity and smoothness will balance the melon's grainy sugars, while the colors make for a stunning presentation.

½ cup fresh lime juice (4 to 6 limes worth)

Zest of one lime

½ cup agave nectar or Simple Syrup (page 186)

1½ cups water

1 tablespoon vodka

Scant ¼ teaspoon good-quality sea salt

⅛ teaspoon ground spirulina (optional, for color)

Whisk together all ingredients until the sea salt is completely dissolved. Refrigerate until thoroughly cold. Strain directly into the bowl of an ice cream maker, and freeze according to manufacturer's directions.

For raw use raw agave nectar and substitute sake for vodka

Lime Juice

I always strain lime juice before measuring. As the fruit is squeezed and the liquid released, the tiny juice vesicles that comprise the pulp burst and release their juice. If left in the juice, the vesicles impart a bitter taste that intensifies on sitting. Using a strainer prevents this, giving you juice that's sour, not bitter.

Chocolate Truffle Cake

Makes 12 to 16 slices

When I want something decadent and impressive to bring to a party, this is my first choice. All the elements of the cake except ganache can be prepared several days in advance and refrigerated. The Chocolate Sponge and Whipped Truffle Mousse also freeze exceptionally well.

To prepare and transfer the cake as easily as possible, use a cardboard cake round, which can be purchased at cake supply stores. Or, make your own: simply cut out a 9-inch or 10-inch circle from sturdy cardboard.

Chocolate Sponge (2 9-inch layers), cooled completely

2 cups Whipped Truffle Mousse (page 181)

2½ cups ganache (page 184), prepared while refrigerating the cake

Using a serrated knife, split the cake layers into halves. Beginning with one of the cakes, slide the blade nearly halfway in, and gently saw back and forth, turning the cake as you go. Continue turning and slicing until the knife goes all the way through. Slide the top half onto a plate or cake round, and set aside. Repeat with the remaining cake layer.

Smear a dab of the mousse onto a cardboard round. Position one of the cake layers on top, and gently press down to secure it. Using an offset metal spatula, spread about ½ cup of the mousse over the layer. Top with another cake layer, and repeat with the remaining mousse and cake, finishing with a layer of cake.

With the remaining mousse, crumb coat the cake: spoon a large dollop on top and spread it very thinly to the edges. It will spill over the edges and begin to slump down the sides. Using the offset spatula, continue spreading filling around the sides of the cake, turning as you do. Be sure to cover any loose crumbs to create the smoothest finish possible. Refrigerate the cake while you prepare the ganache.

When the ganache is ready for pouring, position the cake on a wire rack set over a cake pan that extends several inches beyond the cake's diameter. Pour the ganache in a steady stream over the center of the cake, allowing it to run over the sides. Once the cake is mostly coated, begin to pour ganache over any bare areas. If you must, use an offset spatula to spread it a bit. It's best to avoid this, since working the ganache will ruin its sheen.

Variations

Serve wedges of the cake warm, topped with nondairy ice cream and a sauce of warmed ganache.

Keep the layers unsplit, and stack. Fill with Vanilla Custard (page 180) and fresh berries.

Prepare the cake as directed, filling with Coconut Caramel (page 178) and sliced fresh bananas. Top the poured ganache with curls of coconut and chopped brazil nuts.

Chocolate Sponge

Makes 2 9-inch cake layers

This is the best chocolate cake I know, made even better by its utter simplicity and plain ingredients.

Bake for a Chocolate Truffle Cake (page 222), or spread cooled layers with Whipped Coconut Cream (page 187), and sprinkle liberally with powdered sugar.

2⅔ cups all-purpose flour

2⅔ cups sugar

1 cup plus 2 tablespoons cocoa

1 tablespoon baking powder

1 tablespoon baking soda

1½ cups cold coffee

1½ cups water

3 tablespoons apple cider vinegar

¾ cup vegetable oil

1 tablespoon vanilla extract

Heat the oven to 350° F. Oil and flour 2 9-inch round pans, line with parchment, and set aside.

Measure dry ingredients into a large bowl, sifting or pinching out any lumps in the cocoa or leavenings. Whisk together thoroughly.

In a 2-cup measure or small bowl, whisk together the liquid ingredients. Pour the liquid ingredients into dry ingredients, and gently whisk to combine. The mixture will lighten in color and bubble up slightly, then darken and appear denser. Once the batter darkens, quickly pour into prepared pans. Bake for 45 to 50 minutes, until the top springs back when pressed, and the edges just slightly shrink back from the pan.

Cool for 5 minutes in the pan, then run an offset metal spatula around the cake to release the edges. Invert onto a wire rack, and flip right-side-up to cool completely.

Index

D

About
Joy Tienzo

Joy Tienzo is a mother, writer, believer, adventurer, minimalist, and yoga enthusiast. Whether working as a pastry cook, hosting community brunches, or crafting wedding cakes, she loves bringing people together through food. When not in the kitchen, Joy is on a plane or yoga mat, picking fruit with her children, or creating practices to help people grow.

She lives with her family in Denver, Los Angeles, and all over the world, and can be found online at joytienzo.com.

About PM Press

PM Press was founded at the end of 2007 by a small collection of folks with decades of publishing, media, and organizing experience. PM Press co-conspirators have published and distributed hundreds of books, pamphlets, CDs, and DVDs. Members of PM have founded enduring book fairs, spearheaded victorious tenant organizing campaigns, and worked closely with bookstores, academic conferences, and even rock bands to deliver political and challenging ideas to all walks of life. We're old enough to know what we're doing and young enough to know what's at stake.

We seek to create radical and stimulating fiction and nonfiction books, pamphlets, t-shirts, visual and audio materials to entertain, educate, and inspire you. We aim to distribute these through every available channel with every available technology, whether that means you are seeing anarchist classics at our bookfair stalls; reading our latest vegan cookbook at the café; downloading geeky fiction e-books; or digging new music and timely videos from our website.

PM Press is always on the lookout for talented and skilled volunteers, artists, activists and writers to work with. If you have a great idea for a project or can contribute in some way, please get in touch.

PM Press
PO Box 23912
Oakland, CA 94623
www.pmpress.org

Friends of PM

These are indisputably momentous times – the financial system is melting down globally and the Empire is stumbling. Now more than ever there is a vital need for radical ideas.

In the four years since its founding – and on a mere shoestring – PM Press has risen to the formidable challenge of publishing and distributing knowledge and entertainment for the struggles ahead. With over 180 releases to date, we have published an impressive and stimulating array of literature, art, music, politics, and culture. Using every available medium, we've succeeded in connecting those hungry for ideas and information to those putting them into practice.

Friends of PM allows you to directly help impact, amplify, and revitalize the discourse and actions of radical writers, filmmakers, and artists. It provides us with a stable foundation from which we can build upon our early successes and provides a much-needed subsidy for the materials that can't necessarily pay their own way. You can help make that happen – and receive every new title automatically delivered to your door once a month – by joining as a Friend of PM Press. And, we'll throw in a free T-Shirt when you sign up.

Here are your options:

▶ $25 a month: Get all books and pamphlets plus 50% discount on all webstore purchases

▶ $40 a month: Get all PM Press releases (including CDs and DVDs) plus 50% discount on all webstore purchases

▶ $100 a month: **Superstar** – Everything plus PM merchandise, free downloads, and 50% discount on all webstore purchases

For those who can't afford $25 or more a month, we're introducing **Sustainer Rates** at $15, $10 and $5. Sustainers get a free PM Press t-shirt and a 50% discount on all purchases from our website.

Your Visa or Mastercard will be billed once a month, until you tell us to stop. Or until our efforts succeed in bringing the revolution around. Or the financial meltdown of Capital makes plastic redundant. Whichever comes first.

ALTERNATIVE VEGAN

International Vegan Fare Straight from the Produce Aisle

Dino Sarma Weierman

978-1-60486-508-0 • $17.95

Tofu, seitan, tempeh, tofu, seitan, tempeh... it seems like so many vegans rely on these products as meat substitutes. Isn't it time to break out of the mold?

Taking a fresh, bold, and alternative approach to vegan cooking without the substitutes, this cookbook showcases more than 100 fully vegan recipes, many of which have South Asian influences. With a jazz-style approach to cooking, it also discusses how to improvise cooking with simple ingredients and how to stock a kitchen to prepare simple and delicious vegan meals quickly. The recipes for mouth-watering dishes include one-pot meals—such as South-Indian Uppuma and Chipotle Garlic Risotto—along with Pakoras, Flautas, Bajji, Kashmiri Biriyani, Hummus Canapés, and No-Cheese Pizza. With new, improved recipes this updated edition also shows how to cook simply to let the flavor of fresh ingredients shine through.

Explore your inner chef and get cooking with Dino!

Dino Sarma Weierman was born in New Delhi, India, and immigrated to the U.S. with his family in 1986. From childhood, cooking has been a passion for him. He draws his influences from his mother and the many hours of food shows on television that he watched.

"This is vegan new school, which is really vegan old school, which draws on traditions that pre-date any of us. Cooking can be empowering, no doubt about it."
—Lauren Corman, host of AnimalVoices on CIUT in Toronto

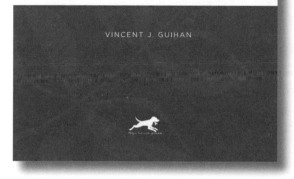

NEW AMERICAN VEGAN

NEW AMERICAN VEGAN

Vincent Guihan

978-1-60486-079-5 • $17.95

New American Vegan breaks from a steady stream of vegan cookbooks inspired by fusion and California cuisines that put catchy titles and esoteric ingredients first in their efforts to cater to a cosmopolitan taste. Instead, Vincent goes back to his Midwestern roots to play a humble but important role in the reinvention of American cuisine while bringing the table back to the center of American life.

Weaving together small-town values, personal stories, and more than 120 great recipes, *New American Vegan* delivers authentically American and authentically vegan cuisine that simply has to be tasted to be believed. Recipes range from very basic to the modestly complicated, but always focusing on creating something that is both beautiful and delicious while keeping it simple. Clear instructions provide step-by-steps but also help new cooks find their feet in a vegan kitchen, with a whole chapter devoted just to terms, tools, and techniques. With an eye toward improvisation, the book provides a detailed basic recipe that's good as-is, but also provides additional notes that explain how to take each recipe further, to increase flavor, to add drama to the presentation, or just how to add a little extra flourish for new cooks and seasoned kitchen veterans.

Vincent Guihan has been a vegan for more than a decade, and was a lacto-ovo vegetarian for a decade prior to becoming vegan. He grew up in a in a very small Midwestern town, where his back yard was the neighbor's cornfield. His parents cooked only sporadically, even though the nearest fast-food restaurants were a 20-minute car ride away and this cookbook is his revenge. He has been blogging about vegan cooking and gourmet topics since 2006. And although not a formally trained chef, he's a formally trained and highly skilled eater.

> "Guihan has a knack for infusing bold and fiery seasonings into fresh produce and vegan pantry staples—creating inventive, novel recipes that will inspire and excite the vegan home cook."
>
> —Dreena Burton, author of *Eat, Drink, & Be Vegan*

"The definitive guide to living as a happy, healthy, and sane vegan."
—GARY L. FRANCIONE, DISTINGUISHED PROFESSOR OF LAW, RUTGERS UNIVERSITY

VEGAN FREAK

Being Vegan in a Non-Vegan World, 2nd Edition

Bob Torres and Jenna Torres

978-1-60486-015-3 • $14.95

Going vegan is easy, and even easier if you have the tools at hand to make it work right. In the second edition of this informative and practical guide, two seasoned vegans help you learn to love your inner vegan freak. Loaded with tips, advice, and stories, this book is the key to helping you thrive as a happy, healthy, and sane vegan in a decidedly non-vegan world that doesn't always get what you're about. In this sometimes funny, sometimes irreverent, and sometimes serious guide that's not afraid to tell it like it is, you will:

- find out how to go vegan in three weeks or less with our "cold tofu method"
- discover and understand the arguments for ethical, abolitionist veganism
- learn how to convince family and friends that you haven't joined a vegetable cult by going vegan
- get some advice on dealing with people in your life without creating havoc or hurt feelings
- learn to survive restaurants, grocery stores, and meals with omnivores
- find advice on how to respond when people ask if you "like, live on apples and twigs."

Now in a revised and expanded second edition, *Vegan Freak* is your guide to embracing vegan freakdom.

Bob Torres holds a PhD in Development Sociology from Cornell University. He's the author of *Making a Killing: The Political Economy of Animal Rights* and co-hosts Vegan Freak Radio.

Jenna Torres has a BA in Spanish and a BS in Plant Science from Penn State University, and received her PhD from Cornell University in Spanish linguistics. She is the co-host of Vegan Freak Radio, a podcast about life as a vegan in a very non-vegan world.

"Vegan Freak is a witty, helpful, wall to wall look at going vegan. A must read for anyone who's felt like the only vegan freak in the room."
—Sarah Kramer, author of *How It All Vegan*

GENERATION V

The Complete Guide to Going, Being, and Staying Vegan as a Teenager

Claire Askew

978-1-60486-338-3 • $14.95

Going vegan is not always easy when you are young. Living under your parents' roof, you probably do not buy your own groceries, and your friends, family, and teachers might look at you like you are nuts.

In this essential guide for the curious, aspiring, and current teenage vegan, Claire Askew draws on her years of experience as a teenage vegan and provides the tools for going vegan and staying vegan as a teen. Full of advice, stories, tips, and resources, Claire covers topics like: how to go vegan and stay sane; how to tell your parents so they do not freak out; how to deal with friends who do not get it; how to eat and stay healthy as a vegan; how to get out of dissection assignments in school; and tons more.

Whether you're a teenager who is thinking about going vegan or already vegan, this is the ultimate resource, written by someone like you, for you.

Claire Askew was born in 1990 and went vegan a few days after her 15th birthday. After growing up in the Midwest, she is currently studying English and gender at a small liberal arts college in Portland, OR.

"An essential guide that covers all bases... this first effort is a welcome surprise"
—*VegNews*

Cook Food

**a manualfesto for
easy, healthy, local eating**

Lisa Jervis

COOK FOOD

A Manualfesto for Easy, Healthy, Local Eating

Lisa Jervis

978-1-60486-073-3 • $12.00

More than just a rousing food manifesto and a nifty set of tools, *Cook Food* makes preparing tasty, wholesome meals simple and accessible for those hungry for both change and scrumptious fare. If you're used to getting your meals from a package—or the delivery guy—or if you think you don't know how to cook, this is the book for you.

If you want to eat healthier but aren't sure where to start, or if you've been reading about food politics but don't know how to bring sustainable eating practices into your everyday life, *Cook Food* will give you the scoop on how, while keeping your taste buds satisfied. With a conversational, do-it-yourself vibe, a practical approach to everyday cooking on a budget, and a whole bunch of animal-free recipes, *Cook Food* will have you cooking up a storm, tasting the difference, thinking globally and eating locally.

Lisa Jervis is the founding editor and publisher of *Bitch: Feminist Response to Pop Culture*, the founding board president of Women in Media and News, and a member of the advisory board for outLoud Radio. Her work has appeared in numerous magazines and books, including *Ms., The San Francisco Chronicle, Utne, Mother Jones, Body Outlaws*, and *The Bust Guide to the New Girl Order*. She is the co-editor of *Young Wives' Tales: New Adventures in Love and Partnership*, and *Bitchfest: Ten Years of Cultural Criticism from the Pages of Bitch Magazine*. She's currently working on a book about the intellectual legacy of gender essentialism and its effect on contemporary feminism.

"*Cook Food* is what you would get if you combined CliffsNotes of Michael Pollan's foodie insta-classic *The Omnivore's Dilemma* with the vegan parts of Mark Bittman's *The Minimalist* cooking column in the *New York Times*, added a healthy pour of DIY attitude and ran it all through a blender. The book's subtitle calls it a 'manualfesto,' and that's just about right—it's a nitty-gritty how-to with a political agenda: to give those of us with good intentions but limited budgets, skills, confidence, or time a chance to participate in the burgeoning local food revolution."

—Salon.com

LICKIN' THE BEATERS 2

Vegan Chocolate and Candy

Siue Moffat • Illustrated by Celso and Missy Kulik

978-1-60486-009-2 • $17.95

The beaters go on—in *Lickin' the Beaters 2: Vegan Chocolate and Candy*, the second of Siue Moffat's fun vegan dessert cookbooks.

Themed around the duality of desert—an angel on one shoulder and a devil on the other—Siue takes chocolate, candy, and even ice creem (vegan alternative to ice cream) head-on with quirky illustrations, useful hints, and a handy "Quick Recipe" indicator to make using this book simple and amusing. With an understanding that dessert should be an indulgence, Moffat provides vegan renditions of tantalizing delicacies, both traditional and original.

Recipes include old favorites such as Caramel Corn, Salt Water Taffy, Pralines, Cookies, Cakes, and Fudge, as well as some brave new recipes like Fabulous Flourless Chocolate Torte and Toll Free Chocolate Chip cookies.

Siue Moffat puts things on paper and film. She loves making vegan candy (she has started a chocolate truffle business) and inspecting beat-up film collections. Radical politics make her eyes light up and *Peanuts* comics make her giggle. Siue lives here and there and has a love/hate relationship with sugar and punk rock.

LICKIN' THE BEATERS

Low Fat Vegan Desserts

978-1-60486-004-7 • $10.95

Don't pass up dessert! If you're vegan or trying to eat healthy, there's no reason to deny yourself sweet treats. Lickin' the Beaters brings you over 80 fabulous low-fat, dairy-free desserts where even the second helping is guilt-free. Breads, cakes, donuts, candies, cookies and bars, pies, ice creams, puddings, toppings, fruity stuff, drinks, and a whole lot more. Illustrated with beautiful linocuts and zany cartoons, you'll find the recipes fun, easy to follow, and so good you'll eat half the batter.

STUFFED AND STARVED

Raj Patel

978-1-60486-103-7 • $14.95 • CD

How can starving people also be obese?

Why does everything have soy in it?

How do petrochemicals and biofuels control the price of food?

It's a perverse fact of modern life: there are more starving people in the world than ever before (800 million) while there are also more people overweight (1 billion).

On this audio CD lecture, Patel talks about his comprehensive investigation into the global food network. It took him from the colossal supermarkets of California to India's wrecked paddy-fields and Africa's bankrupt coffee farms, while along the way he ate genetically engineered soy beans and dodged flying objects in the protestor-packed streets of South Korea.

What he found was shocking, from the false choices given us by supermarkets to a global epidemic of farmer suicides, and real reasons for famine in Asia and Africa.

Yet he also found great cause for hope in international resistance movements working to create a more democratic, sustainable and joyful food system. Going beyond ethical consumerism, Patel explains, from seed to store to plate, the steps to regain control of the global food economy, stop the exploitation of both farmers and consumers, and rebalance global sustenance.

Raj Patel is a writer, activist and former policy analyst with Food First. He has worked for the World Bank, the WTO, and the United Nations, and has also protested them on four continents. He is the author of *Stuffed and Starved: The Hidden Battle for the World Food System.*

> "For anyone attempting to make sense of the world food crisis, or understand the links between U.S. farm policy and the ability of the world's poor to feed themselves, *Stuffed and Starved* is indispensable."
> —Michael Pollan, author of *The Omnivore's Dilemma* (on the book)